Genre Choices, Gender Questions

Oklahoma Project for
Discourse & Theory

OKLAHOMA PROJECT FOR DISCOURSE & THEORY

SERIES EDITORS

Robert Con Davis, University of Oklahoma
Ronald Schleifer, University of Oklahoma

ADVISORY BOARD

Maya Angelou, Wake Forest University
Jonathan Culler, Cornell University
Jacques Derrida, University of California, Irvine
Shoshana Felman, Yale University
Henry Louis Gates, Jr., Cornell University
Sandra M. Gilbert, Princeton University
Edmund Leach, Oxford University
Richard Macksey, Johns Hopkins University
J. Hillis Miller, University of California, Irvine
Marjorie Perloff, Stanford University
Edward W. Said, Columbia University
Thomas A. Sebeok, Indiana University at Bloomington
Gayatri Chakravorty Spivak, University of Pittsburgh
Cornel West, Princeton University

Genre Choices, Gender Questions

by Mary Gerhart

University of Oklahoma Press : Norman and London

In memory of
Mary Weber and William Warthling

By Mary Gerhart

The Question of Belief in Literary Criticism: An Introduction to the Hermeneutical Theory of Paul Ricoeur (Stuttgart, 1979)
Metaphoric Process: The Creation of Scientific and Religious Understanding (with Allan M. Russell) (Fort Worth, 1984)
Morphologies of Faith: Essays in Religion and Culture in Honor of Nathan A. Scott, Jr. (coedited with Anthony C. Yu) (Atlanta, 1990)
Genre Choices, Gender Questions (Norman, 1992)

Figures 1, 3, and 4 first appeared in Mary Gerhart, "Generic Studies," *Journal of the American Academy of Religion* 45 (1977). They are reprinted with permission.

Library of Congress Cataloging-in-Publication Data

Gerhart, Mary.
    Genre choices, gender questions / by Mary Gerhart. — 1st ed.
      p.   cm. — (Oklahoma project for discourse & theory ; v. 9)
    Includes bibliographical references and index.
    ISBN 0-8061-2450-4
    1. Literature, Modern—History and criticism—Theory, etc.
    2. Literary form.   3. Sex.   4. Authorship—Sex differences.
    5. Feminism and literature.   I. Title.   II. Series: Oklahoma
    project for discourse and theory ; v. 9.
    PN771.G47   1992
    809'.03—dc20   92-54152
                                                       CIP

Genre Choices, Gender Questions is Volume 9 of the Oklahoma Project for Discourse & Theory.

The paper in this book meets the guidelines for permanence and durability of the Committee on Production Guidelines for Book Longevity of the Council on Library Resources, Inc.∞

Contents

Contents

Series Editors' Foreword

The Oklahoma Project for Discourse & Theory is a series of interdisciplinary texts whose purpose is to explore the cultural institutions that constitute the human sciences, to see them in relation to one another, and, perhaps above all, to see them as products of particular discursive practices. To this end, we hope that the Oklahoma Project will promote dialogue within and across traditional disciplines—psychology, philology, linguistics, history, art history, aesthetics, logic, political economy, religion, philosophy, anthropology, communications, and the like—in texts that theoretically are located across disciplines. In recent years, in a host of new and traditional areas, there has been great interest in such discursive and theoretical frameworks. Yet we conceive of the Oklahoma Project as going beyond local inquiries, providing a larger forum for interdiscursive theoretical discussions and dialogue.

Our agenda in previous books and certainly in this one has been to present through the University of Oklahoma Press a series of critical volumes that set up a theoretical encounter among disciplines, an interchange not limited to literature but covering virtually the whole range of the human sciences. It is a critical series with an important reference in literary studies—thus mirroring the modern development of discourse theory—but including all approaches, other than quantitative studies, open to semiotic and post-semiotic analysis and to the wider concerns of cultural studies. Regardless of its particular domain, each book in the series will investigate characteristically post-Freudian, post-Saussurean, and post-Marxist questions about culture and the discourses that constitute different cultural phenomena. The Oklahoma Project is a sustained dialogue intended to make a significant contribution to the contemporary understanding of the human sciences in the contexts of cultural theory and cultural studies.

The title of the series reflects, of course, its home base, the University of Oklahoma. But it also signals in a significant way the particularity of the *local* functions within historical and conceptual frameworks for

vii

understanding culture. *Oklahoma* is a haunting place-name in American culture. A Choctaw phrase meaning "red people," it goes back to the Treaty of Dancing Rabbit Creek in Mississippi in 1830. For Franz Kafka, it conjured up the idea of America itself, both the indigenous Indian peoples of North America and the vertiginous space of the vast plains. It is also the place-name, the "American" starting point, with which Wallace Stevens begins his *Collected Poems*. Historically, too, it is a place in which American territorial and political expansion was reenacted in a single day in a retracing called the Oklahoma land run. Geographically, it is the heartland of the continent.

As such—in the interdisciplinary Oklahoma Project for Discourse & Theory—we are hoping to describe, above all, multifaceted *interests* within and across various studies of discourse and culture. Such interests are akin to what Kierkegaard calls the "in-between" aspect of experience, "inter esse," and, perhaps more pertinently, what Nietzsche describes as the always *political* functioning of concepts, art works, and language—the functioning of power as well as knowledge in discourse and theory. Such politics, occasioning dialogue and bringing together powerfully struggling and often unarticulated positions, disciplines, and assumptions, is always local, always particular. In some ways, such interests function in broad feminist critiques of language, theory, and culture as well as microphilosophical and microhistorical critiques of the definitions of truth and art existing within ideologies of "disinterested" meaning. They function in the interested examination of particular disciplines and general disciplinary histories. They function (to allude to two of our early titles) in the very interests of theory and the particularity of the postmodern age in which many of us find ourselves. In such interested particulars, we believe, the human sciences are articulated. We hope that the books of the Oklahoma Project will provide sites of such interest and that in them, individually and collectively, the monologues of traditional scholarly discourse will become heteroglosses, just as such place-names as *Oklahoma* and such commonplace words and concepts as *discourse* and *theory* can become sites for the dialogue and play of culture.

ROBERT CON DAVIS
RONALD SCHLEIFER

Norman, Oklahoma

Preface

This book and I have had the benefit of much collaboration over the past ten years.

It was begun fifteen years ago with an essay, "Generic Studies: Their Renewed Importance in Religious And Literary Interpretation" (*Journal of the American Academy of Religion* 45 [1977]: 309–25). This text grew as my questions outpaced my grasp of the subject of genre. A Fulbright research fellowship to begin the manuscript took me to the John F. Kennedy Institute for American Studies at the Frei Universität Berlin in 1982, and led to the publication of "Genre—The Larger Context" (*Journal of the American Academy of Religion* 49 (1983). Anyone who asked me to lecture or write an article heard about some aspect of genre. Parts of chapter 2 appeared in my essay "Genre, the Larger Context" in *Life on the Borders,* edited by Robert Detweiler (1983). I lectured on genre in the spring of 1983 at the University of Sheffield, the University of Manchester, and in the New College at the University of Edinburgh. A National Endowment for the Humanities Summer Research Grant in 1985 made further research possible. An early version of chapter 4 was first presented in the conference "Empiricism and Hermeneutics: The Invention of Facts in the Study of Literature" at Indiana University at Bloomington in 1986 and published as "The Dilemma of the Text: How to 'Belong' to a Genre" in *Poetics* 18 (1989). Parts of chapter 6 were originally presented to faculty at Hobart and William Smith Colleges in 1987 and published in "Generic Competence in Biblical Hermeneutics," *Semeia* 43 (1988).

The list of names of all the people who directly or indirectly contributed to this book over the years is too long to print here. But some cannot go without saying.

Preface

The following offered invaluable criticisms from their reading of earlier versions of the manuscript: Ursula Brumm, Martin Buss, Kathryn Rabuzzi, Allan Russell, Marianne Sawicki, David Tracy, and Stephen Webb. Claudette Columbus introduced me to the work of Fernando Alegría. David Tracy alerted me to a number of books that supported and clarified my argument. Gregor Goethals and Allan Russell encouraged me to pursue the implications of genre and gender beyond written texts. I also am indebted to my editors Kimberly Wiar and Sarah Nestor for their overall good sense and good management, to the librarians of the Warren Hunting Smith Library for their unstinting resourcefulness, to two sharp anonymous readers, and to the editors of the series, Ron Schleifer (who long ago invited me to send some of my work to *Genre*) and Robert Con Davis.

Finally, however, I bear responsibility for the interpretation of all these suggestions and for the degree to which this book is systematic and effective in its purpose. Its readers will determine whether it is also productive.

MARY GERHART

Geneva, New York

Genre Choices, Gender Questions

Genre and Gender in Public Discourse

Put your discourse into some frame, and start not so wildly from my affair.
I am tame, sir. Pronounce.

Shakespeare, Hamlet *3.325–27*

As more and more texts by women authors are retrieved from oblivion or obscurity, gender as an issue of interpretation becomes increasingly visible. But the relationship between gender and genre is at present only vaguely perceived.[1] Genre and gender as concepts share a history of misreading that ranges on the one hand from their being completely ignored to their being cast into unbreakable stereotypes on the other. This book wagers that once these two concepts are together opened to inquiry, they become central to the process of interpretation and their changing relationships afford a key to understanding.

At one time the question of gender was raised only with respect to the presumed sex of the author. In this framework, literature by women was seen—when it was known or admitted to exist at all—as singular, marginal, and remarkable in its overcoming the odds against its existence. Whenever the sex of the author was in question, as it still is in the case of the anonymously published *The Letters of a Portuguese Nun* (1669), most critics used the excellence of the writing as a major reason why the author could not have been a woman. But to stand in awe of texts because of the sex of their authors is not far removed from ignoring them as texts. Moreover, even though the question of authorial intention in some form continues to be important and relevant, today genre replaces authorial motivation as a key to understanding texts.[2]

3

Genre Choices, Gender Questions

I argue that to ignore genre is to fail to differentiate between the effective and the ineffective framing of discourse, but to link genre too immediately with gender is to ignore much of the complexity and ambiguity that permeate their relationship—two of the features that require interpretation of the text in the first place. This book assumes that to each genre there corresponds a reading of the text, and that in any given historical-cultural context a determinate number of readings are likely to become persuasive. There is, however, not likely to be a "male" reading and a "female" reading of any given text, although it might be expected that at different times available genres have had a different utility for women than for men. Even though the question of author's and reader's intention continues to be important, especially politically and psychologically, the issues of gender and genre are best focused on the texts themselves.

Thanks to the newly visible relationship between gender and genre, reading becomes gender conscious and interpretation becomes genre explicit. Nietzsche's self-sufficient, despairing cry, "Human, all too human" at the end of *Thus Spoke Zarathustra* (1883–91) has a new implication. To read without gender alertness is to engage the category of the "human" at too high a level of abstraction—to make the historically human "all *too* human." Sooner or later, to be critical all reading in the name of the "human" must be checked in a newly constructed history of how "female" and "male" are being understood. Gender reflection raises at least three questions across the multiplicity of genres:

1. What are the conventions by means of which gender is represented, and in what sense is there or is there not equal representation?
2. What values are attached to the representation of gender, and how are such values supported and called into question by specific genres?
3. What are the major contradictions that persist with respect to gender representation and gender valuation, and how does the multiplicity of genres enable readers to avoid, to appropriate, or to resolve those contradictions?

One way to acquire the habit of critical reading is to be alert to the gendered connotations of concepts. In her succinct *The Man of Reason: "Male" and "Female" in Western Philosophy* (1984), Genevieve Lloyd, for example, illustrates how the concept of "reason," too often presumed to be neutral in Western philosophy

4

with respect to gender, has been heavily involved in gender considerations. The association of reason exclusively with males—and the concomitant denial of reason to females—has defied the attempts of well-meaning Western philosophers to correct the problem.[3] The critical reader will be alert to the historical associations of certain concepts with either gender.

Another way to increase the capacity for critical reading is to be alert to the ways in which gender refers to other than two sexes. Gender is far richer and more useful as a social-historical-political construct than as a biological index, and it includes human beings who are androgynous, bisexual, homosexual, heterosexual, and transsexual, as well as those who become eunuchs, celibates, transvestites, and berdache.[4] Some of the most interesting work on the thematization of love—for example, in the Shakespearean sonnets—replaces the presumption of a heterosexual relationship with other hypotheses. Some of the most controversial work done on pornography, a marginal literary genre,[5] provides representations of a variety of relationships between power and sex—relationships variously articulated in our culture.

A third way—one that is more properly the focus of this book—is to attend to the formal written structures by which the gendering of concepts takes place. Such attending, in turn, opens into two foci—the history and the critical alteration of these structures, or genres. In spite of our premise that there is no single "male" or "female" reading of a given text, statistics inform us that certain genres, such as romance novels, are written for and read by a predominantly if not exclusively female audience, and some genres, such as gangster "tragedies," are written for and read by a predominantly male audience.[6] Other genres, such as biography, have been revised in recent years to include women as principal subjects. In *Writing a Woman's Life* (1988, 29), Carolyn Heilbrun, for example, argues that "biographies of women [before 1970] had made certain facts unthinkable. . . . But what has begun to happen in women's biography since 1970 is that the consensus about the author's relation to her work (if she is a writer) has changed, or is changing." Genres, in other words, can be seen to determine (in a negative sense) and to make room for (in a positive sense) what can be thought.

There is another sense in which the study of genre is incomplete without attention to its relationship with gender. The broad interdisciplinary scope of gender studies has already challenged the presumed dichotomy between imagination and reality—a dichotomy often reinforced by the division between the humanities and the social sciences. But the ultimate need to transgress gender distinctions, however useful such distinctions may be to immediate reflection and political action, leads us to expect a similar need for transgression with respect to genric[7] distinctions, however useful such distinctions may be to writing and reading. Can gender and genre together provide a paradigm for a new kind of theory for political action? In her collection of feminist literary criticism, Elaine Showalter comes close to making that claim when she writes that women's writing is not just a "transient by-product of sexism" but a "fundamentally and continually determining reality" (1985, 266).[8] In the same collection, Sandra Gilbert wagers that the "intellectual excitement" encountered in feminist criticism will lift literary studies out of its current "doldrums." What differences might be expected were feminist thought to become the "conscience" of postmodernism?

In the new context of gender studies, genre can no longer be merely an act of classification. Genre as a classificatory device continues to be useful, even indispensable, for some tasks: librarians, publishers, and book borrowers, for example, could scarcely get along without it. Nevertheless, these uses are essentially pragmatic and limited to a particular need. In this book, we inquire into the effect of genre and gender on interpretation. Such an inquiry is not without its problems. Somewhat like Socrates in Plato's *Meno,* we are confronted with a dilemma: how can we presume to know something about genre and gender and at the same time transcend the stereotypes in which both are socially and culturally enmeshed? If we know, we have no need to inquire. If we wish to surpass the traditional classifications, we seem not to be able to inquire, for we do not know what to inquire about. In a process epistemology, however, a relevant question goes (or takes us) beyond what we know, and what we don't know is on the horizon. With respect to gender and genre, one of the results of examining them together will be to make explicit some of the hidden assumptions that obscure or distort our understanding of both. The connections need to be made, however ambiguous the results.

This ancient dilemma of having to inquire without knowing

much about the subject of our inquiry is particularly awkward with the question of genre and gender. Much is known about specific genres and presumed to be known about the conventional genders. Yet there is little agreement about what the concepts of genre and gender themselves mean. Moreover, with the Romanticists' ambition to surpass generic considerations in the nineteenth century and the deconstructionists' effort to dissolve the concept in the twentieth, genre can fairly be said to have come upon hard times. With respect to the question of gender, the uncritical equivalence of gender and biological sex also poses difficulty.

I suggest that, despite misdirected attempts to "get beyond" considerations of genre and gender, they remain at the center of critical interpretation.[9] Generic and gender analysis enable us to become aware of questions that would otherwise go unnoticed. How do generic predispositions set up expectations about the ways in which a text should be read? How do traditions provide both restraints and incentives to the development of new genres? In what senses can a text be said to "belong" to a genre? How does the recognition of genre and gender reduce the possibility of misinterpreting a text and at the same time invite maximum reinterpretation? These are the questions that bind together the already existing reflections on genre and gender, presently scattered among many disciplines.

My method is to gather the central questions that repeatedly give rise to theories of genre and gender and to refract these questions into some state of coherence in order to plot a productive direction for the study—one that will retain answerable questions from classical reflection, formulate new questions from contemporary challenges, and address some of the vexed issues. Finally, this study shows how these questions are operative outside, as well as within, literary criticism—the field in which the concept of genre has traditionally been invoked.

Literary criticism has been the privileged discipline for the study of genre, although even here it has sometimes been treated as an uninvited guest. Like rhetoric and metaphor, having only recently begun again to be taken seriously as processes of knowing, genre has attracted the attention of scholars in many fields. Clifford Geertz's (1980) analysis of "blurred genres" in anthropology, James Kinneavy's (1980) observations on the role of genre in the teaching of rhetoric, and finally, Janet Todd's (1988) notice of the crucial role that gender plays in the history of genres—these examples all include the possibility of understanding genre not merely as a means of classification but as a principle of knowing.

This study is motivated by the conviction that an unreflective understanding of genre and gender contributes to what Bernard Lonergan called "the long decline" in the life of an institution or nation. The inability, in other words, to allow genric and gender insights to enter into our claims about what we know leads to a general impoverishment of knowledge and of the forms in which knowledge is expressed. According to Barbara Johnson (1980, xii), "it is not . . . what you don't know that can or can't hurt you. It is what you don't know you don't know." Critical understanding of genre and gender can help us to discover what Jürgen Habermas (1979) calls the "systematic distortion of communication" so that such distortions can be corrected and communication restored or made possible, perhaps for the first time.

We have all had to make judgments regarding genre—perhaps without being aware that genre was involved. For example, you might be casually reading, say, a magazine piece about driving through the Rocky Mountains. Gradually you get the uneasy feeling that too much time is being spent describing the car rather than the trip or the scenery. Your suspicion is confirmed when, lo and behold, you read, in fine print at the bottom of the page, the word "Advertisement." Genrically, you have been jolted from reading the piece as a travelogue to reading it as a sales pitch. Quite apart from our distrust of the advertisement genre because of the frequency of false claims (e.g., advertising canned tomato sauce as "fresh" when its being canned precludes its being fresh), the foregoing instance of dishonesty is more subtle. It involves using one genre to diguise the use of another. The generic use of male nouns and pronouns to refer to women is similarly an instance of claiming to refer to one gender under the disguise of referring to another.

In place of models of genre and gender as either primary or derivative classifications, I offer models that are epistemological, historical, theoretical, and praxis-oriented. This study is phenomenological to the extent that it attends to the phenomena of genre and gender as potentially present in every act of interpretation. Allowing these phenomena to appear repeatedly in different contexts provides a basis for describing how they function together. The study is also transcendental in the sense that an understanding of genre and gender is already present, gains precision as a hypothesis, and develops throughout the course of the inquiry into an explicit relationship. The grounds for attending to appearances of the two phenomena sometimes singly and sometimes together should be self-evident at the conclusion of the study.

Chapter 1 begins with the idea that genre is a critical process of entering the hermeneutical circle. I argue that the genric process necessarily includes four kinds of reflection. (1) Genres are epistemological because they are constitutive of meaning. (2) Genres are historical, and reflection about them, especially in relation to gender, is itself historical. Genres are no longer, in this theory, regarded as timeless, a priori categories. Instead, because they are constituted by historical reflection, their rise and decline are an intrinsic part of interpretation. Moreover, a particular genre is affected not only by its immediate or explicit predecessor but also by the associations it has with gender in the formal system of structures. (3) Genres are best understood as hypothetical; the process of genre identification is best maintained by genre testing. Replacing both "pure" description and "mere" abstraction, genre is explored as hypothesis to emphasize that "form" is theoretical, as well as descriptive or explanatory. Somewhere between empirical details and metaphysical thematizations lie genric formulations that can assist readers in organizing their responses to the text and in recognizing the probable understanding toward which the conventions of the text are directed. (4) Genres and gender identifications result in praxis. If we understand reading to be isomorphic with authoring, it becomes clear that the reader can no longer be regarded as the self-evident recipient of text signification. The critical role of genre and gender is to transform speech about the text into a reconstruction of the text as a condition for the possibility of the text's having an effect in the world. (Readers who are less interested in historical interpretation are advised to skip or postpone reading chapters 2 and 3.)

Chapter 2 recalls the major traditional and contemporary ways of understanding genre and assesses them in terms of questions pertinent to the issue of gender. The chapter constructs a selective history of the concept of genre in the classical literary critical tradition: from its emergence in classical criticism in the form of a hypothetical debate between Plato and Aristotle, its demise in neoclassical criticism, its static fate in New Criticism, and its survival in morphological criticism, to its expansion by means of structuralism, especially in its application to folklore.

Chapter 3 takes up another strand of genre in relation to gender: that of the biblical hermeneutical tradition, especially in the nineteenth and twentieth centuries. In that tradition, Julius Wellhausen (1878) opened the way for new approaches to understanding biblical texts with his discovery of four different "documents" in the first six books of the bible. Hermann Gunkel (1901) initiated form criticism, which attempted to determine the function of specific biblical texts in their original settings. But Elizabeth Cady Stanton's (1895) efforts to introduce gender criticism into biblical interpretation about the same time with her group-authored *Woman's Bible* was rejected at the time by both women and men. Other, more recent, genre and gender studies of biblical texts illustrate new applications of genre theory and new theoretical developments.

Chapter 4 poses the dilemma of the individual text: how to belong to a genre and a gender. Here, the uniqueness of a text is seen to be the result of its being understood as genric. Three contemporary mainstream alternatives for approaching genre are explored: the traditionalist, the ideological, and the deconstructionist views. Parallel to these views, three alternatives for understanding gender are also introduced: the liberal, the transvaluational, and the horizonal. A revisionist position suggests that the concept of genre is not radically different for the humanities and the sciences and that the concept of gender is not so biologically predetermined as once thought. Finally, metaphoric process is considered as a model for understanding how genres and genders change.

Chapter 5 takes up where the chapters on the history of genres end: on the dispersal of the concept of genre and gender into several new disciplines and fields. Today genre plays a major role in speech act theory, film criticism, anthropology, feminist literary theory and literary history, and the teaching of rhetoric—to mention only a few areas where the issue is explicit. Notice is taken of the differences between concepts of genre that are based in theory and those that are nominalist and primarily pragmatic. The need for the level of theoretical reflection with respect to genre is reinforced by the current new awareness of the need for theory on the issue of gender. A well-publicized debate between Helen Vendler, on one side, and Susan Gilbert and Susan Gubar, on the other, over what constitutes feminist literary criticism alerts us to the shortcomings of trying to do genre criticism without gender criticism, and vice versa.

In chapter 6, I examine the notion of reader competence under three aspects of interpretation: (1) gender and genre testing as multiple hypotheses, (2) gender and genre testing as innovation, and (3) gender and genre testing as modification. I attempt to show how the genric process is operative in readers who may not reflect on genre, and, in addition, may be reluctant to think that gender has anything to do with genre. Correlative to genric competence, the notion of the inscribed reader enables me to view the seductive power of texts in relation to gender. Insensitivity to either genre testing or to gender analysis is likely to result in "overgenred" and "overgendered" interpretations. I conclude that the well-read reader is the genre- and gender-conscious reader.

Chapters 1–6 argue for a highly reflective and critical sense of genre. Chapter 7 applies genre and gender testing heuristically to three kinds of texts: (1) those that lend themselves to inquiry through traditional genres, (2) those that are structured so as to call traditional genres into question and lead to the creation of new genres, and (3) those that are marginal to known genres and lead to the modification of traditional genres. Using the rubrics of traditionalist, ideological, and deconstructive genre theory, I test texts that have come to be known as "new" novels against other genres. Using the rubrics of liberal, transvaluational, and horizonal, I subject my criteria for the best interpretations to gender criticism. I conclude that having a theoretical basis for differences in interpretations makes it more likely that readers will be prepared to make use of those differences in public discourse.

This study does not claim to have the final word on the relationships of gender and genre. But the last word in any argument is sufficient only if it becomes the first word in new, interesting, and more adequate interpretations. Such interpretations require interpreters who appreciate the multiple ways in which speaking and writing are charged with genric and gendered meanings. In the long run, such appreciation may even yield more effective public discourse.

CHAPTER ONE

Elements of Genre and Gender

Images are not made from nothing: one has to begin somewhere.
Adena Rosmarin, The Power of Genre *(1985, 14)*

It would seem as though gender does not have a history. Have there not always been concrete women and men from whose existence the concept of gender derives? In the naive view, not everything needs to be questioned, and for many the issue of gender "goes without saying." Lived experience, however, is limited in its capacity to confirm either the various or the contradictory ways in which women and men live *as* women and *as* men. Feminist thought in particular has taught us the futility of attempts to reify an essence of either "woman" or the collective entity of "women." Such reification may be a necessary heuristic fiction for political action, but it fails to be coherent in thought. Moreover, today we realize that both fictions (and, by implication, "man" and "men" as well) are socially produced. The history of gender discloses the differences in the way the categories "women" and "men" have functioned as social constructs.

Similarly, to define genre it will not be sufficient merely to reject the notion of genre as classification. Perhaps it will not be necessary to reject this notion at all, so long as we are able either to assimilate classification within other more essential functions of genre (such as the constitution and determination of meaning) or to go beyond classification to some broader dimension of genre (such as its historicity or productivity).

As soon as we decide that categorization is not the central feature of genre and gender, however, we encounter an unexpected difficulty. We find that we must *relocate* genre and gender elsewhere than in end products of thought, where they appear as so many "empty" labels waiting to be filled by specific texts. Genre consciousness and gender consciousness are also to be found in the experience of the reader in both the early moments and throughout the process of interpretation.

Initially, we understand genre as a hypothesis regarding an entire text, relating that single text to one or more other texts with similar structures, styles, topics, and effects. Genres, which are constructed to explain individual texts, and theories, which are designed to explain the processes of genre construction, together make up public discourse. By *public discourse* is meant in general any communication that takes place in the public realm. Maximally, public discourse includes communications in both occasional events and everyday institutions. A presidential address, a lecture, a sermon or homily, an editorial, a news item, a talk show, a liturgy, a debate, an ordinance of the city council, a resolution taken in a national professional meeting, a scientific monograph—in short, any form of verbal or written communication intended for an audience of more than one. Minimally, it includes informal speech in the workplace, the market, and even, to some extent, the family. The margins of public discourse are to be found in the situation of one person writing or speaking to one other.

Consider four examples of situations that enable us to perceive the genric process and to reflect on its effects.

Example 1: A resident of New York City receives the following letter:

Dear Mr. Culver:
Please be advised that unless we receive a minimum payment of $10.00 on your VISA bill of January 15, your VISAcard privileges will be terminated. May we hear from you by March 1.
Sincerely yours,
R. Munson
Customer Relations[1]

Anyone familiar with American business practices understands the above letter at a glance. But how might someone who has grown up in China interpret it? Are there any clues that the salutation "Dear" is not a term of endearment but rather a brusque formality? How does the recipient know that the letter is a dun rather than a letter of blackmail or a special offer of goods and services? Consider the general confusion of receiving a letter that begins with a title ("Dear"), which in China is reserved for intimacy, and ends with a greeting ("Sincerely yours"), reserved for courtship. Moreover, the confusion is not restricted to cultures: examples from other periods of one's own national history can be equally puzzling. Such confusion requires a stranger to test more than one genre and to continue testing until one genre or combination of genres yields a persuasive interpretation.

Example 2: If the genre is changed sufficiently, the problem of not being able to read the text before the genre has been identified may arise. What follows is an excerpt from a complex genre. The point of this example will best be made if readers conceal from themselves the identification of its source (given below) until they have struggled a few minutes to make sense of the passage:

> What's needed is a way to examine the parts of a string. Well, you can always look at the display—but that invites human error and judgment. You might be tempted to accept certain four-letter words simply because they are neither obscene, uncouth, inflammatory, nor abusive. That won't do at all, since, by design, the Automatic Censor must be autocratic and arbitrary to a fault.

Many readers may need to be informed that this passage was taken from a computer manual (Stewart, *Getting Started with TRS-80 Basic*) and is an excerpt from instruction for examining the parts of a string (sequence of characters) in Basic memory. The complicated genre, however, is derived from combining instruction with espionage fiction. And since the combination of the genres of instruction and espionage does not have a tradition of interpretation, it poses a problem of readability rather than one of adequate interpretation. Unlike the dun letter in example 1, however, this passage is likely to frustrate most Western readers. They will be unable to make sense of the passage, precisely because an appropriate genre is not apparent on a first reading, nor even perhaps on repeated readings.

Example 3: In his *Autobiography* (1977), Mircea Eliade cites a personal example of the influence of context on genre. When he was a young man, Eliade published what he had designed as a favorable review of a book in a newspaper for which he wrote regularly. He was stunned to be called to the editor's office and

14

to be told that, as a result of the review, all his subsequent copy would have to be read—in effect, censored—by the editors. This new directive puzzled him since until that time his work had never been questioned. He understood only when one of the editors drew him aside and explained, "What you say about Iorga's [the author reviewed] method is correct, but something of that sort must be expounded in a scholarly study; in a newspaper column it is an attack" (119). In other words, in an academic context, a comment about method is appropriate; in a newspaper, even a favorable comment about method takes on quite a different meaning.

Example 4: The following passage is from the preface to Mary Daly's *GynEcology: The Metaethics of Radical Feminism* (1978, xiii):

> Since Gyn/Ecology is the Un-field/Ourfield/Outfield of Journeyers, rather than a game in an "in" field, the pedantic can be expected to perceive it as "unscholarly." Since it *confronts* old molds/models of question-asking by being itself an Other way of thinking/speaking, it will be invisible to those who fetishize old questions—who drone that it does not "deal with" *their* questions.
> Since Gyn/Ecology Spins around, past, and through the coffers/ coffins in which "knowledge" has been stored, re-stored, re-covered, its meaning will be hidden from the Grave Keepers of tradition. . . . It departs from their de-partments.

Readers of Mary Daly's radical feminist theology often find themselves unable to read naively sexist texts again without parodying their "methodolatry." Similarly, some first-time readers of James Joyce's *Finnegans Wake* report that they begin to write and talk in "wakese."[2] One reader who enjoyed a parody of a colleague's decision to leave the teaching profession for a career in computer technology said that for several hours she could not read anything without treating it too as a parody.[3] Although these instances may be extreme, they do alert us to the seductive potential of genres, some with more obvious power than others, but all nudging, pushing, snapping, and teasing us toward a certain horizon of understanding and even toward imitation. Initially hypotheses for reading texts, pretending to be at the service of readers, genres quietly subvert the worlds of meanings that produce them.

Genre Choices, Gender Questions

GENRE AND GENDER AS CONSTITUTIVE OF MEANING

If we contrast the role of genre in each of the foregoing examples with the role of genre in Aristotle's *Poetics*,[4] it becomes clear that the contemporary focus is on the intricacy with which genre is bound up with the meaning of a text. Aristotle was more interested in the effect of a genre, presumed to embrace one kind of text, on its audience. For example, he contrasted the relationship of the hero in tragedy and the hero in comedy in relation to the different ways in which audience perceives itself: in tragedy, the hero is perceived to be better than the audience; in comedy, worse. The all-male and all-Greek constitution of the audience was considered irrelevant in Aristotle's account. Gender considerations in genre, however implicit, function similarly for Plato and Aristotle. Plato, for example, wrote that it is contrary to nature and therefore wholly inappropriate for a male to imitate a female or to be "feminine." This aesthetic directive became a social-ethical stricture that continues to be normative today, with exceptions like Dustin Hoffman in the film *Tootsie* or William Hurt in the film *Kiss of the Spider Woman* "proving"—that is, accentuating—the rule. Classical writers treated genre as an epistemic-rhetorical form, one that exists prior to the interpreted meaning of a literary work. Contemporary theorists are more apt to regard genre as a psychological or a sociopolitical feature, both shaping and being shaped by the interpreted object. Genre, in both senses, however, clearly constitutes, or "makes up," meaning.

The first contemporary genre theorist to express this premise explicitly was E. D. Hirsch, the protagonist in one of the longest and most sustained public debates on the subject. The debate began with Hirsch's *Validity in Interpretation* (1967) and picked up momentum in the 1970s, in a subsequent series of articles by Hirsch with rebuttals and responses by other well-known and lesser critics in the periodical *Genre*,[5] which, although it continues today, no longer deals exclusively with genre theory. Hirsch can be credited with giving the issue of genre its best public exposure in Anglo-American criticism.

For Hirsch, there can be no meaning without genre; that is, verbal meaning is always "genre-bound" (1967, 76).[6] In his most systematic treatment of the subject he distinguishes between "intrinsic genre" and "broad genre." Intrinsic genre is a "shared

16

type that constitutes and determines meaning," and its locus is somewhere between "broad or traditional genre" and the particular meaning of a literary text. In Hirsch's view, Eliade's article commenting on an author's method would be a book review in terms of its "broad" genre, but because the review appeared also as a newspaper column, it had, as a "shared type," a special power—as can be seen in his editor's decision to censor not only that specific article but all of Eliade's subsequent writings.

Both Hirsch and Friedrich Schleiermacher ([1805–33] 1938), one of the founders of the nineteenth-century hermeneutical tradition, thought that any significant interpretation began with misunderstanding.[7] Of the multiple kinds and causes of misunderstanding, one of the most common ways to misread a text is to mistake its genre. On the other hand, a genric misreading opens a space for a different, and possibly critical, interpretation. The newly discovered link between gender and genre could be revolutionary insofar as it suggests that all genres are naively misread where that link has not been recognized.

Some texts force readers to recognize that they have misread the genre. A good example of a text that requires almost all its readers to experience a need to change their genric expectations is Jonathan Swift's *A Modest Proposal* (1729). In his *Rhetoric of Irony* (1975) Wayne Booth argues that Swift's work is designed to "deceive *all* readers for a time and then require *all* readers to recognize and cope with their deception." Initially, that is, the reader will be engaged in weighing what seems to be written in the genre of political legislation, namely, a proposal "for Preventing the Children of poor People in Ireland, from being a Burden to their Parents or Country; and for making them beneficial to the Publick" (the subtitle of the text). Next, having begun to suspect that the genric name of "proposal" couldn't be serious, the reader is at a loss to know what genre to look to next. Only toward the end of the essay does the reader begin to recognize the dominance of irony:

> Different readers will become suspicious at different points. . . . But most will have had their suspicions fully aroused by paragraph 7, and every reader should know, by paragraph 9, that the most wrenching kind of irony is at work. Every reader has thus to some degree been duped—not simply for a fleeting moment of shock and reconstruction

17

that is produced by essays that are ironic from the first word, but for several paragraphs. And every reader has thus been drawn into an engagement of the most active kind: having been driven to suspect, and finally to admit that the voice is speaking a kind of mad reasonableness, one is tricked into an intensely active state. (Booth, 1975, 106–9)

Booth uses this text as an example of the reader's need to be cautious and to avoid deception. But genre testing (see Chapter 7) may also and perhaps more importantly be a key to using such deception productively. In both formalist criticism and form criticism, however, misreading tends to be suppressed as mistaken, most often private, subjective, and idiosyncratic—in any case, an unwelcome experience.

Other texts provide readers with the opportunity for misreading the gender of fictional voices. The following passage, the first chapter of Nathalie Sarraute's *Tropisms,* for example, does not explicitly identify the gender of the characters:

They seemed to spring up from nowhere. . . . They stretched out in long, dark clusters between the dead house fronts. Now and then, before the shop windows, they formed more compact, motionless little knots, giving rise to occasional eddies, slight cloggings.
A strange quietude, a sort of desperate satisfaction emanated from them. They looked closely at the piles of linen in the White Sale display, clever imitations of snow-covered mountains, or at a doll with teeth and eyes, that, at regular intervals, lighted up, went out, lighted up, went out. . . .
They looked for a long time, without moving, they remained there, in offering, before the shop windows, they kept postponing till the next interval the moment of leaving. And the quiet little children, whose hands they held, weary of looking, listless, waited patiently beside them. Sarraute ([1939] 1963, 1–2)

Even though the gender of the human beings is lacking, unwary readers are likely to begin imposing a gender identity on them by wondering: are males or females more likely to be interested in linens and dolls? are males or females more likely to be with children?
Chapter 2 does identify both female and male voices, but from a traditionally male point of view. As a man hears women talking,

fussing, criticizing, gossiping, he "sensed percolating from the kitchen, humble, squalid, time-marking human thought, marking time in one spot . . . going round and round, in circles, as if they were dizzy but couldn't stop. . . ." and thinks, "but perhaps for them it was something else" (Sarraute 1963, 4). In chapter 3 gender identity is again withheld. The remaining chapters (4–24) alternate among male, female, male child, and female child narrative voices, except for chapter 16, which again thwarts gender identification. Occasionally the male voices are sinister in their relationships with women and children and the female voices desperate and compliant. In chapter 8 a grandfather walks with a child in hand, countering the expectation in chapter 1 that the adults walking with children are women.

It is curious, therefore, to find Jean-Paul Sartre writing, "In her first book, *Tropismes,* Nathalie Sarraute showed that women pass their lives in a sort of communion of the commonplace" (Sartre, 1956). Even though Sartre goes on to refer to male as well as female characters in the book, his initial identification of the commonplace with women may be evidence of a gender misreading—a misreading all the more remarkable when it is contrasted to Sarraute's own description of the book in deliberately gender-neutral terms such as the following: "The barely visible, anonymous character was to serve as a mere prop for these movements, which are inherent in everybody and can take place in anybody, at any moment" (Sarraute 1956, vi–ix). Gender theory provides a context for formulating such experiences of misreading as public and historical.

A number of discrete but parallel contemporary analogies support Hirsch's insistence that genric considerations are essential to intelligent reading. Other formulations support the expectation that readers will have to question their initial readings of texts. For Paul Ricoeur, first or "primitive" naïveté is immediacy of belief that today is no longer an option. Second naïveté is belief given through interpretation: "it is by interpreting that we can hear again" (Ricoeur 1960, 351). Ricoeur doubts that contemporary adults can reside in an attitude of unquestioning belief.[8] There is also Paulo Friere's (1978, 298–306) distinction between *prise de conscience* and *conscientization,* in which any awareness of an object always precedes and calls for distancing and objectification in order to achieve a critical understanding. Finally, Hans-Georg

Gadamer's (1975) understanding of "prejudice" entails an initial prejudgment binding a perceived object to the subject's interest as the precondition for authentic understanding. All these formulations suggest that to move from uncritical to critical understanding, from mere awareness to informed understanding, from prejudgments to virtually authentic judgments, requires genre testing and gender questioning. Not all texts, of course, demand such an abruptly explicit judgment on the part of the reader as does Swift's *A Modest Proposal,* but Hirsch's point is thereby strengthened: one of the most difficult aspects of interpreting a text is not only an appropriate determination of its genre but also a recognition that genric reflection is precisely what is needed for understanding.

As many critics have pointed out, Hirsch's major ambition was to make authorial intention normative for the interpretation of a text, and that part of his interpretation theory caused critics to find his concept of genre less than adequate. Nevertheless, his theory is important for two reasons especially. First, he made genre into a principle of meaning: "All understanding of verbal meaning is necessarily genre-bound." Genre is not best understood as an overriding generalization under which individual texts or statements are subsumed. Such a conception obscures the fact that the genric "parentage" of any specific text is often mixed and multiple. If the originating genres of a text are hidden from its readers, we can understand why they may remain indeterminate during the experience of reading. According to Hirsch (1967, 79), "the details of the utterances are not present to consciousness all at once. Only by means of genric considerations do we come to know the range of possible fulfillments and to recognize the probable understanding toward which the conventions of the text are directed. Murray Krieger, in his *Theory of Criticism* (1976), for example, cited the prologue to *Henry IV* as an instance of need for the reader to distinguish between what he called the "broad genres" of history and of poetry. Read as history, the prologue tempts the reader to use one or another sequential model. Read as poetry, however, the prologue leads the reader to "transform the usual meanings of the text from the chronological to the logical" and to "follow the clues of internal relations." In short, reading the prologue as poetry, the reader reconstructs the historical "facts" into "elements that are anything but random for those who have been taught to disentangle and relate them in more ways than their casual before-ness and after-ness would suggest" (156–57). In reading *Henry IV* (or, for that matter, the biblical book of Genesis) as history (a genre favored by the majority), readers are likely to imagine a retrogressive sequence of observed "facts" based in unquestioned assumptions about the genre as well as the elements in the story. But if readers attend to the structure of the elements in the story, they read the text as poetry (a genre which today is held suspect by many).[9] Neither the poetic and historical readings are self-sufficient, of course: both remain in need of gender analysis.

Hirsch's second contribution is his description of the process by which genric considerations lead us to anticipate the wider implications of individual texts. Through the process of discovering the intrinsic genre of a work, we become aware of the "concentrated and symbolizing conventions of the genre itself" (Hirsch 1967, 97). Now, Hirsch himself has less regard for the "wider implications" of genre than we might expect, treating them as only provisional and heuristic. Nevertheless, he exposes the need for a new concept of genre. And although his discussion of genre is flawed by being attached to his impossibly conservative dictum of the normativeness of the author's intention for *the* meaning of the literary work, he nevertheless prepares for an explicitly reflexive solution to the problems he raises.

Such a solution requires that genres and genders be understood not only as provisional and descriptive: they are also historical, theoretical, and praxis-oriented.

GENRE AND GENDER AS HISTORICAL

One of the most suggestive images for understanding the historical dimension of textual analysis is found in Julia Kristeva's (1984) analogy of the text as a texture or textile. Kristeva, a French feminist literary critic and psychoanalyst, defines the text as an interplay of the drives brought to the text by different readers and their societal-cultural-linguistic constraints. A text, in other words, is "a disposition of threads, interwoven, in a perpetual state of flux as different readers intervene, as their knowledge deepens, and as history moves on" (Kristeva 1984, 5). History in contemporary critical understanding, especially in relation to the understanding of texts, is never an ideal relation among events. It is necessarily a form of "historicity."

In order for historicity to be seen as a necessary characteristic of genre, and in turn, genre as a necessary mediation of historical understanding, we must differentiate between "history" and "historical consciousness." History, naively understood, refers to records of events presumed to be correlated to a common chronology. Without exception, formalist approaches in literary criticism, such as the New Criticism in Anglo-American criticism and Russian Formalism, are designed to remove literary analysis and evaluation from the latter kind of biographical and historical "fixing" of literary data. Hermeneutical criticism, too, sets itself apart from naive historicism, but with a difference. Whereas the formalist would like to dismiss historical considerations altogether, hermeneutical criticism requires historical consciousness. It restores history as a matter of the horizons of the interpreters and the historical actors—horizons conceived as public and phenomenal.

Hans-Georg Gadamer's (1975) work has been helpful on this issue. His hermeneutical theory has been extended into literary theory and practical criticism by a number of literary theorists, such as Hans-Robert Jauss. A German hermeneutical philosopher, Gadamer, together with those who use his work, wishes to make explicit the prejudgments (the prejudices) and foremeanings that every interpreter brings to a text. For Gadamer, absolute neutrality with respect to any text is an impossibility. Interpretation, on the contrary, is "the conscious assimilation of one's own foremeanings and prejudices" (Gadamer 1975, 238).[10] Here we can see a difference between Gadamer's and Hirsch's views: Hirsch locates the historicity of genre in the relationship of intrinsic genre to "broader genre ideas"—conventional ideas, he says, that are important only heuristically in arriving at the intrinsic genre. By contrast, Gadamer emphasizes the inescapability of the historical: it is constitutive, he thinks, of the way reflection constantly understands and exercises itself. Although he himself takes no notice of gender, Gadamer's theory leaves room for the recognition that gender in conventional genres is one of the most basic (and therefore least recognized) historical constructs.

Gadamer clarifies his notion of historicity by exploring the various modes of "being historical." In the first mode, persons conceive of themselves as observers and conceive of events and other persons as types and generalizations. History consists of "already-out-there-now-real" (Gadamer 1975, 245–58) facts, to use Bernard Lonergan's (1957) apt phrase for the attitude of naive realism. This conception of being naively historical corresponds to Paul Ricoeur's "first naïveté" and Paulo Friere's *prise de conscience*. It is a prejudgment, an unexamined assumption. It would be to assume, for example, that Harlequin romances are women's novels since they are advertised as representing the romantic ideals of every woman.[11] It would also be to assume that *Alice in Wonderland* is a children's story: wasn't it written for a child?[12] It would be to deny that Shel Silverstein's children's book *The Giving Tree* is without gender implications because it is about a boy and a tree that always provides for his needs.[13] The first mode of "being historical" unhesitatingly roots itself in timeless theories of both genre and gender, to the exclusion of questions about the formation of either concept.

In the second mode of being historical according to Gadamer, persons reflect on their own being but not on their relation to the past. We recognize this second mode in the products of nineteenth-century Romanticism. The Romanticist belief that every historical period is unique prevents both the events of the past and the subjectivity of other persons from being exhausted by typification and generalization. But because it considers every event and person to be unique, Romanticism fosters relativism, another kind of generalization, one that goes unrecognized by the Romanticist. Gadamer criticized this mode of consciousness for its false objectivism: persons in this mode fail to recognize their own role in understanding the past. Their naïveté or their obstinate refusal to see the genric and gender patterns of the past is dangerous, for as a result of treating the past as though it were unique they claim a false mastery for the present over the past.

The third mode of being historical is related to Martin Heidegger's notion of authenticity. This mode does not abuse the past either by claiming to know it objectively or by regarding it as closed to the present because of its uniqueness. This third mode is an openness to what the traditions may have to say to the present. Gadamer developed three paradigms for the third mode of historical consciousness—engaging in dialogue, playing a game, and being overtaken by a work of art—paradigms that have proven helpful in articulating some of the more elusive characteristics of religion and art.

For the issue of genre, Gadamer's example of understanding a "classic" work of literature or art in the third mode of being historical is of special importance. In this mode, the "classical" illustrates the historical process of preservation. The importance of the classical lies in the fact that "its historical domain precedes all historical reflection and continues through it" (Gadamer 1975, 255). In other words, the classical is itself a "foremeaning." This foremeaning is most clear in the sense we sometimes have, in reading texts or in viewing art of being rescued from the immediate present for the sake of the enduring, for a significance that we can't afford to forget, which is understood in relation to all past and future significance as well (ibid., 256). That which we perceive as "natural" with respect to sexual identities is less a product of biological experience than the unreflective acceptance of a classical definition of the relationships between the sexes. Indeed, "sex," according to Judith Butler, is most likely "as culturally constructed as gender. . . . Perhaps it was always already gender"; that is, sex itself is, in its most complex sense, a "gendered category" (Butler 1990, 7).

When we examine classics—those texts that "through the constant proving of themselves" set before us something we recognize as true to our own experience—we notice that they are always representative of literary genres. *Gulliver's Travels, Uncle Tom's Cabin,* and the *Iliad,* for example, are known to us as a satire, a novel, and a classical epic poem, respectively. Classics become classics when, after stylistic ideal is perceived as having been fulfilled at a certain place and time, we have a sense of decline and distance in subsequent works. For some, the sense of nostalgia for the past can paralyze. Read constructively, however, classics are climaxes that articulate "the history of the genre in terms of before and after" and can inspire new creations. Gadamer emphasizes that the climactic points of a genre usually come within a brief period of time. Although genre is therefore history-bound (much more than literary critics usually acknowledge), it is its own uprooting. For as it endures, the classic generates an element of self-criticism: "the classical is what is preserved precisely because it signifies and interprets itself" (Gadamer 1975, 257). That is, the classic is not merely a statement about the past, a witness to what still needs interpretation, but is a communication with the present, a communication that overcomes its own historical distance.

The claim that the classic is its own best critic has incurred its own criticism of Gadamer's theory of interpretation: namely, that it does not allow for any negative effects or for distortions in the process of understanding the past.[14] Whether or not his theory precludes the negative, it is true that Gadamer does not attend explicitly to interruptions in the interpretive process. Because this objection applies equally to his explication of historicity, it is useful to recall Friedrich Nietzsche's essay "On the Advantages and Disadvantages of History Understood as Life" (Nietzsche, [1874] 1980) to construct a more ambivalent view of history. In this essay Nietzsche cites three uses of history: (1) the selection of a time and place past in order to reproduce it in the present; (2) the selection of a monumental event or person of the past in order to emulate it in the present and to achieve something new; and (3) the selection of a monumental event or person of the past in order to deconstruct it and to destroy some present tendency. Nietzsche's third use of history characterizes several contemporary attitudes toward history, including the ideological and the deconstructive views. The ideological in this context refers to the "debunking" or the demystifying of an accepted historical narration in order to destroy its privileged status or to loosen its power over the oppressed. The deconstructive here refers to the demolition of all historical understanding and the substitution of one or another understanding of fiction. All three uses fall within Gadamer's third mode of "being historical." Even his second use of history is different from the traditional view of history, which it closely resembles, in the sense that it is a self-conscious use of the past as distinct from a naive mirroring of past events.

From Gadamer and Nietzsche, then, we obtain a refinement of the broad general notion of genre that Hirsch merely tolerates, namely, its historicity. Both Gadamer and Hirsch wish to get beyond genre as a merely historical species through which all other members are defined and into which they are subsumed. Gadamer's point is that interpretation is best understood, not as an act of subjectivizing, but rather as "the placing of oneself within a process of tradition, in which past and present are constantly fused" (Gadamer 1975, 258).

While Gadamer does help us to clarify the way in which genre is historical, his theory allows the epistemological aspects of genre in interpretation to remain largely unexplored. Let us turn therefore to questions of the status and role of genre in the act of interpretation.

GENRE AND GENDER AS THEORETICAL

As we begin to look closely at the ways genre has been understood in the literary critical tradition, we encounter one major objection. This objection, in principle a rejection of genre theory, accounts for the low repute of any attempt to schematize existing genres. Benedetto Croce (1953) asserts that considerations of genre at worst destroy, and at best jeopardize, the specificity of the literary work. The worst situation is for genre to substitute as a concept for the literary work in itself: "To employ *words* and *phrases* is not to establish *laws* and *definitions*. The mistake only arises when the weight of a scientific definition is given to a word." Nevertheless, Croce does not object to terms like *tragedy, comedy,* and *drama* so long as they are used only "to draw attention to certain groups of works, in general and approximately" (Croce 1953, 38). His objection is to any claim that these terms *mean* anything in themselves or that the terms constitute any knowledge about the texts attended to. Croce's objection is rooted in his assumption that there are two separate ways of knowing: scientific or literary. In his view, "definitions" are formally associated with scientific understanding and therefore precluded from being relevant to literary meaning. Croce's vehement opposition to the constitutive aspect of genre in the interpretation of literary texts comes from his setting the "expressiveness" of the texts over and against the "conceptual nature" of criticism. This schema necessarily excludes genre from any vital role in the literary work itself.

But is Croce's exclusion of "conception" from "expression" logical? In his comprehensive history of genre theory, Klaus Willi Hempfer highlights the epistemological stakes in thinking about genres in relation to literature. He outlines two positions—the nominalist and the realist—and analyzed Croce's work as illustrative of the nominalist position.[15]

The nominalist position is constructed over and against the naive realist position and shares the latter's shortcomings. By relegating genres to the status of "mere" abstractions, nominalists overlook the ways in which genres are operative before, during, and subsequent to the reading of specific texts. Moreover, nominalists seem unmindful that in their claim that the expressiveness of literary texts is unique, they have created an abstraction that both shapes the reception of texts and confines them within a peculiarly narrow history of language.

In *The Fantastic: A Structural Approach to a Literary Genre* (1973), Tzvetan Todorov also answers Croce's objections by explicating how genre functions in the act of interpreting a text. Todorov treats genre as hypothesis and differentiates genre from descriptive and explanatory accounts of the meaningfulness of texts. In his theory, genre is a "principle operative in a number of texts, rather than what is specific about each of them" (p. 3). First of all, Todorov posits that a genre is epistemologically different from an individual text. He insists that the notion of structure is not to be understood as referring to an empirical reality but to a model constructed according to that reality. In Todorov's understanding, the structure that comes to light in a proper generic study does not claim to reproduce the experience involved in writing or in reading the book. What the structure does is to provide a representation, a cluster of meanings—a model constructed after the understanding of the reality. The model provides a context for communicating what goes beyond the particular constitutive meanings of a text. To go from knowledge of a genre to the structure of a given work is not to impose meaning on the empirical reality of a text but rather to incur the original process of arriving at a genre, that is, of distancing, abstracting, or generalizing from the particular and of relating it to whatever else we know. In Todorov's theory there is no necessity that any given work embody its genre—there is only a probability that a work may do so. But, we might add, if the genre and the text are carefully understood, there is a true probability that a text will be better understood by being read in the light of different generic propositions. In addition, any adequate and appropriate under-standing will involve the text in some kind of relation to other texts.

A genre is not, strictly speaking, invalidated by an exception. *Finnegans Wake,* for example, although generally referred to as a novel, has from the time of its publication plagued critics with respect to the way it relates to that genre. Such difficult-to-classify works preserve the integrity of genre as a concept, even more effectively than texts that ostensibly "fit" well-defined genres, in the sense that they expose the simultaneous necessity and limita-tions of genric and gendered considerations. Such necessity and limitation are the gist of Jacques Derrida's classic essay "The Law of Genre" (1980). For Derrida, whether recognized or not, the individual text functions as a "law" of genre. One could say that the individual person functions similarly as a "law" of gender in the sense that she forces the question of what it means to "have" a gender or to manifest those characteristics of what it means to "be" a gender (Butler 1990, 7–8). This view of genre is comple-mentary to that of Todorov, who holds that genre does not define the text and therefore should not be treated as a logical category. Instead genre functions as a hypothesis that calls forth rigorous reflection on the complex factors that make individual works successful or not. In this sense, the empirical reality of a particular text exposes that text's many possible relationships to the genre and gender hypotheses we use to organize our response to it. Genre theory forces us to formulate our own notion of the in-forming principle of texts—texts we might otherwise leave at the level of vague enjoyment or unexamined antipathy.

Genre theory ensures that we maintain a crucial distinction between the genre-specific organizing principle vis-à-vis any read text and the possible genres that can be brought to apply to that text in a particular culture. That Oscar Wilde's *The Picture of Dorian Grey* (1891) has been read as a fable does not preclude other readings, such as that of the literature of paradox. Gender theory ensures that we maintain a crucial distinction between any particular historical-cultural construal of gender vis-à-vis any particular individual and the imaginable configurations of gender that can be realized in that culture. That women in religious orders during the Middle Ages were understood, in their surpassing of prevailing definitions of gender, as men does not preclude other readings of their gender, such as those invoked by an economic analysis of the value of their work or a political analysis of their unavailability for the production of children. Both the actual and the imaginable construals of both genre and gender are time-bound and can change over time and culture. This fluidity makes any distinction between literal and figurative understanding of limited, if not dubious, usefulness. In addition, gender and genre theory enables us to take distance from our immediate experience of a text and to take stock of the ways in which both genre and gender can be said to "produce" something in the world and in the reader's self-understanding. The question of precisely what each produces has a fourth dimension, to which we give the name *praxis*.

GENRE AND GENDER AS PRAXIS-ORIENTED

From Marxist criticism to liberation theology, the notion of praxis has brought about an important correction in the ways we conceive of genre and gender. The term *praxis* calls attention to the practical inseparability of theory from practice. In this sense, praxis supersedes the three foregoing characteristics—genre and gender as constitutive of meaning, as historical, and as theoretical—by insisting that we ask about the ends and purposes of their particular construals. What are the results of any particular genric analysis and of the process of genre differentiation? What are the ends and purposes of any particular gender analysis and of the process of gender identification? Are gender distinctions stereotypical, resulting in mere duplication, or do they clarify or subvert conventional and otherwise invisible forces? With the question of praxis, the author's discourse becomes an explicitly public phenomenon, for it is at the level of praxis that the question of the effect of work becomes an explicit topic of inquiry and debate.

An example of how gender is an issue in the praxis of genre can be found in the history of the novel. As a genre, the novel rose in conjunction with the aspirations and the achievements of the middle class in Europe and Great Britain. In the hierarchy of established genres, the novel ranked low. Not having to prove their mastery of the classical tradition, novelists were regarded as undisciplined popularizers for an audience of the uneducated masses. Not only educated men but women as well became novelists, because the genre could be practiced with the resources women had at hand and because the genre did not demand a classical training, which was inaccessible to most women.

Feminist literary history of the novel brings to light other gender implications of the novel genre:

(1) Whenever the novel has been treated as a substandard genre, it has been systematically associated with feminine traits, which are in turn presented as opposite to reigning male values. For example, the novel is regarded as "soft," "rambling," "homey," whereas classical poetry is "chiseled," "patterned," and "aristocratic."

(2) Contrariwise, whenever the novel has been treated as a serious genre, males have been credited with the major contributions to the genre. Even in Ian Watt's *Rise of the Novel* (1975), for example, which shows uncommon sensitivity to the issue of the representation of women in eighteenth- and nineteenth-century novels, brief mention is made of only seven novels by seven women authors, whereas 148 complete pages are devoted to sixty novels by thirty-eight authors.[16] And yet we know from comments (e.g., by Sir Walter Scott and others) that there were at least as many noteworthy novels by women as by men at that time, possibly even more. Notwithstanding this imbalance, Watt's study documents the way the novel contributed to the growing consciousness of the subordinate status of women in society. Watt was one of the first to notice the reciprocal effects of the production of the novel by and for the middle class: most novelists were themselves of the middle class and were responsible for imagining it as it came to be known. However, Watt does not take notice of a radical decline in the number of published novels by women between 1880 and 1900. This decline, until now inexplicable, has led some feminist critics to seek an explanation in some kind of backlash to the success of women novelists before that period. Could it be that the almost century-long domination of the novel by women was followed by a period during which their work was publicly repressed (Stubbs, 1979)?

(3) Once the issue of the production of the novel in relation to social history was raised, the question of praxis followed. Since the 1970s critics have been increasingly aware that one of the products of the novel (and of popular films and songs) is an uncritical understanding of gender. By fulfilling the expectations of how contemporary women and men act, novels succeed in

attracting readerships. But the novels also create their own reader-ship by confirming the parameters of what behavior is acceptable to be imagined for males and females in a given society. Plato did not solve the problem by his strictures based on gender definitions.

Questions of literary praxis have been raised by theorists such as Georg Lukács, Fredric Jameson, Walter Benjamin, and Terry Eagleton, who apply Marxist theory in literary criticism, at-tempting to distinguish the effects of certain genres as Marxists attempt to specify the effects of different kinds of labor.[17] Genre in relation to praxis is also a familiar notion to contemporary composition theorists, whose attempts to revise the traditional "modes of discourse" (narration, description, exposition, and ar-gument) have emphasized aim or rhetorical purpose as the primary basis for differentiating verbal forms (Kinneavy 1980, 37–52). In sociolinguistics genre is used broadly to refer to different types of recurring, recognizable speech events. Here, the smallest units of speech acts—for example, interjections, opening remarks, excla-mations, questions—are studied for their effect on the context of larger speech events, such as prayers, lectures, arguments, conversations.[18] These speech acts can be said to be rhetorical as soon as they are identified as producing specified responses and results in a given society. Although some literary theorists are more skeptical than others that texts "belonging to" major genres—for example, epic, dramatic, lyric—possess enough specifiable similarities to warrant the expectations that their sig-nificant rhetorical features generate predictable results, these same theorists continue to use familiar genric terms and to create new ones.[19] More recently genre in relation to praxis has come to play a role in some other disciplines as well. In theology, for example, one can find the praxis dimension of genre in Charles Strain's (1978) construction of the genre of "social gospel." One issue of *Yale French Studies* (Johnson 1982), entitled *The Pedagogical Imperative: Teaching as a Literary Genre,* explores the praxis element of genre in the field of education. One analysis of speech behavior according to gender concludes that women frequently ask questions for clarification when they wish to take issue with what has been said. The effect of their substitution of one kind of question for the other frequently produces a perception (some-times by themselves as well as by others) of them as uninformed inquirers rather than as equal participants in serious critical discourse. This gender analysis presumes a significant number of men who conceive of women either as in need of clarification or as potentially equal participants, but not as both.

Paul Ricoeur's work on genre as praxis is of special interest, since he treated genre in the context of some of the most vexed philosophical issues (e.g., imagination and ideology) and offered new arguments to overcome old stalemates and dichotomies.[20] Ricoeur has made two important contributions to the discussion of genre. The first is his notion of genre as a means of production in the *writing* of a text—a notion that offers a basis for my emphasis on genre as a means of production as well in the reading of a text. In his view, genres produce discourse as a work: "To master a genre is to master a 'competence' which offers practical guidelines for 'performing' an individual work" (Ricoeur 1973b, 135). By means of genre, the author's work becomes a public phenomenon. Genre keeps the author's discourse open for "fresh interpretations in new situations" and, at the same time, preserves it from distortions. Ricoeur compares the generative function of grammar, as demonstrated by Noam Chomsky, with the generative function of literary genres: the function of genre "is to mediate between speaker and hearer by establishing a common dynamics capable of ruling both the production of discourse as a work of a certain kind and its interpretation according to the rules provided by the genre." Here, the "dynamics of form" are simultaneously a "dynamics of thought" (ibid., 137). That is, the meaning-oriented content itself is produced at the same level as the corresponding principles of literary genre. To produce a text is to say something *about* something, where the saying shapes what is said by means of genric choices.

Ricoeur's second contribution is his extension of the notion of "work" to both author and reader. For him a "work" is constituted by genric principles of composition and individual style: "Even the term 'work' reveals the nature of these new categories, which are those of production and of labor. To impose a form upon material, to subject a production to genres, and to produce an individual style are ways of considering language as a material to be worked and formed. They are the ways in which discourse becomes the object of a praxis" (ibid., 136). Both the author and the reader can be said to possess a competence with respect to the literary work. Reader competence is similar to authorial competence in the sense that both rely upon genric expectations—in the case of the author, to produce the work, and in the case of the reader, "to perform the corresponding operations of interpretation" (ibid.). The "correspondence" to which Ricoeur refers is complex rather than simple, as the term might suggest. One result of expecting a correspondence, however, is a new basis for calling into question the commonsense notions of "author" and "reader." Ricoeur transposed the notion of author from that of one who speaks to that of one who produces an individual work.

Similarly, we can transpose the notion of reader from that of one who merely listens or follows directions to that of one who produces an individual interpretation. By this transposition, the category of reader becomes as much in need of interpretation as the interpretation produced. For example, the contemporary reader who interprets *Alice in Wonderland* as social criticism is involved in the production of new meaning analogous to the way in which the author produced the original text. The same reader can be said to be a "product" of that interpretation in the sense of having been shaped by what it is possible to think in that historical-cultural context. When someone says, "That question didn't occur to me at the time," they give evidence of the productive power of concepts and interpretations. No longer is Plato's cobbler only the maker of shoes; the cobbler's body and intelligence are marked by what he has made. Gender demarcations of appearances, scent, manner of walking "produce" what we call male or female, feminine or masculine. No longer is the author a self-evident creator, nor is the reader a self-evident decoder of a particular text.

Since 1970 a strong praxis orientation can also be found in French semiotics. In her essay "The Bounded Text," for example, Julia Kristeva wishes to do away with the rhetorical study of genres and to replace it with a "typology of texts" based on the way texts exist in culture and the way in which culture is part of them (Kristeva 1980, 36). She holds that the text "intersects" with the cultural utterances it includes and the semiotic practices by which it refers outside itself. She calls the intersections "ideologemes" (ibid., 37). Genre, in Kristeva's work, is a pattern of choices inscribed in the way the text is written, choices that are both dictated by and reflected in a given historical and cultural milieu.

Kristeva applies this notion of genre to the novel by tracing the shift in the basis for thought from the symbol to the sign in Western literature during the Middle Ages through the late eighteenth century. Although her analysis is too complex to summarize, the results are accessible. Kristeva finds that the novel displays the pre-nineteenth-century pattern (ideologeme) of "closure, non-disjunction, and linking of deviations." By "closure" she means that the conclusion of the novel is "given" in what the reader is told at the beginning of the novel (title, purpose, audience, subject). What is in between makes sense only in terms of what the reader already knows. By "non-disjunction" Kristeva points to the mainspring of the novel: a thematic structure built on the "interplay between two exclusive oppositions," which alternate and advance the plot. By "linking of deviations" she indicates that the two opposing terms are admitted to be irreducible only to the extent that the space separating them is filled with ambiguous combinations of meaning. Sometimes one of the terms is repressed in what is asserted to be "before" the events in the novel; sometimes one of the opposing terms is revealed to be false or ambivalent such that the originally posited opposition turns out to be neither explicit nor logically necessary (ibid., 52). What appeared to be deviations—circumstances calling for affirmation or negation—are replaced instead by a sense of "doubtful positivity" (ibid., 43).

Kristeva holds that the praxis dimension of interpretation is intrinsic to the first reading of the text: praxis is not a separate effort to find what is "ideological" after the meanings have been formulated (ibid., 36–37). Knowing the "production factors" of a work, in other words, directs the choice of analysis—or we could say, the genre—that is appropriate for interpreting the work as a whole.

With Kristeva's analysis of the novel genre we have come a great distance from the notion that the novel is not serious literature because it does not require sophisticated literary prowess, such as only men in Western culture are capable of developing. Can we not also begin to see a relationship between the "doubtful positivity" of the novel and the ambiguities that surround gender differentiations within a critical understanding?

GENRE AND GENDER IN THE HERMENEUTICAL SPIRAL

We are now ready to begin to construct a model of the critical reader in the light of the preceding generic considerations. What

34

characterizes the ideal reader? The hermeneutics of suspicion fashioned by Nietzsche, Freud, and Marx has already demythologized the notion of the reader either as standing objectively disengaged from the work or as innocently engaged. Aesthetic distance has had to make room for aesthetic immanence,[21] which, in turn, has had to incorporate the carnival of inverted relations and endless deferral of meaning. For all that, we have not had a model for a reader who is both engaged with a particular work and knowledgeable of the succession of forms which can be seen to inform it.

Throughout this book the role of the reader is emphasized in relation to the determination of genre—the author as the first reader of the text and the reader as the instantiation of meaning (either constructive or deconstructive) vis-à-vis the text. The model of genre proposed emphasizes the cognitive activity of the reader. The process of genre testing introduced in chapter 6 is grounded in the activity of the reader, and the issue of genric competence is a correlate of the ability to read at all.

Knowing genre in this way, what can we know about authors and readers that is impossible to know without an explicit knowledge of genre? First, we know that authors do in fact tend to invest in a relatively limited number, rather than a multitude of genres. Even when authors do have broad competence with respect to composing in several genres, they are most often known in terms of one genre. James Joyce, for example, wrote drama, short stories, poetry, and essays, but his most recognized work is in the novel. Some correlations between genders and genres can be made,[22] but more recently women have appeared as writers of what were formerly perceived as "male" genres, such as detective fiction and sports stories. Since genre and gender are both imaginative constructs, inextricable from related constructs of identity, such as class, race, and ethnicity, there seems to be no theoretical basis for excluding male or female authorship in any genre, although matter-of-fact necessity can be reasonably invoked for historical examples. To be comprehensive, any assessment of authorial investment in genres would also have to include variations on genders—which ones are opposed and by whom, which perfected, which modified, and which experimented with in the field of genres at any given time. This assessment could include, although it is not limited to, those plot variations called "genres of life-plots," listed by Wayne Booth in *The Company We Keep* (1988, 289):

35

. . . from high promise to happiness to misery; from beginning misery to happiness to misery; from misery to misery to maximum misery) . . . from happiness to happiness to misery; from happiness to happiness to a higher happiness (for example, that rare thing, a reconciled death); from promise to promise to sudden accidental death. And so on. Let your imagination range as freely as you will, add other possibilities ("from virtue to vice to virtue," "from ignorance to revelation," and so on), and you will still fairly soon run out of genres.

We can take Booth's last statement to affirm that correlations between genres and gender constructs are determinable for any given historical-cultural context.

Second, we know that readers in fact may read in either a broad or narrow spectrum of genres. Apart from the study of genre recognition among filmgoers and readers of popular fiction, such as the Harlequin romances, other empirical testing of genres as conditions of production and reception has been conducted by German critics working with Siegfried Schmidt at the Universität Siegen. Readers (and authors as readers) are likely to have developed competence in a broader range of genres than have authors (and readers as authors).

Some readers, of course, evade the question of the epistemological and ethical status of the genres they choose to read and enjoy. Most readers, however, will in fact create priorities among the genres in which they claim competence. Creating priorities responds to the need to make explicit one's reasons for investing intellectually and sometimes ethically and emotionally in some texts rather than others. Such reasons, however difficult to formulate, require some reference both to genre and to gender. With the attempt to formulate reasons, we can expect a better understanding of how some readers adopt several genres as their own.

By means of genric and gender considerations the knowledgeable reader becomes the critical reader, who is in turn capable of questioning how these forms and expressions undergo revision and mutual refinement in the text. In this sense, genric and gender considerations are essential to text interpretation. History is no longer a sequence of events and conditions that provide a context for the meaning of a text, but rather a knowledge of the changing forms of constructs—including those of one's own inquiry—that serve to retrieve and to revivify the text. Genre and gender theory are no longer abstractions imposed on individual texts but rather those self-conscious hypotheses and systematic relations made by the reader-become-interpreter. Finally, reflection on genre and gender may bring about a new role for the reader-become-writer— a role that is no longer passive and receptive but active and suspecting as well as affirming and creative.

People read various texts for various reasons, of course, and not every text requires assiduous analysis. But for anyone who aspires to be a critical reader, some texts will invite sustained and critical attention. For the latter, the critical reader proceeds from naive questions about the text to critical questions of its historicity, its structure, its informing principle, and finally to the most difficult question of all—that of the reader's self-understanding as reflected in the reader's understanding of the text. We might say that any understanding of the text is refracted by means of these questions. But these refractions are held together in a new and more complex hermeneutical model, one best understood by comparing it with alternate models of what critics refer to as the "hermeneutical circle."

The earliest version of the hermeneutical circle is probably that taken from Anselm's famous ontological argument (c. 1070 C.E.). There the formulation is exclusively in terms of the activities of the human subject: "Believe in order to understand; understand in order to believe" (Fig. 1). Anselm argued that to deny the existence of something, one had to have some understanding of it (in his case, God). But aside from the merits of his argument itself, which continue to be debated, Anselm's way of showing the interdependence of belief and understanding retains its cogency. It also postpones indefinitely the dilemma, posed in Plato's *Meno,* of understanding anything, which we recognized in the Introduction as being our problem with respect to genre.

A second formulation of the hermeneutical circle is the conventional literary critical formulation, found in Hirsch's work (1967): a text is always understood in relation to its parts, and the parts are understood in light of the whole text (Fig. 2). A variation of Hirsch's formulation is found in Murray Krieger's notion of the vicious circle, which he invoked in his *Theory of Criticism* (1976, 160). Krieger suggests that readers are disposed to remain entrapped in the process of their own experiencing (Fig. 3). Krieger's exemplary case is Reverend Hightower, the main character in

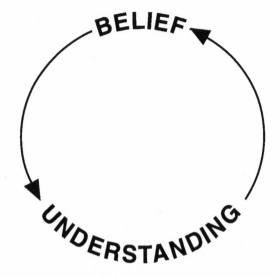

Fig. 1. Early hermeneutical circle based on Anselm's dictum, "Believe in order to understand; understand in order to believe."

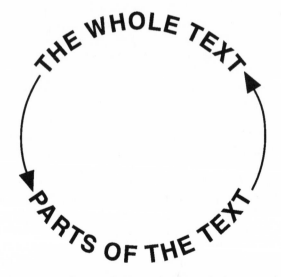

Fig. 2. Literary critical hermeneutical circle based on Hirsch's claim that a text is understood in relation to its parts, while the parts are understood in relation to the whole.

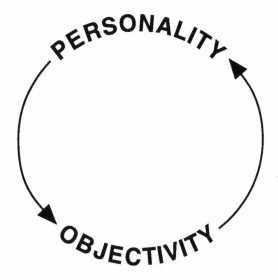

Fig. 3. Krieger's hermeneutical circle, in which objectivity is a deceptive "charade" played out by the reader's own personality.

William Faulkner's *Light in August,* who undergoes a major transformation when he delivers Lena Grove's child. Formerly a recluse, Hightower is converted to action and the ideal of fecundity. This conversion is signified by his giving up reading Tennyson and turning instead to Shakespeare's *Henry IV* for what he calls "food for a man," ostensibly, of course, for the man he has become. "This reference to literature as 'food,' " Krieger writes, "suggests clearly enough the notion that a reader matches his literary work to his prior needs, and then absorbs it into himself, forcing it to serve his own bodily functions." Krieger reformulates this example into a question about the hermeneutical circle: "Are we doomed only to project our own imaginative forms outward . . . turning all works into essentially the same work, even though we persuade ourselves we are but responding to a variety of external features whose uniformity of pattern seems to confirm our hypothesis about them? In his hermeneutic circularity does the critic's every claim to objectivity reduce to this charade played out by his own personality in order to deceive—most of all— himself?" (ibid., 43–44).

If Krieger's way of posing the problem is confined to literary texts, Christopher Lasch (1976) levels a more general indictment with another version of the hermeneutical circle. Lasch describes a "new narcissism"—a "retreat to purely personal satisfactions"—which he considers the chief danger to the political life of the nation: "To live for the moment is the prevailing passion—to live for yourself, not for your predecessors or posterity. We are fast losing the sense of historical continuity, the sense of belonging to a succession of generations originating in the past and stretching into the future" (p. 6). By calling attention to perversions of the act of reading, however, Krieger and Lasch assist in the task of making explicit the principles operative in a reader's critical appropriation of texts. They each show how the traditional model of the hermeneutical circle can be manipulated. Their demonstrations can be clarified by a pair of optical allusions—which, to admirers of Nietzsche, might recall his assertion in *The Birth of Tragedy* that "both art and life depend wholly on the laws of optics, on perspective and illusion; both, to be blunt, depend on the necessity of error" (Nietzsche [1872] 1956, 42). Krieger, for example, is skeptical of the reader's ability to transcend what could become a vicious circle (see Fig. 3), and Lasch charges that the narcissism of his age makes the text into a mirror surface from which only the reader's self-image is reflected (Fig. 4).

Important innovations in the concept of the hermeneutical circle have been made. For example, Ricoeur's best-known formulation of the circle, "The symbol gives rise to thought; thought is informed by symbol," occurs in his early work (Ricoeur 1960, 348–49) (Fig. 5).[23] He later speaks of the dangers of a "too psychological" understanding of the hermeneutical circle: "For behind believing there is the primacy of the object of faith over faith; and behind understanding there is the primacy of exegesis and its method over the naive reading of the text. This means that the genuine hermeneutic circle is not psychological but methodological. It is the circle constituted by the object that regulates faith and the method that regulates understanding. There is a circle because the exegete is not his own master" (Ricoeur 1974, 389).

Bernard Lonergan (1972) acknowledges that the hermeneutic circle is only theoretically a circle, since "coming to understand is not a logical deduction." His model (Fig. 6) represents a "self-correcting process of learning that spirals into the meaning of the whole by using each new part to fill out and qualify and correct

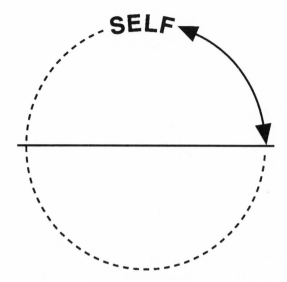

Fig. 4. Hermeneutical circle remnant under Lasch's charge that the text is a mirrored surface that reflects the reader's image.

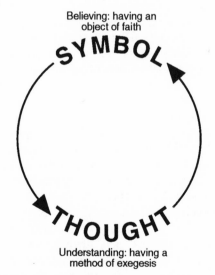

Fig. 5. Hermeneutical circle based on Ricoeur's formulation, "The symbol gives rise to thought; thought is informed by symbol."

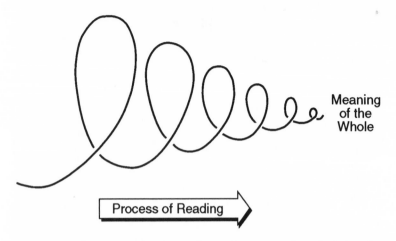

Process of Reading

Fig. 6. Lonergan's hermeneutical "self-correcting process that spirals into the meaning of the whole."

the understanding reached in reading the earlier parts" (p. 159). Ray Hart (1968, 60–68) also shifts to the notion of a spiral and correlates extension and intension, reflection and reflexion in his model. Although none of the foregoing theorists raise the issue of genre explicitly, their concerns include genric considerations. Their analyses point up the need for genric and gender considerations in any new model of the hermeneutical circle.

In our new model, the hermeneutical circle is represented as a spiral (Fig. 7) correlating successive readings with successive understandings of a text. According to this model, we have pre-conceptions of gender when we begin reading a text. Without any knowledge of the text, we bring gender attributes to bear from the first moment of reading, and as we read the text for the first time we formulate an assumption about its genre. The first reading leads to a first understanding focused through first-order genric and gender considerations. The reader's horizon—her capacity for seeing and for asking questions—is likely to undergo the largest change on a first reading of the text because the text constitutes a potentially new field of meanings, both surprising and challenging to the reader. After several readings, the reader's understanding of the text can be expected to stabilize, with each subsequent reading yielding less change in understanding. The reader's horizon expands with each reading of a given text. In the

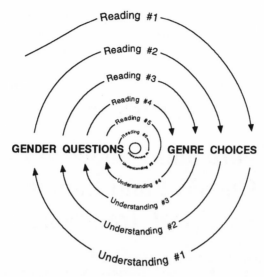

Fig. 7. My model, a hermeneutical spiral, in which successive readings of the text, under the influence of genre choices and gender questions, lead to successively more refined understandings, which finally stabilize as an irreducible interpretation.

absence of other information, however, the understanding will converge on an irreducible interpretation. Some early interpreters conceived of the possibility that one text (e.g., the Bible alone) would be enough for some readers' growth in understanding. In this model of the process of interpretation, the circle at the center is the irreducible understanding of a particular text by a particular reader. Instead of being represented by a single circle as in the traditional model, here the spiral repeatedly curves inward over time. Each loop is only a part of the process of interpretation, and the individual reader is both acted upon and acting.

No longer vicious, the hermeneutical circle now signifies the essential roles of critical thought after naive reading and of informed understanding after thought. Becoming informed by raising genric and gender questions, the reader's understanding is transformed by the fullness and meaning represented by a text.

CHAPTER TWO

Genre and Gender in the Classical and Literary Critical Traditions

The exclusion of the feminine has not resulted from a conspiracy by male philosophers. . . . In some cases it happened despite the conscious intent of the authors.

Genevieve Lloyd, The Man of Reason *(1984, 108–9)*

Genre and gender both have histories. As constructs of thought, both their meanings and referents vary across time and cultures. Nevertheless, they share a common tendency to be overlooked in favor of more imminent reality or to be taken for granted. Too often the relationships between them have been ignored even when made visible. Etymologically, they come from the same root word[1] and hold several family relationships in common. Nouns that appear to be grammatically neuter in English have been gendered for ages in the languages that are the basis of English. "Poetry" in Greek is feminine, for example, while "poet" is masculine in grammatical gender. In the United States, it was not until the 1960s that some publications began to make a systematic effort to be gender-inclusive in pronouns referring to human beings (Miller and Swift 1976; McConnell-Ginet 1980). The ways in which genres have been gender-specific are more varied than ways identified in psychoanalysis, linguistic grammar, and syntax.[2] The relationships between genre and gender are logically fluid but not neutral in terms of value. Feminist criticism has taught us that the history of genre and the history of gender have more in common than we might expect.[3]

44

•

Their coordinate history could be told in several ways. One way would be to show how the dominant gender has exercised control of the major genres. In the classical worlds of both East and West, detailed prescriptions on the subjects and styles of written languages were taught in the schools. In the Middle Ages of Europe and Japan, for example, the male gender was virtually identified with those specific genres promoted and legitimated by the schools insofar as formal instruction in the rules was forbidden to women, the poorly born, and members of minority cultures (Kolb 1989).[4] In Greek and Hebrew writing whose authorship is lost or disputed, texts of lyric poetry are more likely to be attributed to women than are texts of other genres. But the likelihood of female authorship is often repressed in the case of some classical genres, such as medieval songs, for which there is evidence of composition by women. Male domination and defense of the major genres as their creation has produced some embarrassingly sexist arguments. Peggy Kamuf (1980) has given an account of the disputed authorship of *The Portuguese Letters* (1669), showing how the genre issue of whether the letters are authentic or forged is directly related to the issue of gender. Because the letters exhibit literary prowess, they have been most often regarded as fictional (or forged) on the grounds that a woman would not have had the literary skill to produce them. Kamuf argued on the contrary that, notwithstanding historical and cultural probabilities, genre and voice are literary constructs and are not determined by the biological gender of the author. Yet both Mary Ellmann (1968) and Jacques Derrida (1980) have elaborated ways in which the act of writing has been perceived in relation to biological sex. Ellmann, for example, in her early and now classic analysis of a number of sexual analogies, notices that when the "female mind" is discussed, creativity is never mentioned. Discussions of the "male mind," however, readily associate male authorship with the act of giving birth.

Another way of telling the coordinate history of gender and genre presupposes the first but goes further to show how, in spite of the domination of genres by one gender, women's voices occasionally developed into a counterculture that eventuated in new spoken genres and eventually in new written genres. Elizabeth Schüssler Fiorenza (1983) reads the Gospel of John, written a decade or so later than the synoptics, as evidence that exclusively male discipleship was challenged by women and men in the early Christian community. The early Christian tradition was remarkably tolerant of diverse and even subversive genres: the genres of prophecy and speaking in tongues, for example, were at one time viewed as qualifications for the office of bishop. These same genres were later regarded as suspect, to be kept under control by leaders who exercised power exclusively through other genres (Schüssler Fiorenza 1983, 302) and who labored to exclude women from leadership roles.

A radical example of the creation of a new genre as a countercultural revolt is that of amorous epistolary discourse. This genre seems to have developed in opposition to the epic. According to Linda Kauffman (1986, 32), "amorous epistolary discourse is, paradoxically, antigeneric and anticanonical; it engulfs and is engulfed by other languages and other cultures, and it assimilates other genres—Sapphic lyrics, authentic letters, Roman elegies, the soliloquies of tragic heroines." Although he did not invent the genre of amorous epistle, Ovid was one of the earliest writers deliberately to cultivate its subversive potential and to make explicit the relationship between gender and genre. Kauffmann argues that the growing respectability of the love letter, a construct for the disclosure of women's interior lives, brought about a radical displacement in the ranking of classical genres.

To use the lens of gender and genre is to imagine "history wrong side out," as Virginia Woolf put it.[5] This act of imagining is equivalent to reconstructing the history of texts in the light of the newly visible relationships between gender and genre. As Janet Todd (1988, 99) argues,

> The critic emphasizing genre cannot use history simply as a kind of background, as a given from another discipline which will illuminate our own. She is forced to probe ideology in its specific deployment in literary form. Such a method works to deconstruct the powerful ideology of established literary periods or movements, like the Augustan, the Romantic, or the Modern, in such a way that the critic can begin to avoid being dominated by the self-representations of their exponents. The method can also be added to the study of popular culture so that genres that have been despised as popular or feminine can be illuminated and the uncanonized can be connected with the canonized."

New questions arise from the reworking of literary history in the light of gender and genre.

In her own study of the literature of sensibility, *Sensibility: An Introduction* (1986), Todd finds that the concept of sensibility contributed to the decline of the concept of "subject" among both male and female writers. She illustrates how the concept of sensibility, disdained today, formerly aroused brisk philosophical debate. Helen Maria Williams's little-known sentimental eyewitness accounts of French revolutionary events were superseded by Mary Wollstonecraft's later denunciation of sensibility as dangerous and self-indulgent.[6] But Williams's accounts could also be read in conjunction with those of her contemporary Georg-Wilhelm Friedrich Hegel (1977), especially his little-cited chapter "The Law of the Heart," in *The Phenomenology of Spirit* (1807). By making both genred and gendered comparisons in the history of sensibility, we can begin to raise better critical questions, such as whether Wollstonecraft's derogatory account of sensibility succeeded because it was co-opted into the frequently misogynistic link between female and feeling.

Today we have begun to expect that histories of genres will yield some bases for answering these crucial critical questions. It was not always thus. The view that genre can be more than a principle of classification is a relatively recent development. As late as 1965 the article on genre in the *Princeton Encyclopedia of Poetry and Poetics,* by G. N. G. Orsini, concluded by noticing the breakdown of the classical view of genre that had taken place in the last fifty years. Tracing the career of the word *genre* from the time of Plato and Aristotle, Orsini pointed out that the lyric had been excluded from almost all pre-nineteenth-century studies of genre and cited its omission as an example of what he called the fickleness of genric classification. Orsini was pessimistic regarding the prospects for genre as a viable concept in criticism: "The most radical rejection of genre in modern times was made by Croce, who considered them mere abstractions, useful in the construction of classifications for practical convenience, but of no value as aesthetic categories." But Orsini modeled his notion of genric typification on a rudimentary kind of classification and blamed nineteenth-century philosophy for the prolongation of what he regarded a futile categorizing: "It can be imagined to what a riot of dialectic it led in Hegel's Aesthetic, which should have been a warning, but acted instead as an incentive to the metaphysical aestheticians of the nineteenth century, each with his own system of the arts and of the genre" (Orsini 1965, 338). Clearly, for Orsini and, I imagine, for many readers of this influential handbook on literary theory, genre is defunct.

Orsini was not the first to cite the inadequacy of genre as classification. In his brief study of the concept of "genus universum," Michel Beaujour mentions two efforts to surpass genre as mere category in the history of criticism. A first attempt can be seen in the claim that the *Iliad,* the *Odyssey,* and some Romantic texts contain all existing genres and therefore themselves belong to no genre. A second effort to surpass genre as category can be found in the claim that the Bible transcends all genres because divine revelation precludes being genric, that is, bound by any literary form. Why have these two attempts not been persuasive? Today these claims appear to be naive and uncritical: they reject some traditional genres only to reinforce, at the same time, the traditional view of genre by continuing the debate over the same issues and in largely the same terms. The nadir of theoretical studies of genre came in the 1960s when genre theory began to concern itself with issues of classification within narrow fields of study. Such work, which had lost its base in theory, was called "universal journalism," by the poet Mallarmé (Beaujour 1980).

Recent studies of the history of genre theory have led theorists to correct the misunderstanding that genre is mere category. The search for the origins of the tripartite division of literature into epic, dramatic, and lyric, for example, has been converted into a fascinating record of misstatements and partial understandings of genre in the history of thought from Plato to the present. Furthermore, it has been shown that those who research the origins of particular genres often themselves fall into the archaistic fallacy of thinking that once the origins of a genre have been determined, its normativeness has been established.

THE CLASSICAL DISPUTE BETWEEN PLATO AND ARISTOTLE

It has long been stylish to take sides with either Plato or Aristotle on specific issues such as value or virtue. On the issue of genre, however, Plato is seldom recognized even as having a position.

One of the tasks in retrieving the concept from classical thought is to compare and contrast Plato's and Aristotle's views on the topic of genre. There is no evidence that Aristotle referred to Plato on this subject. Nevertheless, since it is likely that Aristotle was acquainted with Plato's position and since together their views continue to prevail in the West, a comparison of their treatments is useful, even if their strategies and ways of thinking about genre are largely incommensurable.

Aristotle's views on tragedy have indisputably been the classical model for understanding genre. In his widely cited systematic study of the history of genre theory from the classical time to the present, Gérard Genette (1977) shows how misunderstandings of Aristotle's *Poetics* gave rise, by the seventeenth century, to the traditionalist tripartite division of genres (narrative, dramatic, lyric). Genette thinks that Aristotle in effect ignores the lyric by restricting his poetics to mimesis. It is legitimate, Genette holds, to attribute to Aristotle alone only two theories: the tragic/comic and the epic. A plausible reason for Aristotle's exclusion of the lyric is that his major concern was to retrieve imitative poetry from Plato's narrow view of it. One should, according to Genette, attribute the genre lyric to Plato, in his category of "pure narrative" (the poet using his own words and thoughts), which Plato distinguishes from "imitation" (the poet using the character's words and gestures instead of his own). Genette argues further that although the tripartite division of genres cannot be attributed to either Plato or Aristotle, there is no good reason to question its usefulness for later theorists.[7] For our purpose, too, the significance of Plato's and Aristotle's work, taken together, is more important than the shortcomings of either taken alone. Together, Plato and Aristotle display two representative attitudes toward literature as well as two complementary views of genre.

If we were to imagine a debate between Plato and Aristotle on the subject of genre, the most explicit motivation for the debate would be the raison d'être of art. A comparison between Plato's and Aristotle's attitudes toward art and poetry might lead us to believe that Plato was conservative to the point of wishing to exclude art altogether from the life of a good citizen and that Aristotle was liberal to the extent of crediting art as a good in itself, apart from its effects. Iris Murdoch reminds us, however, that there may not be sufficient reason to think that Plato was completely opposed to poets. As she writes in her book on Plato, *The Fire and the Sun,* "Plato did not banish all the artists or always suggest banishing any" (Murdoch 1977, 1). Murdoch reminds us also that Plato sometimes associates art with divinity: in *Phaedrus,* for example, he describes artists as being possessed by a madness sent by the Muses, a madness that is, in truth, an indispensable blessing to poets and to humankind (Plato *Phaedrus* 244–45, 249D, 265B).

Nevertheless, in the theory of poetry he develops in the *Republic,* Plato organizes his analysis of poetry around two meanings of imitation. Imitation, in his first reading, is a "form of play, not to be taken seriously." Plato's major objection to the first kind of imitation is that it is done without the imitator's knowing anything "worth mentioning of the thing he imitates" and therefore without his having any "hold" on truth (Plato *Republic* 10: 600–601). In the *Sophist* Plato calls this kind of imitation, "conceit mimicry," which, when it is sincere, is misdirected and, when insincere, is characteristically used by demagogues and Sophists (Plato *Sophist* 267–68). Here is an explicit generic classification, based primarily on the author's intention, although it takes for granted the audience's reception as well.

In the *Republic* Plato gives several reasons for the inadequacy of sincere mimicry. A person's character is essentially too complex to be imitated by anyone else, this fact making any imitation false by deficiency. Moreover, the effect on the actor of imitating too many characters is to disperse himself among unworthy forms and perforce to become like them. Plato gives as the key example to illustrate why such imitation is bad the inappropriateness of a man's imitating a woman's feelings (Plato *Republic* 3.395). He concludes that certain kinds of imitation—such as tragedy, because it incites tyranny—should be excluded from the republic (ibid., 8.568). Changes in genre, for example, in music, are also judged to be hazardous: "A change to a new type of music is something to beware of as a hazard of all our fortunes. For the modes of music are never disturbed without unsettling of the most fundamental political and social conventions" (ibid., 4.424B). All of these examples suggest that, for Plato, imitation is to be bridled.

Notwithstanding all these reservations and cautions, a second kind of imitation appears in Plato: that which is a residue after "ignorant" (unknowing) imitation is subtracted. Plato calls this second type "mimicry by acquaintance," again calling our attention to the intrinsic connection between imitating and knowing. In this type of imitation the actor knows that he is impersonating, has a knowledge of virtue, and is acquainted with the traits and characteristics of the person impersonated. The idea of "production" in the *Sophist,* for example, has two applications: to likenesses (where it is normed by the analogy of a cobbler producing a shoe, which embodies the form "shoeness") and of semblances (where it is required to be actual, as distinct from nonexistent) (Plato *Sophist* 266E). In this passage it is not clear whether Plato's stricture in the *Republic* regarding the object of imitation—namely, that the imitation be a report of the words or the acts of a good man (Plato *Republic* 3.396)—also applies.

How do Plato's views of imitation apply to specific genres? We find one kind of attitude toward genre in the *Republic* when Socrates distinguishes between an actor who speaks in his own voice in a poem and one who only impersonates another. For Plato, only pure "narrative" can be a legitimate genre, because it is an uncompromised expression of the actor's own knowledge. Pure impersonation, however, he regards as dissimulation unless it is mixed with narrative (ibid., 3.394C). Plato's preference for the dithyramb as pure poetry also gives evidence of his belief that nothing should come between the poet's narration and his self-manifestation (ibid., 3.393). We may say that genre, in this view, becomes morphological: it is the direct, uninterrupted extension of a state of self.

Aristotle may have had the Platonic notion of imitation in mind when he tackled the problem of imitation from a different angle. Instead of evaluating imitation primarily on the basis of what is known by the actor, Aristotle values imitation primarily for what it achieves as a process in itself. In this respect, he believes that "to be learning something is the greatest of pleasures." Poetry, in the *Poetics,* provides an occasion for the actor and audience, as well as the philosopher, to attempt "to gather the meaning of things" (Aristotle *Poetics* 1448.15) Aristotle's preference for the tragic and the epic is closely related to this cognitive interest and to his appreciation of the diverse forms of persuasion and imitation, which he elaborates in the *Rhetoric* and the *Poetics,* respectively.

Of major interest in Plato's theory of imitation are the object to be imitated (whether or not it is by the artist and is worthy of imitation) and the resulting imitation (whether or not it resembles the object). Plato's generic considerations are inextricably linked to his insistence on truth by correspondence, a position he himself opposed and surpassed in his practice. Aristotle, by contrast, is careful to detach imitation from existing objects. He says, for example, that even if the object imitated has not been seen before, a pleasurable learning experience can still be had in the execution (the means and process) of the imitation. Improvisation, in the *Poetics,* is evaluated positively: improvisation creates poetry and builds on what was already created (Aristotle *Poetics* 1448.20). Here his notion leads directly to genric considerations. Of central importance is Aristotle's insistence that what is imitated or re-presented is human action and that personal agents are imitated only for the sake of the action. The concept of character—tragic, comic, or epic, as he describes them—enables the reader to ascribe certain moral "qualities" to the personal agent of an action, but character itself is always derivative from the plot or action.[8]

The authoritativeness of Plato's and Aristotle's views on genre for later criticism can be seen most clearly in neoclassical criticism, which is usually remembered for its prescriptive posture toward genres. But neoclassicism also gives ample evidence of a discrepancy between the idealism of its own theory of genre, emphasizing categories—its insistence on "pure" forms—and the prevalence of mixed forms in writing of the same period (Guillén 1971). Post-Renaissance practical criticism diverged even farther from articulated theory than did the neoclassicists, not only by frequently breaking genric prescriptions but, more significantly, introducing some new genres during that period. We may understand this change conservatively, as a discrepancy between theory and practice, or liberally, as does Renato Poggioli, as a distinction between the prescriptions of an age and its "unwritten poetics" (Poggioli 1965, 343–54). This term is especially useful to describe those early periods of criticism whose written poetics did not take emerging genres into account.

Nevertheless, the ideal of "pure" forms recurs throughout literary history. Romanticism, for example, in Philippe Lacoue-Labarthe and Jean-Luc Nancy's study (1980) of the German Romantics, desires to surpass all distinct and determinate genres:

The genre of Romantic poetry is still in the process of becoming: it is its true essence to be always only becoming and never to be capable of completing itself. . . . This inherent impossibility with Romanticism is, of course, the reason why the question [e.g., what is Romanticism, or what is literature] is actually an empty one, and why, under the rubric of Romanticism or of literature, the question only comes to bear on something indistinct and indeterminate, something that indefinitely recedes as one gets closer to it. It is something susceptible to being called (almost) any name, but not able to tolerate any one of these names. . . . Romantic texts, in their fragmentation or even their dispersion, are only the interminable answer (always approximate, neither here nor there) to the question that is really unformable, i.e., always too quickly, too lightly and too easily formulated, just as if the 'thing' worked all by itself. (Lacoue-Labarthe and Nancy 1980, 2)

In some ways, Romanticism is heir to the Platonic impulse on the question of genre. In both, the understanding of genre and gender is held hostage to the determination to keep all things tentative. In both, genre and gender issues are immediately subsumed within the issue of truth. Romanticism and Platonism discourage gender and genre analysis.

The Platonic tradition—whether more than the Aristotelian tradition, one can only surmise—has led English-writing commentators and translators to attach feminine connotations to the noun *poetry* in ways that today appear unremittingly sexist. Eric Havelock, for example, in his widely read *Preface to Plato* (1963), corrects the neoplatonic tendency to reify Plato's observations about the deleterious effects of poetry by arguing persuasively that in fourth-century B.C.E. Athens, "poetry represented not something we call by that name, but an indoctrination which today would be comprised in a shelf of text books and works of reference" (Havelock 1963, 27). Yet Havelock increases the gender bias implicit in the Greek language.

First, he adds exclusively feminine pronouns to translate all and only derogatory references to poetry. Although it is true that the gender of the word *poesis* in the Greek is grammatically feminine, there is nothing in the Greek language that necessarily personifies the concept of poetry as female. In translation it is both possible and more accurate in English to refer to *poesis* as grammatically neuter. G. M. A. Grube, for example, generally translates pronoun referents to poetry as "it." The Bollingen Series, which sometimes uses female referents and other times neuter referents for poetry, also manages to be less offensive than Havelock. Where the Bollingen Series translates line 608B as "he who lends an ear to it must be on his guard fearing for the polity in his soul," Havelock has the following: "We have our city of the soul to protect against her" (Havelock 1963, 5).

Second, Havelock refers to the poet as generically masculine. In this practice, of course, Havelock is not unlike the majority of scholars writing in 1963. Still, the combination of the exaggerated use of the feminine to refer to poetry and the exclusive use of the masculine to refer to poets might have struck an ear even slightly attuned to gender issues as odd even then. Finally, Havelock aggravates the gender bias by introducing anachronistic analogies into his commentary without any clue that they are not Plato's but solely his own. Consider the following passage:

> There has been natural reluctance to take what he says at face value. Plato's admirers, normally devoted to his lightest word, . . . start looking around for an escape hatch, and they find one which they think he has provided for them. Just before this peroration [Plato *Republic* 608B4], has he not said that poetry may offer a defence of herself if she can? Has he not confessed to her overpowering charms? Does he not admit reluctance to expel her, and does this not mean that in effect he recants? He does indeed so confess, but to think that his confession amounts to a recantation profoundly mistakes his intention. Indeed, the terms in which he makes the concession to poetry, to plead her case if she chooses, are themselves damning. For he treats her in effect as a kind of prostitute, *or as a Delilah who may seduce Plato's Samson if he lets her, and so rob him of his strength.* She can charm and coax and wheedle and enthral, but these are precisely the powers that are so fatal. (Havelock 1963, 5, emphasis added)[9]

Even those who recognize that Havelock has imported a biblical allusion may not realize that he both sanctioned and intensified the traditional gender bias against women.

Any account of the influence of Plato and Aristotle on Western criticism would be incomplete without attention to the actual use of genres by Plato and Aristotle. From their extant works, we expect Plato to be the more versatile: He so perfected the genre dialogue as a model of philosophical inquiry that even fourteen centuries later that genre is familiar as the name of his corpus of writing. Within the *Dialogues* Plato uses many other genres, including myth, ethymeme, narrative, anecdote. We know from Arabic sources, however, that Aristotle's dialogues have been lost. What we have of Aristotle's writing is almost entirely in the genre treatise. Vis-à-vis each other, the genre dialogue is more directly based in intersubjectivity and gives the illusion of representing more than one point of view. Its style is conversational. By contrast, the genre treatise is characterized by logic and systematic argument, except when it functions in the hypothetical mode, and its effect is to interrupt or to conclude a conversation.

Ironically, Plato's practice with respect to genre has been far more influential than the theory of genre implicit in his work. His use of dialogue has made that genre second only to that of treatise in the philosophical tradition. His use of myth, even though it was subsequently rejected as inappropriate to philosophy, is nonetheless important in his own work.

With respect to Plato's and Aristotle's theories, however, we recognize two polar tensions that have persisted in the understanding of genre to the present. The initial position, the Platonic argument, holds that the only legitimate genres are those that serve an immediate expression of the knowing and truth-seeking self. The position generates an antipathy to all genric considerations that are not immediately concerned with self-expression. The second position in the debate, the Aristotelian argument, holds that different genres mediate distinct meanings, themselves capable of being analyzed systematically. From this position, literary forms are distinct and require an interpretation that is species-specific and that has as its ambition an explanation of how the literary work operates. Instead of asking, "Whence comes the power of this work?" this second kind of critic asks, "How is the power of this work generated through its particular form and meaning?" The first pole of the debate taken alone generates errors such as that of regarding the speaker in a lyric poem as the poet, rather than as a persona created by the poet. The second pole of the debate taken alone results in formalism.

The theory of genre developed in this book attempts to place the Platonic and the Aristotelian positions in a dialectical relationship. Questions about genres in relation to self-expression are most pertinent to the Platonic view of genre. Questions about genres in relation to other genres are most relevant for the Aristotelian view. But each set of questions is incomplete without the other and without gender analysis.

In the twentieth century, New Criticism was not reluctant to be proclaimed the legitimate heir of classical Aristotelian criticism. Two kinds of formalism presided in the New Criticism, which dominated Anglo-American criticism from 1920 to 1960. For those most opposed to Romanticism—critics such as Richard McKeon and R. S. Crane—the Aristotelian categories of plot, character, imitation, and words as the "matter" of poetry were the major tools of analysis.[10] The later, even more "formalist" New Critics attempted to account for the power and meaning of a text entirely by means of rhetorical concepts such as tension, ambiguity, and objective correlatives.

But for all its dedication to formal analysis, New Criticism strikes one as having been at odds with itself on the issue of genre. Although the New Critics were intent upon what Murray Kreiger calls "formulating a new 'apology' for poetry" (Krieger 1969, 3–28), they were uninterested in exploring the continuities between ordinary and nonliterary language on the one hand, and poetry and nonliterary genres on the other (ibid., 109–14). As a consequence, literary genres, although explicit, were essentially unproblematic for the New Critics as an issue in interpretation. R. S. Crane and Sheldon Sacks argued, for example, over the way a particular text is best understood—whether Jane Austen's *Persuasion* is best read as a "love tale" or as serious comedy (Crane 1967, 89) and whether *Emma* is best read as satire or as represented action (Sacks 1967, 15–20)—but they assumed that genres are formal categories, for the most part adequately defined in the history of criticism. Critical gender reflection is lacking, as can be seen in the use of quotation marks for "love tale" and in contrasting this genre with *serious* (my emphasis) comedy.

As a reaction against the biographical and historical usurpation of textual criticism, the New Criticism concentrated on tensions within particular texts. This restriction had a twofold effect. One effect, the differentiation of literature as literature from other

56

kinds of texts, was conceived as one of the major tasks of literary criticism. R. S. Crane's well-known dictum reigned: there was literary criticism, and then there were criticisms with "extra-literary interests," exemplified, he thought, by myth criticism (Crane 1953, 109–14). Crane and the first generation of New Critics were interested predominantly in poetry and took it to be normative for other kinds of literature. The second generation of the New Critics broadened the scope of inquiry to include narrative and drama.

Nevertheless, both groups were attracted to novels that lent themselves to a kind of rhetorical unity. The New Critics' long-standing reluctance to deal with the emerging genre of "new" novels disclosed one limit of New Criticism itself, however. It could not account for texts that lacked a positive principle of unity.[11] With respect to the issue of gender, this principle of organic unity could sometimes be waived if the author were famous and male, for example, in the case of Edgar Allan Poe's "The Pit and the Pendulum" (1843), which concludes with a deus ex machina in the form of the Foreign Legion. In the case of a famous female writer, however, a lack of ostensible unity was criticized as evidence of the author's ineptitude. Male critics were unable to perceive the narrator's use of distorted syntax and faulty grammar as an objective correlative of her descent into madness at the conclusion of Charlotte Perkins Gilman's short story "The Yellow Wallpaper" (1892).

The hallmark of the New Critics—the reconstruction of the text into an organic whole—the "sense of an ending," as Frank Kermode (1968) spoke of it—continued implicitly with the herme-neutical critics, but was challenged by the ideological critics and rejected by the deconstructionists. The latter especially objected to the celebration of the classics as a virtually timeless presence in the tradition, waiting only to be invoked by a reader.

A second effect of the New Critics' concentration on the inner tensions of texts was a certain nonchalance toward genres—a tendency to accept them as given and to take them for granted. In his classic essay "Tradition and the Individual Talent" T. S. Eliot, for example, did not once mention genre (or gender),[12] dealing instead with the issue of new texts in terms of thought and emotion. Although he was willing to confront the issue of "change" in literary traditions, change, in Eliot's conception, came about by the addition of new *texts:* the question of new *genres* seems not to have arisen for him.

Although genre theory was not programmatically dismissed by the New Critics, it was benignly neglected insofar as it was taken for granted in the act of criticism. Their expectation was that if one were to analyze the individual text carefully and precisely, comparisons of texts in terms of their genres would be largely gratuitous—except of course, in literary history, which, again from their perspective, was a dubious enterprise. On the positive side, we might say that in New Criticism, an *epoche* of genre theory occurred for the purpose of testing the definitions inherited from classicism.

Russian Formalism can perhaps be best characterized by its tendency to ignore "thematology," that is, the definition of literature in terms of major themes—especially the favorite New Critical theme of the relation between appearance and reality—in order to focus almost exclusively on compositional patterns (Erlich 1969). They had much in common with Anglo-American New Criticism, with the major difference that, whereas the strength of the New Critics was in their ability to discern patterns of imagery and to relate these patterns to the meaning of a work as a whole, the Russian Formalists confined their interest to linguistic structure.

Instead of imagery, the Russian Formalists, following Roman Jakobson, were interested in the difference between "figures of similarity" (metaphor) and "figures of contiguity" (metonymy). Both Russian Formalists and some of their successors, the structural linguists, assumed that linguistic analysis is unbiased and objective, and as such that it can provide a complete inventory of the patterns in a literary work (Culler 1975, 57). In both Russian Formalism and structural linguistics, genres are conventions that provide "possibilities of meaning" for a text. A text, in other words, is "naturalized" by being brought within the discursive order by the critic, who justifies elements of the work by explaining their function. One might explain Alain Robbe-Grillet's *The Voyeur,* for example, by identifying the narration as pathological speech and therefore making it intelligible in terms of pathology. Reading, in this view, is the act of making the strange familiar. It is conceivable, of course, that a text might belong to more than one genre. Ben Jonson's "Inviting a Friend to Supper" can be read as an invitation to supper or as literature. Whereas speech act theory would emphasize the continuity between the two genres, Russian Formalism, the New Criticism, and structural poetics would all claim that by becoming a part of literature, the poem "becomes a formal device rather than thematic centre, and what might have been explained as elements of an invitation are given another function" (ibid., 147). The lasting effects of Russian Formalism have been its contributions to versification. Russian Formalism altered the genres of poetry in the sense that the relationship between sound and sense is now accessible through linguistic analysis. The earliest Russian Formalists, like the Anglo-American New Critics, tried to free the literary work from biography, psychology, or social significance. The later Russian Formalists were unsuccessful in their attempt to include sociological considerations in their work.

THE MORPHOLOGICAL TRADITION

The morphological critics, by contrast, were preoccupied with genre theory. The eighteenth- and nineteenth-century classical figures in German literature—Goethe, F. Schlegel, A. W. Schlegel, Schiller, and Herder—had debated both the question and theory of genre.[13] Their successors, the late twentieth-century German morphologists, were interested in finding continuities between literary genres and subjective forms, for example, between the literary form of the genre dirge and the grieving subject. They conceived of the human being "as a self-contained whole which unites rational understanding with the irrational unconscious." They recognized in the nature of the human as well "a predisposition to become integrated in the universally human," i.e., across time and geography: "By establishing an ontology which has ultimate reference to the metaphysical basis of human existence, it becomes possible to understand the individual literary work as the synthesis of all its levels of concretization. . . . It is precisely this "synergetic" quality that characterizes the artistic mode of presentation" (Weissenberger 1978, 320). In the morphological approach, discussion of how the literary work succeeds is subordinated to what it can be taken to say about human consciousness.

Morphological criticism claimed its specific origins in eighteenth-century Germany with Goethe's *Naturformen*, which Karl

Viëtor (1952) converted in his own theory to *Grundhaltungen*. Contemporary morphological criticism has as its basic assumption that genres are fundamental attitudes that, in the poet, shape ordinary experience into a created object. In this assumption we recognize Plato's belief that certain literary genres are linked inextricably to basic human propensities, such as tragedy to tyranny. The crucial difference is that whereas in Plato "attitudes" are immediately ethical-political, those of morphological criticism are claimed to be psychological, linguistic, or phenomenological.

The twentieth-century morphological tradition, as represented by Emil Staiger, Wolfgang Kayser, Käte Hamburger, and Walter Muschg, illustrates a major effort at "naturalizing" genres, that is, of establishing their roots in an ontology of human existence. Muschg's poetics, for example, were derived directly from his typology of poetic attitudes: for example, he correlated the magical with the pronoun *I*, the mystical with the pronoun *you*, the mythical with the pronoun *it*. The "language of the I" has as its prototype the language of the Orphic poet, the shaman, or the magus, who is in harmony with nature such that the "I expands and becomes one with the universe." The language of the *you* has its archetype in the mystic, who tries to escape the experience of earthly limitation in a vision of divine limitlessness: "The tension within the 'I' increases to the point of displacing the focus of existence to a point outside the world." The language of the *it* is exemplified in the singer imbued with the mythical imagination and a "hunger for things of this world" (Muschg 1969, 241–43).

Emil Staiger (1956) developed a correlation between the triad lyric-epic-dramatic and stages in the development of language. For him, the lyric, like the syllable, is pure expression; both the lyric and the syllable aim at identity of signifier and signified. The epic, like the word, conceptualizes objects. The dramatic, like the sentence, requires comprehension of the total action to make sense. Staiger also correlated the same genric triad with time. The lyric, which eschews time and space, is the past, from which all distance has been eliminated. The epic, with its presentation and recording of events as present, is the present. The dramatic, with its projection of the historical into timelessness, is the future. Hamburger and Kayser both agreed that the major issue of criticism was that of the relation between genres (or "forms of presentation" as Joseph Strelka called them) and natural forms—both critics emphasizing the transformative power of the literary creation (Hamburger 1973; Kayser 1959). We find Platonic echoes in most morphological criticism, for example, Hamburger's dual classification of lyrical-existential (experienced as the "I" of a statement-subject) and fictional-mimetic drama (which lacks a statement-subject but refers to a fictive statement-subject).

Klaus Weissenberger synthesized the typologies of the foregoing morphological critics and applied them to lyric poetry in an attempt to show how the morphological approach can be used to inform an understanding of lyric poetry and its subforms. He chose to do this for the lyric because it seemed to him to be most simple and straightforward. Weissenberger admitted that morphological criticism is better at explaining the origins of lyric than its effects, which he spoke of in terms of its "teleological character" (Weissenberger 1978, 245–46).

The morphologists forced criticism to confront the difference between the classical way of classifying according to genus and species and the contemporary ways of understanding genre. Claudio Guillén praised the morphological critics for having provided alternative terms for *genus* (he mentioned universals, ultimates, types, *Naturformen, Grundhaltungen*). He called attention to an important change in terminology: "What we call genre today was once considered more specific than genric, and . . . we are left without an accepted term for genus." Guillén considered this loss fortunate, however, because it permitted the concept of genre to be "properly isolated and understood": the change in terminology forces a recognition of the need for a new theory of genre (Guillén 1971, 118–19).

The morphological critics attempted to retrieve and reformulate the essential link between different genres of literature and ultimate "states" of life. They were untroubled by what appears to be a fundamental ambiguity in their understanding of the relationship between genres and universals. Guillén tried to clarify the relationship by asserting that "Universals and genres belong to different orders, and can only be grasped by means of different criteria." In his view, "only the genre is a structural model, an invitation to the actual construction of the work of art" (Guillén, 119). Universals, in other words, are a higher level of abstraction than are genres.

Gender distinctions in morphological criticism are masked by the stated focus of morphological critics on "universal" or gender-neutral states of consciousness. Nevertheless, the progression from lyric to epic to drama is also a progression from emotion to logic, a progression that parallels many nineteenth-century renditions of the hierarchy of values associated with gender. Staiger, for example, uses Ernst Cassirer's three stages of language to explain the progression from lyric to drama: "language in the phase of sensuous expression, language in the phase of concrete expression, language in the phase of conceptual thought" (Weissenberger 1978, 232). Although in morphological theory the lyric is never explicitly associated with women, nor drama with men, gender stereotypes are difficult to avoid in the application of the theory.

Morphological criticism is not alone in attempting to show continuities between forms of life and literary genres. Another promising attempt at showing the continuities among literary genres, ordinary experience, and language appeared in Barbara Herrnstein Smith's book *On the Margins of Discourse: The Relation of Literature to Language* (1978). Smith distinguished between "natural discourse" and "fictive discourse" and examined the creation of fictive objects and events, such as Hallmark greetings and verbal "make-believe," which are to be found on the "edges" of both artistic and natural discourse (Smith 1978, xi, 41–75).

THE STRUCTURALIST CONTROVERSY

Just when Formalist criticism almost succeeded in creating a closed world of literature—a world theoretically unaffected by and only diffidently affecting the epistemic procedures of other disciplines—structuralism arrived on the scene. Meaning, according to structuralism, is derived from a text or made explicit by the use of binary oppositions, the terms in opposition resolved by a third term. Structuralism seemed at first to further the aims of New Criticism by isolating the text from conditions and contexts presumed to be foreign to it as a work of art. But soon structuralism brought about such radical differences in the reading of texts that it was perceived as a serious threat to literary criticism in both its historical and its New Critical forms.

The major threat levied by structuralism had to do with the status of literature as a special language. Because the methods of structuralism were the same regardless of the genre of the text, literature appeared to be indistinguishable from other kinds of writing. Like Formalist criticism, structuralism endorsed the banishing of history and authorial intention from critical inquiry. But structuralism overturned the Formalist belief that just because there is no necessary relationship between genric concepts and the conditions that gave rise to them, those conditions are irrelevant. And although structuralism continued to ignore the role of the reader, it set the stage for reader-centered criticism, which was to follow in its wake.

For some structuralists, the expectation that certain patterns existed in nature, however variable in their actual occurrence in texts and in cultural signs, was intensified. Structuralism provided a new agenda, new ways to account for the details of literary works. Networks of variable relationships were developed and studied in structuralist analysis. Vladimir Propp (1958), for example, codified relationships among action verbs in a series of stories and organized them in terms of oppositions and resemblances. A. J. Greimas (1970) extended Propp's work and specified six sets of character functions in Slavic fairy tales. Of more general use in literary criticism was Gérard Genette's (1979, 1981) four categories for understanding narratives: order (the direction of action toward or away from the present), duration (the relative length of the episodes), frequency (the relation between the number of times events happen and the number of times they are narrated), and mood (the distance between the narrator's voice and the materials of the text).[14]

Following are the major tenets of structuralism in terms of their effect on genre theory.

1. In the structuralist view, a text is a structure, arranged hierarchically, within which elements are systematically organized in both conflictual and harmonious relationships. Organic unity is no longer a prime criterion in the definition of genre or in the ways texts belong to genres.

2. Instead of immanent texts, structuralism posited autonomous texts, which can be interpreted with different interrelationships of structures so long as the analysis is consistent with the text. Such autonomy of texts suggests that texts can be successfully interpreted in the light of different genres. Arguments in terms of genre understood traditionally, such as that between Konstantin Stanislavsky, who argued that Chekhov's major plays are

    tragedies, and Anton Chekhov, who insisted that they are comedies, become moot within structuralist criticism, where Chekhov's plays can be argued to be both tragedy and comedy.

3. Structures in literature and criticism are both synchronic and diachronic. As genres evolve, their elements can be analyzed systematically.

4. Although structure is functional, many structures can be discerned in one text, and the structures can be reordered hierarchically in subsequent analyses. Unlike the ontologically "given" progression of genres in morphological criticism, genres in structuralist criticism can take different positions of dominance and recessiveness (Winner 1978).

Because of these tenets, one might expect structuralism to have broken free from undiagnosed gender affiliations. Unfortunately, such freedom was not that easy to achieve. Because binomial oppositions were at the basis of structuralist analysis, male-female dualisms, uncritical and value biased, continued to prevail in the application of structuralist criticism.

Claude Lévi-Strauss's (1970) structuralist approach to the study of primordial societies in terms of opposing categories was a novel methodology that eventually cut across all of the disciplines. In literary and other text criticism, structuralism put genre theory on a new footing: form (i.e., structure) was elevated to an interdependent status. The ambiguity regarding the role of form was finally resolved with a new dogma: "The content is determined by the form." This dictum also settled one issue of the Plato-Aristotle debate. The suitability of certain actions or behavior for artistic representation was subsumed within the question of *how* those actions were presented.

One reason for the ease with which structuralism became a dominant theory was that structuralism provided a means for understanding genres outside the classical triumvirate of epic, dramatic, lyric. Only the most tenuous relations to classical genres have been found for texts like myths, folktales, and various narrative forms other than the novel. Accordingly, the efforts to use classical genre theory to interpret them have been minimally successful. One might argue that "high culture"—which as late as the Enlightenment admitted only classical genres to the domain of reason and knowledge—constitutes itself by definition over and against those genres that do not fulfill classical generic expectations. In this argument, structuralism as a theory illuminates those genres made exceptional by classical genre theory.

The rapid dissemination of structuralist theories in accounting for folk literature also illustrates how different genre theories have peculiar capacities for particular kinds of literature. Formalist genre theory and New Criticism worked best and almost exclusively, for example, with short poems, drama, and "well-wrought" novels, whereas reader-reception theory has focused primarily on symbolist poetry and pre-twentieth-century novels.[15]

It is clear in retrospect that the fascination with structuralism aggravated old wounds at the same time that it opened new possibilities for genre theory. With its origins in the social sciences, structuralism, like morphological criticism, affirmed the ties that human artifacts have with their social and natural environment. For structuralism, however, the arbitrariness of meaning is attached to other givens: for example, the specific language system within which one is speaking or writing (as well as the system itself within a network of other language systems), or the structures of production and consumption within a specific society (as well as the society itself within a network of other societies). Meaning is "determined" only in the use of these "givens." Meaning, first of all, is inscribed by means of conventions known, for example, by speakers of the language or by inhabitants of a country. Just as important for structuralist criticism, meaning is inscribed in generic conventions—ways that stories and pictures are constructed, begun, ended; stock characters; central themes; titles; ways that representations are linked together; turns of phrase, implicit judgments, clusters of images and events.

For the structuralist, meaning is inscribed not only in conventional genres; it surpasses them by working against them, in other words, by working in their perceived absence. Structuralism affirmed (with Freud and other masters of suspicion), the ways in which meaning is "overdetermined" by the desires, fears, and obsessions—not least those having to do with sex and gender—latent in our most considered articulations. Whereas in Romanticism meaning was understood as a projection of one mind to others and of an intentional act on the part of a creator, in structuralism meaning is understood as signaled and responded to, with or without recognition by the signaler or receiver.

One of the most paradoxical effects of structuralism is in its denial of genre for the sake of larger genres. In his "Against Genres: Are Parables Lights Set in Candlesticks or Put under a

Bushel?" Edmund Leach, for example, objected to genres on the grounds that they introduce unnecessary distinctions among texts that have essential similarities.

> The thesis which I am maintaining . . . is that this kind of fragmentation of the textual materials into genres of different kinds is radically misleading. Text is text. We shall only understand the text as a whole if we recognize that some sections are structural transformations of other sections. But these transformations cut right across the conventional genre-distinctions to which I have referred. In any case the genre-distinctions are much less precise than many people suppose. (Leach 1983, 93)

He protested that disciplinary definitions of parable were so narrow that they precluded likeness with genres from other cultures. Leach objected also to traditional New Testament scholarship that, by defining parable as a subclass of the verbal teachings of Jesus, made unnecessarily discrete claims about Christian parable. Leach thought that the most appropriate way to understand the Christian gospels was to recognize their function in the context of ritual. Only in this context, he thought, might the literal-mindedness of orthodox understanding be broken. Understanding the gospels in the context of ritual made it possible to recognize that "the time of the gospel stories is mythical time, in which no one event happens before or after any other event. . . . The gospel story does not have a beginning and a middle and an end; it all exists in synchrony as in a dream" (ibid., 110, 98). Leach's work shows the extent to which structuralists were aware of the shaping power and status of genres and of the necessity of trespassing disciplines and genres in the search for adequate understanding of texts.

There were losses and gains with the advent of structuralism. What was lost was the unquestioned authority of literary historical "facts" that described genres in relation to common sense and to the received canon of texts. What was gained was a relativizing of several canons in relation to one another. Meaning, in the structuralist perspective, was the product of certain shared systems of signification that cut across time and space.

In the end, the terms the structuralists substituted for traditional genres were subject to the same kinds of fragmentation as those of traditional criticism. Leach observed that

> as knowledge accumulates, the sheer bulk of the available data leads to specialisation and this in turn leads to demarcation disputes and the over-elaboration of definitions. The two processes proceed in parallel. Within the general area with which we are now concerned, scholars who specialise in the study of myths distinguish themselves from those who concern themselves with folktales . . . so myths, and folktales and fairy-tales must be given definitions which make the categories mutually exclusive. Before very long people begin to believe that the distinctions, . . . reflect 'real' discontinuities in the total field of that under review. (ibid., 111–12)

This same criticism of genric definitions, of course, can be made with respect to gender definitions–namely, that the search for distinctions has too often led to categories that are mutually exclusive. History relates only too well the results of the belief that gender distinctions reflect discontinuities in the total field of human action. But when Leach concludes that "if we want to know what the text means we must consider the text as a whole" (ibid., 96), we must add that the question of the text "as a whole" is also a genric and a gender question, regardless of whether or not it is resolved satisfactorily and without further complications.

New criticism, morphological criticism, and structural criticism each developed either the Platonic or the Aristotelian assumptions about genre. The New Critics accepted Aristotle's legitimation of imitation and, accordingly, of the role of genre in shaping literary meaning, and they rejected Plato's demand that all imitation be rooted in the self-expression of the narrator and his condemnation of genres that involved inappropriate impersonation of another person. Morphological critics built on Plato's demand that there be an explicit and immediate link between an actor's being and imitative action, and they rejected Aristotle's "distancing" of genres from the actor's intentions. Structuralists, by refusing to offer a persuasive rationale for the links they posited between forms and sources of forms, incurred the criticism that they were neoplatonic and obscurantist.

It does not seem too surprising, then, that for lack of confronting the epistemological issues assumed in each position, the debate continues today. Meanwhile, the understanding of genre slips into new protean oppositions, such as "real" versus "nominal," "intrinsic" versus "extrinsic," or "heuristic" versus "essentialist." The trick will be to get a grasp on how genres have functioned in relation to gender in the interpretation of a major text in the West in order to assess their best potential for the future.

CHAPTER THREE

Genre and Gender in the Biblical Hermeneutical Tradition

There is no such thing as generic homo religiosus.
Caroline Walker Bynum, "The Complexity of Symbols" (1986, 2)

The Bible presents a special resource for exploring the relationship between genre and gender. Together with the Qu'ran, the Hebrew Bible and the New Testament have had by far the widest readership and, at the same time, the most complex and sustained history of interpretation of books in the West. As a single book of scripture, the Hebrew Bible incorporates an amazing variety and number of genres. The New Testament, too, although only a quarter as long, includes a number of genres. Most readers are unaware either that many of these forms were new genres at the time of their origin or that their transmigration from their original cultural setting into our own poses a genric problem of interpretation. In his classic study of the New Testament modes and genres (1971), Amos Wilder recognizes the problem and argues that these forms— such as the gospels, acts and letters, and midrash—were best understood as drama (or dialogue), narrative, and poem.

Although the genres of both testaments are fairly well known today, only recently have gender issues had a prominent place in their interpretation. Too often, gender and genre analysis have gone separate ways.

TWO HERMENEUTICAL TRADITIONS

When interpretation *as interpretation* became explicit as a problem in the late nineteenth century, two traditions of interpretation were recognized: besides the tradition of classical hermeneutics, as described in chapter 2, there was the distinct tradition of biblical hermeneutics. One would like to know that the best thinkers, from the Common Era on, appreciated both traditions and found ways to draw from both and even to draw them together. Some did: Augustine in the fourth century was primarily responsible, in *De dottrina christiana,* for making explicit that there were two traditions, each of which might claim a peculiar logic, and liberally cited from both, for example, in *The City of God.* Yet even Augustine, like most other classical thinkers, chose to develop one (in his case, biblical hermeneutics) while forfeiting the other.

In the nineteenth century, biblical studies and philology were surpassed in a different level of reflection, called general hermeneutics, which, as its name suggests, was able to offer more widely applicable concepts of "text" and "interpretation" than was possible in the specializations of either biblical studies or classical philology. One might argue that the subsequent discipline of literary criticism owes to nineteenth-century hermeneutics the expectation that it be applicable to all texts. The debt of literary criticism to biblical and philological studies, however, is less apparent, even though several literary critics—Frank Kermode, Robert Alter, Julia Kristeva, Judith Berlin, and Northrop Frye, to name only a few—have published interpretations of biblical texts. Many biblical scholars today continue the "two-tradition" approach by regarding themselves as "borrowers" of literary methods. Other scholars, such as Mieke Bal, see their relationship as far more reciprocal:

> Relations between biblical and literary scholarship tend to be limited to the question of "literary readings of the Bible"—to the question if and to what extent, the Bible can, deserves, and needs to be read "as" literature. But that question is wrongly put and betrays an attempt to separate religious from secular concerns. Such an attempt is futile. The Bible, as at least partially a religious document, has been formative of Western culture. . . . . Literature, the cultural need of literary texts and of literary "life"—in other words, the literary attitude, ideology, or way of life—is similarly an undeniable part of the same culture. Hence, the Bible is both entirely religious, whatever that may mean, and entirely literary. (Bal 1989, 374)

70

Bal suggests that the best approach is to redirect attention from the question of literature to the question of reading. What is distinctive about the biblical hermeneutical tradition? Reader-reception theory has begun to make explicit what Paul Ricoeur (1971) in general hermeneutical theory called "the arch of interpretation," which has been a definitive characteristic of the biblical tradition. In this tradition, one can see the full range of understanding reading—from reading as a solitary act in a historical vacuum to reading as always already "vectored" in and before the moment it gains our attention. One frequently finds the text functioning as a sacred icon—a bridge, as it were, between the acts of imagining and thinking.[1] Most biblical scholars today assume that biblical texts have been redacted and read in different ways by different communities.[2] In this sense, the privileging of the text over readers—a privilege which has been called into question by the reader-reception critics (Jauss 1978, 143)—has been less of a problem in modern biblical scholarship than in modern literary criticism, especially in the latter's formalist expressions. In addition, how the repeated question of "Which genre is this?" has been answered provides a valuable historical record of different readings based on different genres, and of the kinds of genric questions generated by historically different concepts of genre.

Before the nineteenth century, when interpretation became a common focus for both, there were few borrowings by one hermeneutical tradition from the other. With some exceptions, scholars were trained in either classical or biblical studies, and only exceptional scholars devoted equal time to both fields. With the advent of historical-critical method in the late nineteenth century, the Bible was no longer thought to surpass all genres (and therefore to be unique and incomparable)—as it was by the Romantics fifty years earlier—and some methods came to be applied in both fields. It has taken longer for literary critical methods to be accepted in biblical studies. Indeed, in a review of recent books on the Bible, Robert Polzin (1989) complains that, regardless of what they call their approach, many biblical scholars continue to do historical text criticism: that many are not doing literary *interpretation,* even when they say they are employing literary critical methods.

Nevertheless, in biblical studies as in the field of classical and literary critical hermeneutics, there exists a plurality of methods and approaches and a history of method in each discipline roughly approximating that in the other. More to the point is Polzin's observation that the great divide today may lie not so much *between* the tradition of classical hermeneutics (including contemporary literary criticism) and the tradition of biblical hermeneutics as it does *within* each field. With the plurality of methods and approaches in each tradition, the fault lines within each tradition are often ignored until the question, "What are the meanings of the text?" is raised. Then the structuralists vie with the New Critics, the hermeneutical critics with the deconstructionists—within each tradition.

To a certain extent but with variations, then, the history of biblical hermeneutics parallels the selective history of classical and literary criticism in the previous chapter. One exception is current narrative criticism as employed by scholars of the gospels—an enterprise which, Stephen Moore (1989, xxii) claims, "differs significantly from anything to be found in nonbiblical literary criticism."[3] He locates this difference largely in biblical scholars' attention to the multiple ways in which a plot develops within narrative genres. Moore is also hopeful that feminist criticism of the Bible might yield important results, yet he cites no examples.

Some scholars continue to think that literary critical methods are limited in their applicability to biblical texts. They fault structuralism, for example, for removing the necessary ambiguity from texts as read in traditionally religious senses. They point out the lack of "fit" in the application of structuralism to some biblical texts—a deficiency perhaps not so noticeable in nonbiblical applications. But good interpreters never merely "apply" methods. Using Propp's morphology of the folktale (Hero, Helper, Originator, and Opponent), Roland Barthes (1974) proposed a variation on a structuralist analysis in his reading of Jacob and the Angel in Genesis 32:22–32. In Barthes's application, both the Originator and the Helpers (such as animals or a woodcutter) can step in and assist the Hero, and whereas according to Propp the Originator is present again at end of quest, in Barthes's analysis of the Jacob story the Opponent and Originator turn out to be the same. By means of Barthes's analysis, one might be tempted to claim that the distinctiveness of the Bible is in the way it exploits genric conventions traditionally conceived in structuralism. Others would say that any good text does the same. Still others hold that religious classics (which include but are not limited to scriptural texts), as well as other classics, exceed conventional expectations (Tracy, 1981).[4]

ORIGINS OF GENRE AND GENDER CRITICISM IN BIBLICAL INTERPRETATION

We might expect that the use of genre as a tool for critical inquiry in biblical hermeneutics would reflect its similarities with and differences from classical literary hermeneutics. This expectation is fulfilled in the paradigmatic use of genre for interpreting biblical texts by Hermann Gunkel.

Gunkel, who lived from 1862 to 1932, agreed with the basic claim of Julius Wellhausen's documentary theory ([1878] 1983), which was that the Hexateuch (Genesis, Exodus, Leviticus, Numbers, Deuteronomy, and Joshua) comprised four main "documents" (a genre that took on new meaning in his theory), which Wellhausen labeled J, E, D, and P, written in that chronological order and woven together by later redactionists. J and E were early narrative accounts, according to Wellhausen, which he dated in the ninth and eight centuries B.C.E, respectively. Document D was a redaction of J and E and at least chapters 12–22 of Deuteronomy, which he dated after 680 B.C.E. Document P, written about 450, covered the Exile through the reforms of Ezra and Nehemiah as recorded in the Pentateuch. Nevertheless, like many other biblical scholars, Gunkel was dissatisfied that the applications of Wellhausen's theory were restricted to a critique of the sources of the texts and yielded so little exegetically (Suelzer, 1968).

Gunkel (1910) proposed to retrieve the question of understanding the authors and their work by identifying the separate preliterary traditions from which the texts originated, for example, the ritual-cult settings of many of the psalms, taunt songs, dirges, and folk legends. His idea was to use established genres to bring new understanding to texts that otherwise had no reference group. By means of Gunkel's theory, other scholars noticed that Deuteronomy, for example, is not very close to either vassal-treaty or wisdom literature, as he had originally proposed, but that both genres help in the interpretation of the whole text and of key passages, such as, "Thou shalt love the Lord thy God." Gunkel thought that by working slowly and methodologically with every text, borrowing from archeology and from other Near Eastern literature, it would be possible to know how each text had come to be incorporated in the Bible—for example, as part of Hebrew rituals. Again, we see in Gunkel's work, and in form criticism in general, a reaffirmation of what has traditionally been the goal of biblical exegesis: to interpret individual texts in the light of a presumed whole.

Documentary theory and Gunkel's genre criticism (which came to be called form criticism) were the most important achievements of the early twentieth century. In both approaches, the author and history are seen as determiners of the meaning of a text. For example, in form criticism, the hypotheses of Karl Graf and Wellhausen were used primarily to shed light on ancient Israel's religious institutions, that is, the relation of postexilic to preexilic faith. Establishing document P as the latest, rather than the earliest, source helped distinguish preexilic Yahwism from later Rabbinic Judaism. Gunkel's genre criticism was used to learn more about the particular setting out of which the text emerged—for example, the cult songs that gave rise to the Book of Psalms (Gunkel 1928). In other words, Gunkel made genre visible in a way that has been sustained by subsequent scholarship.

The success of documentary theory can be seen in the way the Hexateuch is read today: some form of documentary theory is adhered to by most biblical scholars. Nevertheless, fine tuning the relationship between form criticism and documentary theory continues. For example, closer literary analyses of the Hexateuch has revealed that the documents were probably composed by several authors from previously existing documents. The importance of the work of redactors became recognized and their creativity was affirmed. A new emphasis on oral transmission has pushed the actual dates of the creation of the four documents much earlier than Wellhausen's. At the same time, Gunkel's investigation of *Sitz im Leben* (i.e., the function of a genre for its first audience) as represented by the text provided for the identification of discrete genres—the ready lists of genres taken for granted today, including creation stories, genealogical lists, proverbs, and etiological tales, in addition to those mentioned before.

One of the earliest insights that gave rise to Wellhausen's documentary theory was the observation that the northern tribes of Israel called God "Elohim" and the southern tribes called God "Yahweh." About the same time that Wellhausen was formulating his theory, Elizabeth Cady Stanton observed that the Bible was the basis for the teaching that woman is inferior to man and therefore subject to him and that this teaching was to be found in "civil and canon law, church and state, priests and legislators . . . political parties and religious denominations" (Stanton et al. 1895, 7). Although Stanton's gender differentiation did not sort out and distinguish distinct strands within the biblical text according to origin, as did Wellhausen's geographical differentiation, it could have sparked equally far-reaching consequences.

Stanton formed a Revising Committee of twenty North Americans and five Anglo-Europeans to "revise only those texts and chapters directly referring to women, and those also in which women are made prominent by exclusion." They estimated that this description fit one-tenth of the Biblical passages, and that "these texts, with [our] commentaries, [could] easily be compressed into a duodecimo volume of about four hundred pages" (ibid., 5). The project was completed as planned. *The Woman's Bible: Part One, Comments on Genesis, Exodus, Leviticus, Numbers, and Deuteronomy* was published in 1895, and *Part Two: Comments on the Old and New Testaments from Joshua to Revelation* was published in 1898, with a total of 377 pages.

The Woman's Bible is remarkable for many reasons, not least that it does not fit easily into any recognized genres. Its title suggests a text written for a female audience, that is, something that appeals to women's interests of the early twentieth century, such as housekeeping or cooking. It has echoes of popular journals, such as *Women's Home Companion,* current at the time. But if taken in these senses, the title is misleading, because the book is the first systematic study of gender relations found in the Bible. The commentaries have a "threefold character": (1) the translation and meaning of particular words and texts in the original; (2) the provision of a context from biblical history, old manuscripts, and the latest theories for the meaning of occult passages; and (3) comments on the most widely quoted English version of the selected passages. As an academic study, the book has relevance for audiences of both genders.

In her description of the project in her introduction to part 1, Stanton reports that several distinguished Hebrew and Greek scholars (women) invited to do the translation expressed fear "that their high reputation and scholarly attainments might be compromised by taking part in an enterprise that for a time may prove very unpopular" (ibid., 9). Indeed, the enterprise proved so unpopular that shortly after publication it was disowned by the National Association of Women, who had initially sponsored the project, on the grounds that it was too radical. The group also withdrew its support for Stanton as president of the association and elected someone else.

Given *The Women's Bible*'s unpopular reception and its marginality to recognized genres, what genric claims can be made for it? First of all, the controversy unleashed by the book indicates that the text did not fit comfortably within any one genre. Moreover, the contrasting expectations set up by its title and its composition make it difficult to know how the text should be read. In addition, the controversy reveals the challenge laid down by an explicitly gender-based text that calls into question the unrecognized gender bias of accepted genres and texts. Within fifty years many of the comments in the *Women's Bible* had been further researched and became the basis for more conventional scholarly publications.[5] Although *The Woman's Bible* was derided when it was published at the turn of the century, today it can be seen as evidence that a genre that is marginal can also be highly productive.

EFFECTS OF GENRE CRITICISM IN BIBLICAL INTERPRETATION

Genre criticism became the mainstream of biblical interpretation early in this century, while gender criticism continued to be idiosyncratic within scholarly circles until the 1950s. Subsequent developments of genre criticism include redaction criticism, for example, which focuses on the traces of editing and composition by those who arranged the original documents into the biblical text. The genius of redaction criticism is best seen in its handling of aspects and portions of biblical text that are least attractive to the general reader. Whereas source critics are drawn to rambling, repetitious, narrative form, redaction critics like to work with seemingly incoherent collections of unrelated sayings, formulas, and genealogies, such as the Table of Nations in Genesis 10 (Childs 1979; Barton 1984, 89–103). Redaction criticism had its best results in the New Testament and in the P source of the Hebrew Bible, mostly with its archival lists. Redactionists often found a function in the position of these lists: for example, to link the tribal history of Abraham to the primeval history of preceding chapters of Genesis. In redaction criticism, Israel emerges as the climax and chief purpose of history of the whole world; creation no longer belongs to a mythic, timeless realm but is connected with a worldly time scale. God appears as responsible both for creating and for directing subsequent history.

One shortcoming of redaction criticism is that, by using literary criticism indiscriminately, it appears to preclude asking religious questions of the text. As a result of this perceived shortcoming, canonical criticism was developed as an attempt to heal the breach between theology and biblical studies. Canonical criticism is concerned with what the text means rather than what it meant. Brevard S. Childs adds a question about meaning at the canonical level to the agenda for biblical criticism: can the study of an Old Testament text be regarded as complete until we ask what it means now that it is part of the Old Testament canon, as well as what it meant at a precanonical stage?[6] The question reveals a greater affinity between canonical criticism and structuralism than between canonical criticism and form or redaction criticism. Both abandon the author's intention and the setting in which the text was composed as determining the meaning of the text, and both locate meaning in the text as read.

In the light of the subsequent criticisms of the results of Gunkel's work, one of the significant contributions of form criticism is in danger of being overlooked: a major shift in the multiplicity of genric considerations that were made. The Psalms, form critics argued, were not only lyric but also liturgical; Deuteronomy was not only a divine/human covenant but also a feudal contract; the Song of Songs, not only allegory but also epithalamium. Nevertheless, in both Gunkel's conception of the link between particular genres and their historical origins and Hirsch's notion of the multiple parentage of genres, the question of genre is bound either to original authors or original audiences. Gunkel and Hirsch both held that genres were there "before" individual texts and were altered by individual authors. We would add that genres also persist after the author and even after their reconception by subsequent readers.

A final result of Gunkel's work is the recognition of the implicitly religious and theological assumptions in genric criticism. His methods assume, in other words, that the question of belief originates as a question of interest. Why one is interested (for positive and negative reasons, or for both) intrinsically has theological implications.

Gunkel enriched the hermeneutical tradition when he turned his familiarity with classical texts and philological methods to biblical texts: genre criticism turned out to be a noteworthy and lasting contribution to biblical studies. Genre criticism, along with redaction and form criticism, has played a crucial role in the retrieval of reliable texts and understandings of them as texts. Gunkel's expectation that only one model for each of the texts is correct limited the success of his insight and resulted in the presumed origin of the text determining its meaning (Buss 1979). Nevertheless, the explicit use of genre theory in form criticism yielded important information about biblical texts, and despite criticism from literary critics like Kenneth Burke (1961) and reservations from biblical scholars like Gerhard von Rad (1965, 330) on its use for particular kinds of texts, the notion of genre continues to be useful.

One example of a challenge to the single antecedent model—in this case, for the genre gospel—can be found in Charles H. Talbert's *What Is a Gospel? The Genre of the Canonical Gospels* (1978). Talbert does not accept Rudolf Bultmann's evidence for the thesis that "literary form *gospel* developed out of the kerygma." Instead Talbert introduces evidence of his own that suggests likenesses between the gospel form and Greco-Roman biographies. He delineates a system of biographical classifications based on social functions:

A. Works that "provide the readers a pattern to copy"
B. Works that "aim to dispel a false image of the teacher"
C. Works that attempt to "discredit a given teacher by exposure"
D. Lives of philosophers that trace "the living voice" after the period of the founding teacher
E. Lives of philosophers that explicate the teacher's doctrine

78

Talbert sees Matthew as a Type E, Mark and John as Type B, and Luke-Acts as Type D. Since Talbert's book was published, several studies of the genres biography and autobiography, such as that of Janet Gunn (1982), have suggested alternatives to Gunkel's and Talbert's overdependence on the question of origins. From the perspective of biblical studies it makes sense to construct several different genric hypotheses for specific groups of texts in order to bring out to the fullest the mainsprings of their uniqueness. Talbert's genric study provokes further theological and philosophical questions, such as, in this case, "What is the significance of reading the Gospels as if they were biographies as well as kerygma and myth?

Whereas Hermann Gunkel and other scholars of the late nineteenth century had focused on the *Sitz im Leben,* other scholars used genre self-consciously as mediating the contemporary meanings of texts rather than as a means of identifying an original situation. Rudolf Bultmann and other New Testament scholars of the early twentieth century, for example, argued that the central figure of the gospels was mythical because divine, rather than biographically and developmentally human. The gospels were myths told for religious purposes and as such were to be understood in the light of philosophical-theological truth rather than in literally biographical terms (Bultmann 1941). The debates over the proper genre of biblical texts had the effect of preventing further scholarly speculation and investigation until the late 1970s.

GENRE AND GENDER IN BIBLICAL NARRATIVE

Besides work on individual genres, the study of biblical narrative in general has produced considerable changes in the field. Recent studies force the question, How does a postcritical theory of narrative differ from a precritical one? Thomas Wilson described precritical biblical criticism in his handbook *The Arte of Rhetorique* (1553). Wilson's account answers questions considered to be appropriate for a precritical understanding of narrative: who, what, where, with what help, wherefore, how, at what time? These precritical questions focus on the character, considered to be the replica of a person. These questions presume also that only one time is significant in the explication of narrative, namely, the action described in the plot. Furthermore, the action is conceived of in terms of a naive realist epistemology. The action appears as an "already, out there now real," and does not include the operations of consciousness of the one who conceived of the action, that is, the explicator. Finally, the action is conceived of in terms of the effect it has in itself, that is, apart from the work it accomplishes by means of the reader's activity.

In the "higher criticism" of the Bible, including Gunkel's genre criticism, the ambition was to identify the *sub*genre of specific texts—such as gospel, midrash, story of the Living Oracle, parable, and so forth. Most of these subgenres are sufficiently established so that the evocation of a genric identity concomitantly sets in motion certain expectations for the reader. With respect to biblical narrative in general, however, it is more difficult to specify just what these expectations are.

Notwithstanding this difficulty, some expectations are made evident whenever we try to read a text aloud and find ourselves adopting certain tones or ways of expression rather than others. We are also made aware of such expectations whenever we are led to ask what mode of cognition is represented by narrative in general. Finally, in postmodern theory we may ask, What is the cognitive status of narrative in relation to other major modes of cognition designated by discipline as philosophical, scientific, historical, fictional? What is its status among the modes of thought viewed as binary oppositions cutting across several disciplines: oppositions such as linear/hermeneutical, synchronic/diachronic, reductionist/transformative, apodictic/polemical, theoretical/commonsensical, analogical/metaphorical, mimetic/impressionistic, male/female, and so forth? We find that narrative participates in more than one mode of cognition, viewed either as a discipline or as a binary opposition, and it overarches many of the traditionally designated literary genres. Of all the oppositions, that of gender denomination is the most recent and one in most need of attention. In short, narrative surpasses both the class "major modes of cognition" and the class "major literary genres" in ways that none of the other members of either class does.

Narrative belongs to, and therefore is, both a mode of cognition and a genre at once. A phenomenology of narrative, constructed along the lines of what Paul Ricoeur (1984, 1:52–94) calls the "competence" each of us has for following a story, will make explicit the cognitive character of narrative. In Ricoeur's hermeneutical theory narrative persuades neither by means of formal logic nor by the results of thought brought directly to judgment, but rather by multiple means, such as juxtaposition of qualities, reinforcement by images, jarring of assumptions by means of metaphor, suspense, coincidence, failure of logic, sympathy, identification, repulsion, and appropriate and inappropriate instances of abstraction. Narrative employs the same tactics to create gender constructs, or our expectations of what it is like to be male or female. As we saw in Plato, these constructs or portrayals become normative in a culture for what it is possible to think or imagine about gender. The conception of narrative as a distinctive mode of thought clarifies the indispensability of a literary analysis of narrative and the recognition that the narrative mode of thought may not be substituted for without remainder by other modes of thought.

The notion of the competence every reader must have for following a story is intrinsic to a postcritical theory of narrative. This notion objectifies the minimal conditions for the act of intelligent reading and brings to light what will be our first premise, namely, that a narrative "whole" is located between the text and the reader's reconstruction of its parts. Next, it discloses a second premise, that there are, according to Ricoeur, minimally two time elements in a narrative: the time of events told about and the time of telling. Narrative sentences refer to at least two time-separated events, and explicitly aim to describe the earliest event to which they refer. It is this time separation that accounts for the essential difference between literary-historical narrative on the one hand and philosophical-scientific explanation on the other. This factor also has the potential for overcoming the naive realist expectation that an event has a fixed meaning, which can be recorded by a perfect witness, who can give a full description of it as soon as it has occurred. A narrative sentence, then, describes an event A by making reference to a future event B, which could not be known at the time when A occurred.

This factor of the time separation of the events to which the text refers from the event(s) of narration is familiar to us, of course, especially from redaction criticism, which has, as its first objective, to distinguish narrated events from the event(s) of narration. In redaction criticism the time of narration is as important as the time of the events referred to in a text.

Ricoeur's analysis is especially helpful for instances in which the time of narration is presumably singular and in which events A and B can be understood to be related in terms provided only by hypothetical circumstances belonging to the time of narration. These are *hypothetical* circumstances because, strictly speaking, both the narrated events and the original narration are inaccessible to the reader except through "texts" and must be reconstructed in interpretation. Robert Alter makes this kind of hypothesis (although not explicitly) when he observes, for example, that in traditional criticism the story of Tamar (Genesis, chapter 38) has been treated as an anomalous fragment inserted into the Joseph story between Genesis, chapters 37 and 39. By paying close attention to the language of narration, however, Alter perceives certain coincidences between the verbs that describe Jacob's recognition of Joseph's coat brought to their father by his other sons and Judah's recognition of his own seal, cord, and staff brought to him by his servants from Tamar. These coincidences lead to the awareness of larger similarities of plot in the two stories and eventually disclose a link between the stories of Joseph and Tamar. This link is the uprooting of the law of primogeniture, which Alter finds to be at the heart of both stories (Alter 1981).

We can say, then, that the precritical notion that a narration is merely the reenactment of what characters originally thought, felt, or did must be replaced with the postcritical realization that actors' actions are described in the light of events that they did not and could not know, as for example, the reason for Judah's being singled out in the first episode in the story of Joseph. According to Ricoeur, it is frequently the case that the conditions for understanding an event may not be sufficient until after the time of the original event.

We know from the nineteenth-century hermeneutical critics that we are drawn to read narratives because they are about human action. What is represented in narratives is, in the largest sense, human actions. However far these particular human actions may be from the reader's present feelings or interest, by means of the plot the actions attract the reader's basic interest in the human realm. But this ultimate interest in human beings and actions is not enough. In Ricoeur's theory, a narrative lures the potential reader into reading because in narrative, human actions have been radically disintegrated. Narrative constructs a felt need to reintegrate these actions into the continuity of a narrative. The reader's own life project, which the reader is constructing, comes into view when the reader begins to explain the relations of the parts to the whole, and vice versa. The entire process of understanding a narrative begins with the reader's reconstructing its plot.

The act of reconstructing the plot brings us back to the issue of genre. Readers are aware, if only minimally so, that the text contains certain clues that lead to understanding it in one way rather than another. In *Fiction and the Shape of Belief,* Sheldon Sacks argues, for example, that Henry Fielding's *Tom Jones* needs to be read as "represented action" rather than as satire or apologue (Sacks 1964, 1–69). In fact, whenever we understand a text, we understand it *as* a particular genre. By means of its genric disposition, narrative produces effects in the world in ways similar to other work in the world. We recognize this "praxis dimension" of different kinds of narrative, for example, in the abbreviated typology of the effects of myth, parable, apologue, and satire in John Dominic Crossan's *The Dark Interval* (1975, 9): "Story establishes world in *myth,* defends such established world in *apologue,* discusses and describes world in *action,* attacks world in *satire,* and subverts world in *parable.*" However limited such typologies are in their ability to provide an overarching sense of the work that narrative in general does, they do remind us that biblical narrative "works" in multiple ways. Narrative is designed to generate new meaning, to manifest meaning in nascent form, and to lure us into recognition of ways of being in the world other than our own.

GENRE AND GENDER IN DECONSTRUCTIONIST BIBLICAL INTERPRETATION

Until the nineteenth century, genre had two major uses. It was used incidentally to identify texts. Many of the names of the books of the Bible have come to be associated with genric designations: Leviticus (laws), the Book of Psalms (songs), Genesis (an etymology of tribes and of the known world), Jeremias (jeremiad), Apocalypse (a prophetic, usually disastrous, revelation). Exegetes used these traditional designations as frames with particular functions in relation to the overall plan of a providential God. But beyond this incidental use, the genre of narrative played a synthe-sizing role by subsuming all subgenres into itself. Genre allowed the book to be read as a whole—in this case, as the *story* of human salvation. This assumption has provided the informing principle throughout the history of biblical hermeneutics (even for those who rejected or tested its validity), much as the theory of evolution has provided the informing principle for twentieth-century biolog-ical studies.

Deconstructionism, as the last example of a literary interpreta-tion of biblical narrative, is a type of criticism that turns its attention against philosophy to suspend its power and logic for the purpose of examining the complicity between thought and rhetoric. As Christopher Norris observed in his commentary on Paul de Man's *Allegories of Reading* 1979: " 'Literature' is pre-cisely what results from philosophy's inability to *think through* its own constitution in textual-rhetorical terms" (Norris 1982, 104).[7] In the context of biblical hermeneutics it is useful to add a corollary: "Theology" is precisely what results from the inability of the Old and New Testaments to *think through* their own consti-tution in partial and provisional cognitive terms.

Although Derrida, the foremost deconstructionist, occasionally claims no more for his work than that it "baffle and provoke rather than to reach any common ground of discussion" (Norris 1982), and another American, Geoffrey Hartmann, boasts of a "wild" arbitrary kind of deconstructionism, this approach nevertheless provides a serious alternative for the illumination of texts and forces critics to reexamine assumptions they would otherwise accept uncritically.

Deconstruction, more than any other literary critical approach, calls into question the assumption that there is a "whole" that can or should be the goal of interpretation. Nellie Furman's "His story Versus Her Story: Male Genealogy and Female Strategy in the Jacob Cycle," a good example of deconstructionist analysis of a familiar biblical text, allows us to reflect on the ways that deconstructionist criticism differs remarkably from structuralist and other kinds of literary criticism. Compared with Altman's analysis of the same text above, Furman's reading, which is explicitly gender conscious, provides a different way of under-standing how the text demands a theological response.

Furman examines the role that pieces of attire—coats, staffs, girdles, jewelry, veils—play in the lives of males in selected biblical narratives as contrasted with the roles these articles play in the lives of females. In her introduction she redefines the biblical text as any "conceptualization" or reading of it. "It is the perception of the reader which creates the text," she writes: "its coherence is in the eyes of the reader and not in the intentionality of the author(s), narrator(s) or editor(s)" (Furman 1989, 141). In this view, the primacy of the reading takes precedence over any given text: the deconstructionist methodology is designed to "weave and waver" through a substratum of meanings that undermine the surface readings of any story. Furman concludes that for males, clothing functions in the story as an extension of the wearer's power and status and for females, as a means of regaining what belonged to them by law.

Using Furman's reading, let us compare a structuralist and a deconstructionist analysis in order to understand how each challenges both classical and traditional methods and readings.

1. In a structuralist analysis, the categories that become binary oppositions and mediators are general categories and retain an uncritical relationship with nature and human beings as they appear in the story. In a deconstructionist analysis, the categories are derived from a hermeneutics of suspicion, that is, from a hunch that what one sees in approved readings is a reinforcement of the status quo (which has a stake, perhaps, in the suppression of minority interests) and from an insight that there are unapproved associations of elements in the text worth pursuing. Furman, for example, chooses the seduction scene (Genesis, chapter 39) to begin her analysis: "it beckons the interest of the [deconstructionist] reader for it deals with two contrary interpretations of one event, two seemingly antithetical readings"—one by Potiphar's wife and another by the anonymous narrator and Joseph. The suspicion aroused by the opposing points of view within the text calls into question the genre of the text as well.

2. In a structuralist analysis, the intention of the author is ignored as being irrelevant to what appears in the text. In a deconstructionist analysis, the intention of the author functions as a norm against which opposing readings are constructed.

3. In a structuralist analysis, the perspective of the reader is hidden under the assumed neutrality of the categories chosen, the meanings of which are presumed to be self-evident or self-

authenticated by their closeness to the text. In a deconstructionist analysis, the perspective of the reader is alluded to and is understood to prevail over that of the author. For some deconstructionists there is no end to the regress of further deconstructions upon deconstructions. For others, like de Man, however, a limit of deconstructionism is reached in fact in the sense that the texts themselves must provide the invitation to deconstruct (Norris 1982, 106).

4. In a structuralist analysis, the selected text is considered to be a unitary whole, a traditionally defined genre, and the analysis by means of binary operations serves to exhaust the meanings of the text as charted by these specific terms. Theoretically, however, the text is open to other structuralist analyses using different binary oppositions. In a deconstructionist analysis, the texts are selected for their ability to conduct a hermeneutics of suspicion. Only those threads that sustain the suspicion are attended to. The analysis is complete whenever the interpreter decides that enough illumination has been played out from the texts. Closure of the analysis of the text is neither claimed nor desired.

5. Both structuralism and deconstructionism are evidence of the emphasis in contemporary literary criticism on formal structural analysis rather than historical meaning.

When we attend to the differences between structuralism and deconstructionism, the old conflict between literary criticism and biblical exegesis seems far in the past. It is easy to forget that hardly a century and a half ago, notwithstanding his own aesthetically complex use of different genres, Søren Kierkegaard (1843) dismissed the aesthete as a dilettante.[8] Nor was Rudolf Bultmann (1941), who more recently demanded a philosophical "demythologization" of Christian scriptures, a particular friend of myth or narrative as genres, although he did force a new question about the relation of these genres in biblical interpretation.

Among recent literary critical approaches to the Bible, genre studies have a small but increasingly diverse representation. In the early 1970s the Society of Biblical Literature Seminar on the Gospels formed a Task Force on Genre. As a member of that group, William G. Doty did a comprehensive review of the then current theories of genre and of the status of the concept. After several observations, he concluded that "the main propaedeutic role of genric classification lies in the training of the interpreter to comprehend adequately (a) the associational complexes in which a work appears [and] . . . (c) the preperceptions about the type of writing which the interpreter carried forward out of his own context, and which hinder or aid interpretation" (Doty 1972, 29). His comment is noteworthy in that, at a time when genre was known to most scholars as a tool for historical-literary analysis, Doty saw genre as clarifying the horizons of both reader and text.

In the late 1970s a group of scholars attempted a systematic study of apocalypse as a genre. They regarded genre as "an attempt to bring some order into a rather chaotic area of study" (Collins 1979, iv). In this study, genre was used as a "heuristic device" to show both the distinctive elements and the "recurrent features" encountered in apocalyptic texts. The editor, J. J. Collins, observed that "interpretation already involves an implicit notion of genre" and that although similarities among texts identify genres, "similarity does not necessarily imply historical relationships" (ibid., 1). He acknowledged "widespread opposition to any attempt to define [apocalypse] as a literary genre" and saw the study as restricted "to the initial stage of literary analysis" (ibid., 4). In 1986 a sequel (edited by Adela Yarbro Collins) to this work continued the attempt to define apocalypse and to extend the definition to the social functions of the genre in various settings (Collins 1986). One contributor noticed that until then, paradigmatic studies (those that group features in hierarchies) had prevailed over syntagmatic studies (those that use text-linguistic methods to analyze meaning), and that the weakness of paradigmatic studies is the "tendency to remain taxonomic and static" (Aune 1986, 33). From these studies it is apparent that today genre criticism is central to biblical interpretation. Gunkel's ambition to achieve a complete knowledge of the origins of the texts has given way to several ways of understanding genre, with a variety of questions and outcomes.

GENRE AND THEOLOGICAL REFLECTION IN
BIBLICAL INTERPRETATION

Consideration of the genre narrative leads to the recognition (1) that narrative generates meaning; (2) that those meanings inform the worlds that shape readers, and readers, them; and (3) that the forms of explanation employed to interpret narratives are themselves genrically constitutive of the reader's understanding. When we question a narrative and allow it to question us, new questions arise, questions of *which* meanings to affirm and of *how* to relate those meanings into "meaningful *wholes*," or what Fredric Jameson calls "master stories."[9] In other words, to ask and to attempt to answer such questions regarding the selection of texts, genres, and criteria is to engage in activities that can be seen, in terms of the hermeneutical spiral, to generate the reader's understandings of self and world.

To say that narrative is genrically theological is equivalent to the claim that a biblical interpreter cannot fail to engage in implicit theological reflection. Most minimally, by choosing to read biblical as distinct from, or in addition to, other texts, the reader makes an investment in what they express. But what do biblical texts express? One theologian specifies the object of religious texts as follows:

> For the Jewish, Christian and Islamic traditions, [the] experience of the whole is an experience of a who: a loving and jealous, living, acting, covenanting God, a God who discloses who God is, who we are, what history and nature, reality itself ultimately are . . . scriptures are themselves only a relatively adequate expression of the earliest . . . community's experience. . . . They remain open to new experiences—new questions, new and sometimes more adequate responses for later generations who experience the same event[s] in ever different situations. Yet throughout the . . . tradition these scriptures will serve as finally normative: as that set of aspirations, controls and correctives upon all later expressions, all later classical texts, persons, images, symbols, doctrines, events that claim appropriateness to the classic witnesses to that event. (Tracy 1981, 248–49)

David Tracy's statement is an expression of *explicit* theological reflection on the scriptures. We notice, however, that even in this maximal (i.e., an explicit act of taking a position before the text, of allowing the text to become a "whole" in front of the reader), no threat exists either of translating narrative into some other mode of cognition, such as doctrine, or of substituting some creedal statement for any of the multiple genres that constitute the original text and its original interpretations. The implication is that narrative (as well as other biblical genres) serves as the relatively adequate originating expression and norm for God's self-manifestation. Every other mode, however appropriate and expeditious, is subject to the same need for interpretation, genric differentiation, and evaluation.

But is it not true that by certain choices of texts, interpretations, criteria, we preclude other choices? Is it possible to be a Proteus of the scriptures, appropriating them all, thereby maintaining for ourselves a pluralism of texts and interpretations? Furthermore, does not every expression of a "whole" tend "in spite of itself to give the impression of a facile totalization, a seamless web of phenomena"? Such is the charge made by Louis Althusser, a Marxist revisionist critic. In examining Althusser's criticism and his counterthesis that a text "is a process without a *telos* or a *subject*," Fredric Jameson admits that the Althusserian critique is irrefutable on its own terms: "It demonstrates the way in which the construction of a . . . totality necessarily involves the isolation and privileging of one of the elements *within* that totality (a kind of thought habit, a predilection for specific forms, a certain type of belief, a 'characteristic' political structure or form of domination) such that the element in question becomes a master code or 'inner essence' capable of explicating the other elements or feature of the 'whole' in question" (Jameson 1981, 27–28).

Althusser's claim represents a limit of thought for Jameson, one he finds appropriate to accept because it corresponds to our experience of reading texts. There is a difference, therefore, between a "pluralism" that refers to "the coexistence of methods and interpretations in the intellectual and academic marketplace" and one that is used as a "proposition about the infinity of possible meanings and methods and their ultimate equivalence with and substitutability for one another." Jameson concludes: "I suspect, indeed, that there are only a finite number of interpretative possibilities in any given textual situation . . . : to forestall that systematic articulation and totalization of interpretive results . . . can only lead to embarrassing questions about the relationship between them" (ibid.). Interestingly, Jameson finds Americans especially unhearing with respect to what he calls "an upper methodological limit."

There are those, of course, who, like Althusser, decry any kind of closure to thought, but on different grounds. Some find narrative a "reactionary" form in the sense that it imposes an *illusory* order upon an essentially chaotic reality. Others use certain kinds of narrative, such as narratives of the memory of suffering, to challenge bourgeois expectations of order. All denials of closure implicitly affirm the limits of the genre of narrative—a genre that like other genres gives rise to thought, sometimes religious and theological thought.

Nevertheless, theology has frequently been suspect—by biblical scholars, literary critics, and philosophers alike—of substituting itself as self-evident meaning in place of existing texts. Paul de Man, for example, makes his suspicion explicit when he locates hermeneutics traditionally in the "sphere of theology . . . [and] its secular prolongation in the various historical disciplines." He explains his position by comparing poetics and hermeneutics: "Unlike poetics, which is concerned with the taxonomy and the interaction of poetic structures, hermeneutics is concerned with the meaning of specific texts." De Man summarizes his suspicion in the following charge: "In a hermeneutical enterprise, reading necessarily intervenes but, like computation in an algebraic proof, it is a means toward an end . . . : the ultimate aim of a hermeneutically successful reading is to do away with reading altogether" (de Man 1982, ix–x). As long as this suspicion is not addressed, theology will necessarily be at odds with one of its major sources for reflection.

The "necessity of reading" cannot be dismissed, however, if one pays attention to genre. With genric analysis there is no temptation to translate genred discourse such as narratives, liturgical hymns, or aphorisms into nongenred discourse, as philosophy and theology are misunderstood to be. With genric analysis, theological work can be seen to be a mediation between and among genres. Itself embodied frequently in argument, analogy, and treatise, theology also requires "reading," that is, genric analysis, no less than the recognized genres of literary and biblical texts. In addition, genric analysis is capable of disclosing to authors and readers their own predilection for one or another genre, analogous to the ways in which biblical scholars construct a "working canon" by privileging one or another genre.

Genric analysis makes clear the probability that genres are not indigenous to nature nor perhaps only to one culture. Nevertheless, they do indicate a capacity to make and to recognize rules of reading behavior in response to culture-dependent and culture-transcending bonds. Genric analysis can also alert the reader to tired genres. When genres become too familiar, successful writers alter the genre by introducing new elements, new endings. Chapter 7 demonstrates how interpreters can revitalize genres by testing texts in the light of more than one genre.

GENRE AND GENDER IN THEOLOGICAL REFLECTION

The Woman's Bible demonstrated at the turn of the century that both the biblical text and the methods of interpreting the Bible were seriously deficient with respect to an appropriate understanding of gender. When Stanton and her coauthors claimed that the Bible and its interpretation were sexist, they were making an implicit theological statement in the sense that the referent of the statement pertained both to the character of "the whole" and the conditions for its being other than it was at that time.

Since the 1960s gender issues have come to the fore in biblical interpretation. Their importance can be estimated by the number of references, in relevant biblical publications, to Elisabeth Schüssler Fiorenza's monumental study of the New Testament, *In Memory of Her* (1983), and Phyllis Trible's studies of the Old Testament. Both Schüssler Fiorenza and Trible are explicitly theological. Indeed, although she is less clear about the results of her gender reflection for human beings of both genders together, Schüssler Fiorenza understands her interpretation of the New Testament to be the basis for what she calls "woman church," an alternative to an ecclesial body in which males are designated solely by gender to hold office. Trible, on the other hand, relegates "theological disputation" to footnotes, keeping her focus on the many meanings that the text proposes rather than on the issue of appropriating them. Both Schüssler Fiorenza and Trible treat genre explicitly as well. Schüssler Fiorenza attributes the success of her interpretation to its reliance on the genre narrative as a method of investigation (Schüssler Fiorenza 1983, 152). Trible is attentive to the intricacies of genre delineations, such as in the ways that repetition within a text may signal a shift in genre.

Presuming, then, that gender analysis is today a sine qua non in biblical criticism, let us explore the effects of genre reflection, or the lack of it, in gender criticism. First, let us recall an interpretation in which neither gender nor genre is a critical issue. The following passage is from Francis Quarles's seventeenth-century book of emblems interpreting the Canticle of Canticles. Here is his description of the opening scene of the text:

> a female figure, conventionally signifying the human soul, standing with a flat candlestick in her hand by a bedside; she is turning down the bed-clothes, and appears surprised to find nothing inside them; while on the floor, hidden from her but visible to the reader, is the figure of the Saviour, in the attitude of one who has tumbled out of bed. (Quoted in Moulton 1899)

James Moulton comments that "no irreverence, of course, is intended; but such ludicrous literalism would be impossible to anyone reading the poem as a piece of literature" (ibid., 6). But to determine what is literal and what is other than literal is a problem that is not so easily settled, as can be judged by the disputes between the Alexandrians and the Antiochans in the High Middle Ages and the differences between metaphor theorists today. It is more to the point to observe that Quarles simply assumed that the text is a drama and that the gender designations are without implications. Indeed, his interpretation is precritical, not only in the sense of its being unself-conscious about the act of interpretation (as we saw above), but also because it is devoid of both genric and gender reflection. Most readers today would agree that the dramatic scene he presented is not congruent with the text in specific parts or as a whole. Marcia Falk's interpretation of the Canticle of Canticles, by contrast, carefully assesses the genre of the text. On the grounds that the traditional genres used to interpret this text—drama, cycle of wedding songs, fertility liturgies—result in "forced" readings, she argues instead for treating it as a collection of different types of love songs drawn from different sources and containing some Arabian genric fragments called *wasfs*. She also calls attention to the ways in which the text challenges gender stereotypes, namely, by the avoidance of gender stereotypes in the selection of analogies and by having women initiate love relationships and take active roles throughout the story (Falk 1988, 525–26).

Harold Bloom, a major literary critical deconstructionist best known for his theory of the "influence of anxiety," has published a remarkable study of the first five books of the Old Testament, *The Book of J*, which consists of a 55-page introduction by Bloom, a 115-page new translation of all the passages in the Yahwist strand by David Rosenberg, followed by a 162-page commentary by Bloom. The novel hypothesis proposed by Bloom is that the Yahwist strand of the Torah in Wellhausen's theory may have been written by a woman. Traditionally read piously and in a normative sense, the Yahwist story, when read ironically as the invention of a woman respected in the life of the court, Bloom argues, suddenly takes on new dimensions of meaning and calls into question many of the conclusions previously drawn about it. The basis for Bloom's claim is his discovery that the character Yahweh is treated ironically throughout the texts in the J strand. Bloom thinks it reasonable to suppose that a woman has more reasons to portray Yahweh ironically than a man. Moreover, according to Bloom, the J strand is the only account of the formation of a human female in all the extant related Near Eastern literature, and the creation of the human female is given six times more space than that of the human man.

Bloom credits feminist criticism for his new understanding of the "extravagant strangeness" of the character Yahweh: "It was only in the last year that I began to wonder whether the voice I encounter in the text is that of a woman. My starting point of wonder came when I heard yet once more the familiar contention of feminist criticism that my own theories of influence are patriarchal. Why, I reflected, are the portraits of the Patriarchs and of Moses so mixed, and even at moments so unfavorable, in what the older scholarship found to be the Yahwistic, or earliest, portion of the Pentateuch?" The leap to explain the "strangeness" of Yahweh comes suddenly for Bloom: "It is perfectly clear to me that J neither loved nor feared her Yahweh" (Bloom 1990, 34). Indeed, for Bloom, the author of J "simply was not a religious writer" (ibid., 31).

Bloom dismisses genre considerations with the assertion that "the world's strongest authors are precisely those who violate known forms." The proof is in history: "Shakespeare wrote five-act dramas for stage presentation, yet Shakespeare wrote no genre. What, again, is *Troilas and Cressida?* It is comedy, history, tragedy, satire, yet none of those singly, and more than all of them together. What is Dante's *Commedia?* Is it an epic, a comedy, a spiritual autobiography, or a prophecy . . . ? J mixes everything available to her and produces a work so comprehensive and so universal that the entire Hebrew Bible, Greek New Testament, and Arabic Koran could be founded upon it" (ibid., 18).

Bloom's attempt to take gender criticism of his own work seriously by reversing the gender of an ancient author is daring and imaginative. But it is difficult to find his claims, lacking the discipline of genre reflection, to be as plausible as they are imaginative. Moreover, even if he believes that the presumed author of J had no religious interest in what she portrayed, Bloom's own interpretation of Yahweh as a playful, unpredictable god is at the very least implicitly theological. Yet because his theological position is couched in the genre of ironic treatise, it needs further interpretation for what it implies about the character of the whole of existence.[10]

Radical feminist theologians provide an interesting example of interpreters who bring an insightful gender analysis to bear upon biblical texts but who frequently fail to take genre issues into account. Feminist critics of biblical traditions, such as Mary Daly (1978) and Daphne Hampson (1990), argue that the structures and the central doctrines of Judaism and Christianity are irremediably androcentric. Hampson, for example, criticizes reformist feminists—those who think that it is possible to revise the religious traditions—for wanting to change only the actors rather than the play itself (Hampson 1990, 162). She holds that the damage done to women by the symbolic meaning of Christianity is so extensive and continuous that the most ethical contemporary response is to develop a post-Christian religion with new, nonsexist myths and symbols.

Although Hampson's criticism of Christianity is well founded, her own post-Christian position is surprisingly innocent of reflection on the function of genric structures. She writes that Christianity is irremediably sexist because it is based on the Bible, which is entirely sex-biased: "how could one transform Christian imagery to its very core while Christianity remains rooted in the biblical texts?" (ibid., 108). But the meaning of "rooted in the biblical texts" is not as self-evident as Hampson seems to presume. The meanings of biblical expressions can range from common interpretations to creative interpretations that allude to or even subvert the original texts (Tolbert 1983). Examples of creative interpretation of biblical texts include Judith Plaskow's "Lilith" (1979) (the story of the "other" woman in the Garden of Eden) and Rosemary

Ruether's (1983) midrashic re-creations (of the Creator God/ess or of the disciples' behavior after Christ's death). In addition to the range of the interpretation of biblical texts, changes can be made in the readings of the texts: by understanding critically what it means to "belong" to a genre, by testing for different genres, and by comparing the differences among texts that can be argued to belong to the same genre.

Hampson concedes that the "reworking" of patriarchal myths of biblical literature "may be effective for women immersed in Judaism and Christianity" (Hampson 1990, 110). But her claim that the myths are meaningless for other women underestimates the power of myth. Myths characteristically appeal to people of diverse backgrounds, including people unacquainted with the traditions in which the myths originated (O'Flaherty 1988). The power of the myth of Adam and Eve in Genesis, for better or worse—depending on how it is interpreted—continues in the wider culture among those who may not care whence it comes. Western readers' perennial attraction to Greek myths and their growing appreciation for the myths of Eastern religions illustrate the ability of myth to surpass its origins. Even though ancient Greek religion no longer exists in its original forms, Greek myths—especially as they were originally transformed from Homer and from Hesiod's *Theogony* into the Greek tragedies— continue to exercise a hold on the contemporary imagination, especially as they reappear in new classics, such as Eugene O'Neill's *Mourning Becomes Electra*.

Gender criticism has already had important effects on the way of doing theology in the Christian traditions (Schüssler Fiorenza et al. 1991), thanks to the work of revisionary feminist theologians, whose work is to reform the tradition, and the radical feminist religious thinkers, whose work has been to critique the tradition and often to construct alternatives to the tradition. Thus far these two directions, like gender and genre criticism in biblical interpretation, have diverged. But the point of divergence is specifiable. Whereas the revisionists have for the most part taken genre seriously, the radical work is largely uninformed by genre considerations. One of the revisionists' major contributions may be the creation of new religious expressions. Indeed, they affirm the meaningfulness for themselves of new genres—such as womanist hymns of praise, myths of birth and death, and ritual prayers—

as they occur in new religions. But they do address neither the issue of the status of these genres outside the new religions nor how they may be related to traditional religious genres. Do the new texts have meaning only for these new religions? This is an epistemological question that needs to be addressed.

Among biblical interpretations that take explicit account of both gender and genre issues, Mieke Bal's work is exemplary. In her *Lethal Love: Feminist Literary Readings of Biblical Love Stories* (1987), for example, Bal examines four well-known biblical stories (the stories of Samson and Delilah in Judges, chapters 13–16; Tamar in Genesis, chapters 37–39; Adam and Eve in Genesis 2:4b–3:27; and Ruth in the Book of Ruth) in the light of the three contrasting models of interpretation: "frame theory," the "semiotics of form," and "narratology," which she treats as a variation of the structuralist approach. Bal agrees that both frame theory and the semiotics of form are adequate enough in terms of literary critical considerations. But she goes on to demonstrate how both models "fail the critics" at crucial moments in their reading of the texts: the critics assume what is relevant with respect to gender in Hebrew culture but then overlook a crucial "gap" in the text" (Bal 1987, 35). Bal argues that it is possible to avoid opting for either a sexist or a feminist reading—she refers to both as "equally false"—and instead finds in the text "traces of a *problematization* of man's priority and domination" (ibid., 110). Genre and gender considerations are here woven through the interpretation, and the two kinds of issues mutually inform each other.

Most of the examples in this chapter bear out the claim that in biblical interpretation, gender and genre criticism for the most part have gone separate ways. Bal's work, together with that of a few others, makes it possible to think that the divergence is only a temporary state.

CHAPTER FOUR

How to "Belong" to a Genre or a Gender

Animals are divided into: (a) belonging to the Emperor, (b) embalmed, (c) tame, (d) sucking pigs, (e) sirens, (f) fabulous, (g) stray dogs, (h) included in the present classification, (i) frenzied, (j) innumerable, (k) drawn with a very fine camelhair brush, (l) et cetera, (m) having just broken the water pitcher, (n) that from a long way off look like flies.
Jorge Luis Borges, as quoted in Michel Foucault, The Order of Things
(1970, xv)

At first glance, the question of how to "belong" to a genre or a gender seems to pertain to two different groups. After all, do not texts belong to a genre and people to a gender? Is it not self-evident that certain texts are novels or poems and that certain persons are male or female? It is true that the everyday world appears to run on these unquestioned assumptions. Movies, for example, are classified and marketed by production studios according to established genres. But even the Arts and Leisure section of the Sunday paper documents that traditional ideas about gender and genres change: The bildungsroman, until recently presumed to be about the growth and development of a male hero, is reported to have been modified and now includes the growth and development of females as well. Even if we set aside cultural variations on how "male" and "female" are understood, the classification of gender into male and female ignores a significant part of the human population, persons who are, for example, hermophrodite, androgenous, or sexually ambiguous. The purpose of this chapter is to challenge what seems to be self-evident about genre and gender when they begin to inform the act of interpretation.[1]

97

Genre Choices, Gender Questions

GENRE, GENDER, AND THE USE OF DIAGNOSTICS

When we locate the terms *genre* and *gender* etymologically in a family of meanings across several disciplines, we find that they share family resemblances. The family to which both *genre* and *gender* belong includes words such as *general, gender, genre, genes, genus, generic, generation,* and *generative.* This family of *genre* and *gender* carries two general senses: the categorial and the productive. The categorial sense pertains to the meaning "of a kind or sort" (in the case of *gender,* the sense of differentiation according to biological or grammatical constructs; in the case of *generation,* the sense of differentiation according to spiritual, biological, chemical, or physical form). The productive sense means "of or pertaining to the act of rooting, begetting, bearing, producing." The productive sense is analogous to what is referred to as the "praxis dimension" in chapter 1. With respect to gender, production only partially, and only for some human beings, pertains to the production of children. Even in this instance, biology is one of several fields of differentiation and not necessarily the dominant.

By placing the terms *genre* and *gender* in their larger family of resemblances, we see that the problems of understanding genre and gender are not unique to the discipline of literary criticism. The double meanings of differentiation and production in the whole family of terms suggests that exclusive emphasis on differentiation as the meaning of the terms *genre* and *gender* is clearly an aberration—an aberration, moreover, that has resulted in both terms losing their epistemological (knowledge-in-process) dimension.

Despite their common family of meaning, *genre* and *gender* have quite different relationships within different fields of meanings. For the notion of genre, the differences between its use in literary criticism and the notion of species in biology, the field that is most often compared with literary criticism, are emphasized. In his *Literature as System (1971),* Claudio Guillén notes that what was regarded as a species in Renaissance criticism is today understood as a genre, and that the classical expectation that a genre contains things that are "specifically different from one another" has by and large been lost in literary criticism. This loss is reflected in the commonsense understanding that in literary criticism the individual text is of greater importance than the genre, and that in biology the species and genus are more important than the individual organism. With respect to the notion of gender, however, biological differentiation is often presumed to be sufficient and exhaustive.

There is some evidence, however, that there need not be a disciplinary split on the issue of what it means to "belong" to a genre or to a gender. In both literary criticism and biology, the initial stage of understanding is to sort, to classify, and to identify by similarities and differences. In other words, to claim that something or someone belongs to a gender or genre begins by observing how one something or someone *behaves* as a genre or gender. In everyday life, how do we decide if someone is a man or a woman?[2] Aside from some biological information (which we don't ordinarily possess), we depend on behavior—clothing, hair, body shape, gait, and activities. Our first guesses are sometimes wrong or we cannot decide, because personality that expresses itself as gender is a composite of features. Do not texts behave in the same way? In some sense they can be said to have a personality, which expresses itself in genre. The person or text as advertised (by associates, friends, blurbs) do not always turn out to be as we expected. This process of gender testing goes on all the time and allows for biological males to be of the female gender and vice versa. The way in which we experiment with—and break—the presumed link between sex and gender provides us with a model for genre testing as well.

Because theory is largely inexplicit in gender and genre testing, we may be tempted is to think of species as "real" objects and to think of genera as "unreal" abstractions. Indeed, in biology the concept "species" is understood as having corresponding referents, whereas the concept "genus" is understood as being an arbitrary generalization that does not refer to any real objects. Genera in biology seldom, if ever, change. They have an equivalent in morphological literary criticism, where the genus is alternatively understood as "universal," "type," or "mode of representation"—all understood as being essentially unchanging.

What distinguishes categorial from productive understanding in the long run is the presence or absence of theory. In both literary criticism and in biology, it is possible, of course, to arrange individual items into progressively more and more inclusive groups, without referring explicitly to the theory that accounts for both the pattern and its sequential construction. In both literary criticism and in the sciences, however, categories are in the service of an explicit or presumed hypothesis. In biology, for example, the categories are determined by the extent to which they contribute to the theory of evolution—a theory that since 1930 has been the general organizing principle of biology (von Mayr 1963, 1:17). Genre and gender in biology today thus reveal themselves to be under the guidance of explicit presuppositions and assumptions. Literary histories, too, are organized around explanatory theories—theories that struggle against one another and that change the historical process as it changes them.[3] The range of theories in literary criticism in wider than that in biology, notwithstanding several versions of the theory of evolution; the composite human subject gives rise to multiple, and frequently conflicting, meanings.

In biology we are eventually compelled to ask what were the conditions under which evolutionary hypotheses were developed, on what grounds are they accepted, or rejected, or modified, and what criteria of truth are applied to them. In literary criticism, largely as an effect of ideological criticism, we are brought to ask how genres and genders are constructed, what do they accomplish, and what are the grounds for their effectiveness in particular times and places.

It is sometimes thought that the criteria for acceptance of a hypothesis differ radically in the sciences and the humanities. Even in the sciences, however, the continued support of any hypothesis can be explained in two ways by using different understandings of theory. In the first way, theories are understood to be *classes of statements,* some of which are established as true or as false by empirical means. "Empirical" here means testing and sampling for appropriate "fits." This is sometimes called the "statement view," a position held by philosophers of science such as Karl Popper and Imre Lakatos. The statement view invokes criteria of validity (fulfillment of appropriate methods and warrants) and verifiability (certification by more than one person). In the second way of supporting a hypothesis, a theory is a "composite mathematical structure together with a class of intended applications" (Stegmuller 1976, 14, 19). This is known as the "nonstatement view," a position taken by Thomas Kuhn. The main feature of the nonstatement view is that it depends "not upon the *truth* of scientific statements so much as upon their *applicability* to empirical states of affairs (Schmidt 1982, 6). A live explanatory hypothesis receives continued support, in this view, not so much because newly gathered evidence continues to "correspond" with the theory, as because the theory provides the best "functional consensus" for most applications; that is, it is most coherent and offers the best account of our overall experience (ibid., 7). It is claimed that the nonstatement view of theory, which invokes the criterion of viability, cannot be verified or falsified because its truth is of a more comprehensive kind than can be measured by any test. The nonstatement view is an apt description of validation and verification in the humanities as well as in the sciences.

Some of the same problems in the application of categorization exist in both the natural sciences and in literary studies. Species in biology and genres in literary criticism can easily fall prey to a forgetfulness of the theory and of the comprehensive situation in which it is enacted and maintained. These lapses yield positivist or classicist views of species and genres—views in which concrete texts and objects are taken to be the sole determinant of what is the case. The oversights of positivism and classicism are strikingly similar in that they both ignore the processes of theory making and theory maintenance.

But if no hidden biases obscure the level of theory and hypothesis, it is possible to understand the categorial and the productive senses of genre and gender as interdependent. Having learned from philosophy of science that categorizing is the major activity in the early stages of a science, we will understand categorizing as a kind of empirical diagnostics, in which new observations and data are tested in the light of implicit theory and in the context of established genres and species. But beyond categorizing there is the productive activity of science and literary criticism, which focuses on explicit theory making and interpretation. In terms of productivity, genre testing and gender reflection are central to both science and literary criticism.

"BELONGING" TO A GENRE OR A GENDER

We are now prepared to extend the history of genre that has already been constructed in chapter 2—a history informed primarily, though unevenly, by Platonic and Aristotelian philosophy, morphological criticism, formalism, and structuralism.[4] In this chapter we consider contemporary options for understanding how to "belong" to a genre and then how to "belong" to a gender. Notwithstanding the diversity of contemporary theories of genre, three basic views can be distinguished as responses to the question of "how to belong" to a genre in literary criticism, that discipline most committed—although not unequivocally so—to genre theory. These positions are the traditionalist view, as illustrated in Fowler 1982; the ideological view,[5] as understood in contemporary discourse theory; and the deconstructionist view, a special form of the ideological view, as represented by Jacques Derrida (1980). We compare the traditionalist belief that genres never transcend their localities[6] to the ideological belief that genres are always systematically biased in their approximations of reality, and to the deconstructionist belief that genres always exceed their stated rhetorical purposes. To make explicit the ability of this new concept of genre to include live and emerging as well as conventional genres, genre is redefined as a process analogous to metaphoric process. Finally, we take up parallel options for understanding gender.

The Traditionalist View

In the traditionalist view, genre theory is built on the tension between singularity and commonality, between individual and species. Its major concern is that of safeguarding the uniqueness of the individual text. Traditionalists are skeptical of genre theory. That they often use it prescriptively, however, reveals that they regard it as a necessary tool for understanding. At the same time, traditionalists resign themselves to the dilemma that neither belonging nor not belonging to particular genres *guarantees* that all of a text's features will be understood or even recognized, since theoretically there would have to be as many genres as there are texts to attend to every variation in kind.

Cyril Birch gives us a striking analogy for understanding the traditionalist presumptions in his collection of essays on several different genres in Chinese literature. In his effort to introduce Western readers to unfamiliar texts, he makes the following analogy: "A literary genre is a comfortable saddle. The writer-rider once installed has the assurance that he will be in full control of his mount; the reader-rider who follows need not fear being bounced and shaken beyond endurance. . . . Expectations of form fulfilled leave us freer to contemplate the total meaning" (Birch 1974, 4). This homey image, this idea of manufactured leatherware, form-fitted to the size of an animal (as well as the human body), schemes to domesticate text by means of genre. The author's mount is, of course, the text, which seems to need some kind of control in order for the reader-rider to arrive at some understanding of the ride as a whole. A second reading of the passage alerts us to a pattern of key terms: "comfortable"; "assurance"; "full control"; "no . . . fear"; "form fulfilled." Genre tames and "controls" the text and, we might add, the reader, just as the saddle does the horse.

The point of traditionalist genre criticism is stated clearly: "Happiest of all will be the literary critic-historian, for he will be able to determine where the work 'belongs'." The patterning is conclusive: "happiest," "determine," "belongs." Although Birch is aware that the rider might, on occasion, be thrown out of the saddle—Birch notes that "All will canter smoothly until the genre itself changes, or splits, or falls to pieces and is replaced" (ibid.)— it is apparent that neither the emergence nor the "falling off" of genre is vital to Birch's understanding of genre. Indeed, in the traditionalist view, the emergence and the decline of genres are negative instances, or failures, of genre.

Birch was interested primarily in literary history as an uncontested report of information known or capable of being discovered. An implicit question does seem to be signaled by Birch's use of quotation marks in the phrase "he will be able to determine where the work 'belongs.' " Yet the model for the text's "belonging" is taken from stabilized genres, and while there is a recognition that genres change, this fact does not enter into the problem of "belonging," since each historical period is discrete. In Birch's analysis, genres are heuristic devices—to use E. D. Hirsch's terminology (Hirsch 1967, 78, 88, 110, 116f, 271)—that enable readers to "handle" otherwise unmanageable, unique texts. Genres may also constitute historical facts insofar as they are descriptions of groupings that have occurred. But in the traditionalist view, they do not constitute any systematic understanding of either literature in general or of particular texts.

The bias in favor of the individual text, considered as unique—the bias that militates against any correlation with scientific understanding—can be seen even more clearly in Alistair Fowler's introduction to genre theory: "Literature cannot be counted the material of a critical science, the material of mechanical engineering, or puddings of a branch of domestic science. There are gods in literature's machines, who are said to metamorphose and multiply beyond knowing. . . . The *materia critica* should not be thought of as a group of objects. It is literature subjectively encountered, individually and in part variously constructed, interpreted, and valued, within the institutions of societies that change" (Fowler 1982, 1).

We notice, first of all, the caricature of a "critical science" (machines and puddings) that betrays at worst a misunderstanding of science or at best an effort to emphasize the nonempirical over the empirical ("gods in literature . . . multiply beyond knowing"). We notice also the prejudice toward the unique in Fowler's opposition of "literature subjectively encountered, individually and in part variously constructed" to literature as a "group of objects." Although genre theory, in Fowler's view, mitigates the absolute individuality of texts, still the major concern is to preserve their uniqueness. In the traditionalist view, whatever similarities may be found among texts, their *differences* are the determining factors of their identity.

On the basis of these two fairly characteristic treatments of genre—one, an example of applied criticism and the second, of theory—we may say that basic to the traditionalist view is the assumption that every noteworthy text aims and succeeds at being unique. Indeed, it is difficult to find exceptions. Jorge Luis Borges (1962) created the inimitably imaginable case of what it would mean for a twentieth-century author to compose anew the seventeenth-century novel by Cervantes *Don Quixote*. Borges's author, Pierre Menard, completes only two or three chapters of the masterpiece. But even these chapters, written with identical words, are understood differently because the chapters appear four centuries later than the original, when the language no longer has the same meaning. It seems reasonable to believe that, aside from the highly improbable circumstance designed by Borges, the goal of being unique is achieved by every book—whether the referent of a work be some state of affairs, such as the act of writing about an unhappy family in Vladimir Nabokov's *Ada* (1969); some idea, such as "nothingness" in Samuel Beckett's *Stories and Texts for Nothing* (1967); nonsense, as in Ghanic folktales;[7] or even the act of writing itself, as in John Barth's *Lost in the Funhouse* (1969). A text aims to represent its referent in such a way that what is said is (1) a new saying of the already-said, (2) a saying of the not-yet-said, (3) a new denial of the already-said, (4) a denial of the not-yet-said, or (5) some combination of these ambitions.

Yet to be understood at all, a text must belong to a network of texts. The goal of originality is ever, at best, only partially realized. Hence, the dilemma of the text in the traditionalist view is that, in spite of its uniqueness, a text *must* belong to a genre. In this sense, belonging to a genre is rather like relativity—motion must be *with respect to* something.

A first step toward the resolution of this apparent contradiction is to notice that the dictionary definition of *unique*—"one of a kind"—has certain epistemological limitations.[8] Logically this definition is self-contradictory: if something is only one of a kind, it is not *of* a "kind" at all; it is *its own* logical type, *sui generis*. This definition precludes our imagining other members of the type. Based on the assumption of existence, then, the last surviving object of a type—say, the last existing crane—can be said to be unique. What is usually meant by this first definition, however, is that within a group of similar things, one object is different enough to call attention to the differences it has with the others, often at the expense of its likenesses, which are ignored or subverted for the purposes of identifying the thing *as* unique. This way of understanding the first definition of unique is supported by its second dictionary definition: "having no like or equal," in other words, matchless and unequaled. The second definition does not incur the contradiction present in the first.[9]

One of the unfortunate results of traditionalists' overemphasis on the uniqueness of the literary text is the common conclusion that scientific and literary/artistic inquiry must have radically different objects. Traditionalists presume that literary and artistic interest maximizes differences between one object and another, and that scientific interest focuses on similarities among objects. The event of experiencing the individual object in all its concreteness is considered to be intrinsic to literary and artistic interpretation. Attention to such experiencing is too frequently neglected in scientific inquiry.

In what sense is the traditionalists' claim—that a work of literature or an art object is unique—legitimate? Originality is not sanctioned by history, since the ancients sought not to be original but to do more perfectly what had already been done. Nevertheless, the claim is epistemologically sound insofar as it pertains to an object that so fixes our attention that we must suspend our attention to other objects (whether similar or dissimilar) and permit the object to give rise to spontaneous questions and reflections. For an object or phenomenon to fix one's attention so exclusively, it must stand out from among all others. In the case of *all* phenomena, whether traditionally conceived as literary or scientific, the *experience* of the perceiver must be presumed and ideally will be made explicit.[10] If such experiences of phenomena remain private and do not enter into public discussion and attention, the object is likely to remain unknown or marginal in a particular period or epoch. Reader-reception theory has taught us that an object may be central to its immediate audience (for example, Charles Dickens's David Copperfield and Marie Curie's discovery of radium) or it may not be central until a later generation (as was the case for Gustave Flaubert's *Madame Bovary*[11] and Gregor Johann Mendel's expression of the laws of heredity). In either case, an object becomes understood and accepted by means of generic considerations—considerations that constitute literary and artistic as well as scientific knowledge.[12] In no case does unique mean exclusively unlike: if anything is completely unlike everything that we know, it is likely to be either rejected as meaningless or not even perceived. All knowing is with respect to something. At the moment of encounter, of course, any object can be apprehended as unique: Every blade of grass is unique—and not only for Walt Whitman—and every text is likely to be unlike any other. If I have seen only one iceberg, *that* experience of seeing and hence *that iceberg* is unique (to me, of course). But uniqueness is meaningless unless we differentiate between the differences that are trivial and those that are significant. Both persons and texts can be unique in significant ways. But such uniqueness ordinarily does not preclude, indeed it may even be verified by, their being apprehended in relation to other objects in some genric terms.[13] Recent reflections on the role of the "other" points up the complexity of this relationship.

In the sciences, the epistemological situation is not significantly different. However unique individual objects may appear to be to an individual or group of observers, what is significant is what can be *known* about the object—that is, one or several forms or aspects that are understood in relation to those same forms or aspects in at least one other object.

The notion of "style"—understood as characteristic traits of an individual author's work—has also been used to buttress the claim that literary/artistic objects are unique. But this understanding of style leaves no room for the expectation that certain techniques may be the shared possession of more than one author and that it is in the particular *constellation* of techniques that the differences lie. Furthermore, it is possible to study the components of one author's way of handling certain technical problems, choice of words, imagery, syntax, and resolution of tension (e.g., Kermode's "sense of an ending"), so that the concept "author" comes to mean "style" in the totality of the senses in which style has been understood (Ricoeur 1973b, 136–37). In the sciences, style is not as diverse a phenomenon as in the humanities. This is not to say that style is not a factor: "elegant" solutions and "parsimony" as a canon merely take precedence over all others, sometimes to the apparent exclusion of all others.

The history of the science of stylistics throws more light on the way in which style is derivatively known only as a relationship. Corresponding to the ancients' disregard for originality, stylistics was largely prescriptive and normative until the mid-nineteenth century. Its object of study can be any text—an author's corpus, a single passage, the works of a particular historical period, or, most recently, texts differentiated by gender. The science of stylistics is used to compare texts, to evaluate the coherence of perceived traits, to determine authorship, and to date texts. One school of thought, *Stilforschung,* associated with the poetics of Bernadetto Croce, concentrated on what can be known about the "inner form," the spirit or psychological attitude of the author, by means of "outer form," or artistic phenomena (Wimsatt and Brooks 1967, 502–3). This form of stylistic inquiry has been judged most reliable when applied to the authors of a particular period or nation.

The differentiation between genre and gender on the one hand and style on the other can be made in such a way that style is not relegated to the private or to the unique. *Style* is a genric term, and one that is gendered as well. Even in the humanities it is applied to periods and schools as well as to individual authors or artists.

The Ideological View

The second view of belonging to a genre is built on the tension between texts and social contexts. Ideological critics are concerned with disclosing the inevitability of that tension in such a way as to prevent the substitution of nonliterary explanations for the literary texts themselves. Ideological critics select genres on the basis of their power to explain social privilege or oppression. They employ genre almost exclusively as a tool of negative criticism: For ideological critics, even the concept "genre" is understood to privilege the primacy of the text over readers. In this sense, they believe, traditional genres betray a romanticism that they think needs to be unmasked as false consciousness (Jauss 1978, 137).

In contrast to the traditionalist view that genres are region- and time-specific, ideological critics believe that genres transcend regional boundaries. Besides being rooted in specific cultures, genres, for ideological critics, are also inscribed in opposing social relations—oppositions that depend on one another and that exhibit large commonalities across specific cultures. An example of such an opposition is the privileging of individual experience at the expense of shared and common human experience (Bal 1984).

Ideological critics do not limit their work to analyses of particular genres in order to demonstrate how they are, without remainder, reflections of a ruling class's interests. Indeed, the term *ideology* is used by critics in several different ways. From the time of its origin in the French Enlightenment, the term signified a general attempt to explain a historical-social phenomenon by its origin in specific ideas. Religion was explained in early forms of ideology critique as arising out of the desire of the ruling classes to perpetuate their privileges. Early analyses of ideology came to be identified with "deception theory," a term that referred to the "false conscience" of those who originated an ideology and who promulgated lies to keep themselves in power. Later forms of ideology critique focus less on the duplicity of originators and more on the complicity of all participants in a given superstructure.

In particular, the Marxist version of ideology shifts the focus from ideas to economic structures that are understood to distort reality and to perpetuate a false consciousness in those who maintain as well as originate such systems. A good example of an ideological analysis of structures in relation to questions of genre is Theodor Adorno's and Max Horkheimer's description of how nineteenth-century interpretations of *The Odyssey* exploited the irrational by seeing it merely as a mythic element that was overcome when myth was incorporated into the genre epic (Horkheimer and Adorno 1972, 43–80, note 10). A second example can be found in feminist critiques of the readings of the Hebrew Book of Genesis as genreless and timeless truths, rather than as narrative calling for interpretation. The feminist critiques call into question patriarchal exegesis that, by reading Genesis as etiological myth, promotes the idea of male domination and female deviousness and perpetuates the oppression of women in religion and society (Trible 1973).

Literary criticism sometimes combines sociology of knowledge with a form of ideology critique. This combination of methods is based on the assumption that all human knowledge and thinking are the result of social processes. Although this combination of ideology and sociology of knowledge removes the stigma of a false conscience, the claim that analyses done in this mode of thought are themselves "value-free" has been challenged. By abjuring questions of truth or falsity, sociologists of knowledge obscure the processes and results of their own judgments and abandon the question of truth and evaluation to positivist-empiricist thought.[14] Other forms of ideological critique can be useful in making explicit values that are assumed but not argued for in the descriptive analyses of social histories, such as in Arnold Hauser's *Sociology of Art* (1957).

A similar method can be found in recent reconstructions of the genre of autobiography, for example, that argue that nineteenth-century readings of eighteenth-century autobiographies were flawed inasmuch as they presumed a unified self and overlooked the inconsistencies, contradictions, and equivocations that suffuse eighteenth-century autobiographical writings (Nussbaum, 1986).

Again, this kind of genre history is not itself value-free. The twentieth-century ideological critiques of eighteenth-century autobiographies, for example, have their own investment in the idea of a disunited, disoriented self that emphasizes societal processes at the expense of critical decisions. These critiques would seem to be ideological themselves to the extent that they fail to argue why the idea of a unified self is an ideology and fail to question what kind of ideology is the idea of a disunited self. Indeed, this is the major question for ideology critique: if every critique of ideology itself is merely in opposition to an ideology, doesn't the critique perpetuate, rather than correct, the structures of reality?

In one sense, the problem of freeing oneself from an ideology resembles the problem of freeing oneself from a genre. In both situations, there is the recognition of an undesirable but inevitable fact. In the introduction to his collection of essays, *The Politics of Interpretation* (1982), W. J. T. Mitchell describes the predicament of those who employ ideology critique. He does not know how interpretation can be a viable route to understanding, he says,

> unless it wins for cultural work some common ground for negotiation and struggle between ideologies and disciplines. The staking out of this common ground may well be the most controversial and difficult objective that these essays could attain. For it is precisely the appeal to a background of relatively neutral commonplaces, criteria, and concurrent practices that tends to be denied by a concern with the politics of interpretation. Any such appeal is likely to be denounced as a disguised grab for power, an attempt to seize the political high ground by laying claim to some reserve of scientific, aesthetic, or ethical "purity." But we also need to ask ourselves what the cost will be of failing to acknowledge some principle contrary to the political, some dialectical antithesis to the social, cultural, and historical world that [human beings make around themselves]. Some obvious candidates for this position are God, Nature, Logic, and the Individual, notions which are usually dismissed by interpretive politicians. If these notions cannot be recuperated, then we will still have to answer [the] question: [Ideology] as opposed to what? (Mitchell 1982, 5)[15]

So long as those who employ ideology critique fail to address the question of the inevitability of themselves having an ideology, they are themselves apt targets of ideology critique.

Louis Althusser, in his essay "Ideology and Ideological State

Apparatuses: Notes towards an Investigation" (1970), gives a first reasonable response to this dilemma that ideology has with itself. Althusser points out the "double struggle" of ideologies—that they arise from social conflicts and, by means of prevailing practices, reproduce those conflicts. Discourse theorists have taken this insight and shown how the same language in different genres can be used as a weapon in opposing ideologies. In her book *Theories of Discourse* Diane Macdonell notices that in England in the forty years after the French Revolution, "words were a weapon of struggle so that, for example, what might count as a 'hymn' became an issue of importance" (Macdonnell 1986, 24). Shelley's *Hymn to Intellectual Beauty* (1817), for example, although clearly a poem employing orthodox Christian vocabulary ("grace," "spirit," "hope,") could be read as a humanist, atheist manifesto:

> Love, Hope, and Self-esteem, like clouds depart
> And come, for some uncertain moments lent.
> Man were immortal, and omnipotent,
> Didst thou, unknown and awful as thou art,
> Keep with thy glorious train firm state within his heart. (as quoted in
> Mcdonnell 1986, 25)

Macdonell uses Althusser's work to show how ideology is always rooted in material and social constructions. She argues that to be a force for change, ideology can no longer simply maintain the struggle—thus reproducing the conflict—but instead has to negotiate the terms of the struggle. Her own contribution is to show how the "struggle of discourses changes their meanings" (ibid., 51). By means of the ideological view of criticism, we are able to see that when genres or genders are involved in a struggle with (as distinct from a reaction to) other genres or genders, either to preserve or to destroy meanings, they are changed in the process. In terms of the ideological view, genres are more appropriately viewed as changing rather than as static.

The Deconstructionist View

Deconstructionist criticism is here understood as a form of ideology critique that shifts the focus of critique from social structures to the *language* of ideas, structures, and knowledge. To those who would explain social-historical phenomena by their origin in specific ideas, the deconstructionist critics insist that writing both precedes and takes precedence over any specific ideas. To those who see the world as the dialectic of materialism and oppression, Jacques Derrida—together with Julia Kristeva, Giles Deleuze, and Michel Foucault, on the basis of their different analyses of the relation of textuality to representation—critiques all body-images of power and presence (Bloom et al. 1979, vii). And to those who claim to be value-free in their analysis of human beings as the product of social processes, the deconstructionists employ semiotic analyses of texts showing how words constantly betray their users' stated intentions.

Deconstructionism reveals a fundamental ambivalence in the relation of texts to genres. On the one hand, Derrida, for example, affirms a role for genre: every text participates in one or several genres, there is not a genreless text, there are always a genre and genres, yet such participation never amounts to belonging (Derrida 1980, 212). (Can we not say also that there is not a genderless text, there are always a gender and genders, yet such participation never amounts to belonging?) These claims are only partially dependent on the plurality of genres and genders. For the deconstructionists, genres are destroyed by individual texts. "Making genre its mark" means that the text puts itself in a position to be "marked" by a genre, *and* that it targets genre to destroy genre in the same act that genre destroys the text. In Derrida's view, the act of genrification is a necessary death for both texts and genres:

> The clause or floodgate of genre declasses what it allows to be classed. It tolls the knell of genealogy or of genericity, which it however brings forth to the light of day. Putting to death the very thing that it engenders, it cuts a strange figure, a formless form, it remains nearly invisible, it neither sees the day nor brings it to light. Without it, neither genre nor literature come to light, but as soon as there is this blinking of an eye, this clause or this floodgate of genre, at the very moment that a genre or a literature is broached, at that very moment degenerescence has begun, the end begins. (ibid., 213)

The end begins, that is, when the act of writing or reading the text ends in the beginning of genric understanding—which understanding is also one of the "ends" of the text itself.

In Derrida's view, the individual text is analogous to a word in the system of language; each text is a unit synchronous with other units, together forming a system of texts that parlay (*parle!*) their own and one another's meanings. Texts permit themselves to be related to one another, now in this way and now in that, but never to "belong" to one or another group (genre or kind). In contrast both to the traditionalist view (in which the writer and reader are in control) and the ideological view (in which readers collaborate with authors), the deconstructionist views written texts as controlling writers and readers. Applied to gender, the deconstructionist view of texts runs parallel to the view that a person's gender is constituted (or controlled) by the texts of one's culture.

Deconstructionist critics work in opposition to traditionalist genre theory in the sense that their mode of analysis unravels the genre or conventional "intent" of the text by subversive word associations from across the disciplines. In his analysis of Rousseau, for example, Derrida plays with Rousseau's word *supplement* to undo Rousseau's stated purposes (Derrida 1974, 141–64, 269–316). Disciplines are similarly unboundaried *as genres:* Where traditionalist and ideological criticism retain the literary as a discrete field, in deconstructionism "writing is 'littérature et philosophie melée" (Hartman 1981, xviii). The effect of treating philosophy as another genre is to deny philosophy the prerogative it has traditionally assumed for itself—that of surpassing genric considerations—and to reduce philosophy to a lesser genre, namely, commentary, which in turn is understood not on its own terms but as derivative from and parasitic upon literature. Emerging and declining genres are not major issues for deconstructionist criticism, since their inquiries are limited to the arbitrary and constantly changing synchronic relations among and within texts.

Deconstructionist criticism ignores the sciences or dismisses them as equivalent to positivism. Geoffrey Hartman, for example, concludes his commentary on Derrida's *Glas* with the following statement about his own method:

> I have tried to recover a sense of "the wound in the word" in relation to "the word in the word." . . . I have wished to describe rather than explain; and I have used mainly literary examples. I cannot find it in myself to worry the question of the relation of empirical evidence to theory and, in particular, to the hypothesis of a primal word-wound. I always slip back to a historical or psychological starting point

mediated by literature. My field of inquiry is bounded by language and its intricate relation to human development. (ibid., 154)

But just how successful is this deconstructive critique of empirical knowledge? Hartman gives a name to Derrida's method—*"discours prophetique et pare."* But Hartman goes on to comment: although Derrida's word plays—elisions, convolutions, and genetic associations—are proclaimed to eschew "all allegoresis, all ideologizing moves, it remains an open question whether [such discourse] . . . can resist being in the service of political power" (ibid., xxv). Like other forms of ideological criticism, deconstructionism relativizes history and, in so doing, constitutes a new phenomenon, capable of being known and dealt with in ways other than it intends or anticipates, for example, politically and literarily. Nor does deconstructionism seem capable of maintaining indefinitely the conditions necessary to its own survival, namely, a plurality of texts and meanings and the freedom to associate this plurality in multiple ways.

The deconstructionists force us to raise the issue of genre as knowledge. First, by relinquishing the pursuit of "positive" meaning in literary texts, the deconstructionists make the formal aspect of knowledge (in this case, language) its ultimate referent. In so doing, they radicalize the question of meaning and the cognitive status of *all* texts. Second, by claiming to untangle "the inherence of metaphysics in nihilism and of nihilism in metaphysics" (Miller 1979, 230),[16] deconstructionist criticism makes explicit the interdependency the relationship between texts and commentaries on texts. Miller calls this interdependency the inseparability of host text and parasite (ibid., 220ff). Because it transgresses the boundaries of the text in new ways, deconstructionism treats genre more arbitrarily than either traditionalist or ideological criticism.

From our study of contemporary options regarding the understanding of genre theory, we are now prepared to draw three conclusions. First, historical description is no longer a sufficient basis for defining genre theory. History and description are always accompanied by "extralogical" interests—interests that in fact provide leading threads for one or another reading and that call for articulation whenever such interests impede dialogical progress. More importantly, the deconstructionists have taught us that logic can always be defeated by attending to the hidden counterlogic always present within it. Second, genre theory must take into account the roles of author, reader, spheres of discourse, and text—making the necessary allowances when exploiting one at the expense of another in the act of interpretation. Genre theory will present each element of interpretation as producing and being produced by the other elements. Third, claims to uniqueness made on behalf of art and literary texts must be related to the claims for and against the uniqueness of other epistemic objects. Ideology critique assists us in overcoming the naïveté endemic to classical genre theory—a naïveté that manifests itself under exaggerated notions of uniqueness. By means of ideology critique, texts reveal their similarities and differences and lend themselves to critical analysis so that it is reasonable to claim (*pace* Alastair Fowler) that genres, as well as texts, do transcend their localities in determinate and significant ways. Is it reasonable to make a similar claim for gender?

CONTEMPORARY OPTIONS FOR UNDERSTANDING GENDER

How adaptable are these foregoing contemporary options for understanding genre: the traditional, the ideological, and the deconstructionist? Although existing genre theories, such as Northrop Frye's (1969) mythic correlations, Gérard Genette's (1981) structures of literary discourse, and Mikhail Bakhtin's (1986) speech genres, do not correspond to any one of these options without remainder, the options nevertheless provide for systematic relationships among the theories and their applications. In turn, these relationships disclose features of the theories, features that otherwise are hidden or obscured by other considerations.

It is possible to understand gender according to the same three options. Several elements in this topology apply to gender as well as to genre with similar results. The traditional way of understanding gender according to biological constitution has been challenged by the realization that traditionalism does not account for the ways in which persons and things are gendered by cultural processes. Even the more recent distinction between sex and gender—sex referring to the biological distinction, which is applicable to all but a very few human beings, and gender referring to the varied cultural determinations of what counts as "male" and what counts as "female"—has come to share a similar criticism, namely, that it is unable to account for variations across cultures that are related to class and race. The ideological view of gender introduces an important historical-critical element in understanding the effects of gender indicators in particular cultures, but the ideological view taken alone is less able to account for changes within particular ideologies and is pessimistic if not dismissive of efforts to surpass ideologies, even when they become conscious. The deconstructive view of gender reveals the negativity at the heart of any attempt to claim a determinative meaning for gender identity, but the deconstructive view taken alone results in a devastation of meaning that ultimately is incompatible with much of our experience of lived reality. In other words, like existentialism, deconstructionism has been indispensable in chastising the substantialist perceptions of gender based on classical metaphysics. At the same time, like analytic philosophy, deconstructionism is a field of inquiry so restrictive as to be rendered next to useless for understanding the more crucial and (equally, if not more) interesting ways of constructing selves and meanings on the whole.

We can derive a more appropriate typology for what it means to "belong to a gender"—one that is similar to but not the same as the one we have used for "belonging to a genre"—from Julia Kristeva's notion of "Women's Time" (1981).[17] Kristeva observes that the women's movement can be understood to have had three phases or generations. The first phase is characterized by women's claim on an equal part of traditional benefits of being a member of society: the right to vote, to participate freely in public as recognized professionals, to receive equal pay for equal work, to decide for themselves whether to bear children or not. Generalized with respect to gender, this revised traditional view of gender is comparable with the traditional view of genre in the sense that male and female categories are for the most part left unquestioned while a liberal political goal of equality for both sexes is pursued. We shall call this first phase "liberal" to signify that equal rights and opportunities, regardless of gender, is the central issue.

In the second phase, characteristic of French feminism after 1968, for example, women are suspicious of the public realm represented primarily by males. Feminists of the second phase seek to replace androcentric values with gynocentric ones and to transvaluate the perceived attributes of feminine from negative to positive. Generalized with respect to gender, the second phase is roughly comparable with the ideological approach to genre in the sense that male and female categories are viewed as culture- and interest-bound, and the privileging of male over female is judged to be largely the result of the manipulative use of power on the part of males. We shall call this second phase "transvaluational" to signify that once equality has been achieved, the question of the value of elements marked as female and male must be addressed.

The deconstructiveness of Kristeva's third phase starts off with a comment on the notion of phase itself. The three phases or "generations" of the feminist movement, according to Kristeva, are not so much chronological (although there is a reciprocal relationship between key historical events and the growth of consciousness regarding gender) as they are "parallel" and "interwoven" in time. In the United States, for example, women in liberationist groups quickly discovered that working for a common political goal did not in itself result in gender equality. Understood in terms of horizon growth (or in terms of the hermeneutical spiral—see chapter 1, fig. 7), the phases provide an analogue for Kristeva's proposal for understanding gender. From the first phase she proposes to retain the aspiration of each sex to embody the whole. But her guess is that if each sex aims only for a "hypothetical bisexuality," those identifying themselves as the dominant sex will aspire to bisexuality and the other sex will merely assist that ambition. We shall call this third phase "horizonal" to signify that once gender equality has been achieved and gender values transformed, gender differentiation becomes the work of the individual consciousness.

With respect to the second phase, Kristeva encourages the destruction of sexism (which she thinks has already taken place) and with it the classical dichotomy of male/female. Denise Riley finds textual evidence for an explicit justification of that classical dichotomy in the "formal alignment of sex against sex" in fourteenth- and fifteenth-century treatises, among which she also finds a new "genre of women's defenses against their vilification" (Riley 1988, 10). But if the classical dichotomy of male/female is overcome, there results a problem of logic: What can "identity," even "sexual identity," mean in a new theoretical and scientific space where the very notion of identity is challenged?

In the third phase, Kristeva would move conflicts based on gender from the site of publicly sanctioned oppositions—the first two phases of feminism have successfully challenged the truth and adequacy of those public meanings—to the site of "personal and sexual identity":

What I mean is, first of all, the demassification of the problematic of *difference,* which would imply, in a first phase, an apparent de-dramatization of the "fight to death" between rival groups and thus between the sexes. And this not in the name of some reconciliation—feminism has at least had the merit of showing what is irreducible and even deadly in the social contract—but in order that the struggle, the implacable difference, the violence be conceived in the very place where it operates with the maximum intransigence, in other words, in personal and sexual identity itself, so as to make it disintegrate in its very nucleus. (Kristeva 1981, 52)

This third phase has much in common with Riley's observation that "any attention to the life of a woman, if traced out carefully, must admit the degree to which the effects of lived gender are at least sometimes unpredictable, and fleeting." Riley speaks of the phenomenology of possessing a sex as "odd" and asks, "How could someone 'be a woman' through and through, make a final home in that classification without suffering claustrophobia?" (Riley 1988, 6). In this phase, the struggle for gender and individual identity is to be carried out in the lives of individuals—at the nucleus of the conflict and its most crucial ground.

One might ask, to what extent does Kristeva's third phase escape the endless wordplay of deconstructionism, or absence of being, at the interior of texts? The orthodox deconstructionist denial or dismissal of questions of reference makes deconstructionism as a political vehicle for change finally as barren as the New Criticism of the first half of this century. Deconstructionism retains, of course, the significant power of a vacuum. In this it also resembles existentialism: both have tellingly revealed the power of negativity in the face of a metaphysics understood positivistically. But after their message has been assimilated, other bases than negativity for decision and political action must be sought.

Because it calls on individuals to enter this "signifying space," which is "a both corporeal and desiring mental space" (Kristeva 1981, 51), Kristeva's analysis builds constructively on the shifting quality of gender relations. Her analysis also assumes the indispensability of the first- and second-generational contributions to a new understanding of gender, an assumption that many of her best critics (e.g., Riley, 109–11) do not take sufficiently into account. Finally, she regards the "generations" less in a chronological than in a "signifying" sense, implying that individuals must continue to appropriate the contributions of the first two generations.

METAPHORIC PROCESS AS MODEL FOR UNDERSTANDING GENRE AND GENDER

The issues of genre and gender are at the heart of the epistemological struggle between the way artists and scientists understand their work. There is a need for an inclusive epistemology that can illuminate equally the role of specificity (understood as an obstacle in the sciences) and the role of abstraction (understood to be an obstacle in the humanities). Whereas the scientist thinks of coming-to-know as the overcoming of specificity, the literary critic thinks of coming-to-know as the overcoming of abstraction. To show how coming-to-know is the same in both instances, we need an epistemology that will preserve the tension between articulated past understandings of an object (as those understandings presently differ in the arts and sciences) and the availability of that object for future inquiries.

Some progress toward the solution of this problem was made by Bernard Lonergan in his *Insight: A Study of Human Understanding* (1958), where he develops the notion of empirical residue. In the course of coming-to-know, Lonergan says, we pose questions to understand objects. The fulfillment of conditions set forth in the questions does not exhaust our knowledge of the object, because the object retains an "empirical residue" with a potential for new questions to be asked about it. "Empirical residue" points to the resistance made by specific objects to being contained within prevailing abstractions (Lonergan 1958, 86–102). Making explicit this resistance, Lonergan in a sense "saves" the specificity of the object from being confined to successive abstractions. To come to knowledge in both science and art is ever to withdraw from relatively inadequate understanding and to move to new knowledge, which is itself always only relatively adequate in its own and subsequent contexts.

A more specific process, however, is needed to account for the creation of new genres. A more specific account may redress the mistaken equivalence of "originality" and "uniqueness" in the humanities and the presumed suspension of attention to specificity in the sciences. In another book, *Metaphoric Process: The Creation of Scientific and Religious Understanding* (Gerhart and Russell 1984), a scientist colleague and I develop a theory of metaphor directed at the problem of new understanding in science and religion, a theory that can be extended to the creation of genres.

In *Metaphoric Process* we distinguish between analogy and metaphor. Analogy, we argue, is the enlargement of knowledge by the application of something known to a new situation. In analogical understanding we come to know the unfamiliar by comparing it with that which is familiar. An analogy, in this view, relates a known to an unknown. In the analogical process, new meaning is not significantly different from what we know in the first place. In terms of form and general shape, analogy—for example, Aquinas's use of the known concept "habit" to understand the unknown concept "grace"—enables us to understand the latter in terms of the former. The comparison involved in analogical process ordinarily terminates with an understanding of the unknown. Comparisons come into play whenever critics are puzzled by new genres. The "new" novel in French literature, for example, has been analogously understood in relation to "holocaust" literature, "detective fiction," and the philosophy of "things."[18] In each case, what is known about established genres provides the basis of a model for understanding the identity and function of a "new" genre and extends knowledge about the known to the unknown. The same holds true whenever critics are puzzled by expectations with respect to gender.

Metaphor, on the other hand, in the theory of metaphor developed in our book, is the forced equivalence of two knowns. Unlike analogy, in which an unknown is understood in terms of a known, metaphor is founded on two knowns, which are forced into equivalency. In Shakespeare's Sonnet 73, "bare ruin'd choirs" force "branches" to be the same as "choirs."[19] Because each of the terms is firmly rooted in a "field of meanings," the move toward equivalence meets resistance. "Branches" comes from the field of biological plants or of geometric angles; "choirs" comes from the field of musical performers or of architectural structures. In metaphoric processes, the fields of meanings to which the concepts belong are distorted, thrown out of lexical and semantic shape, when two concepts rigidly embedded in these fields are asserted to be the same. The distortion of the fields of meanings creates new meanings for old concepts. Metaphoric process also incites a potential for ontological change in the sense that an individual's "world of meanings," weltanschauung, or cosmology, also undergoes a metamorphosis.

As concepts, genres and genders are embedded in fields of meanings. A subgenre in the field of fantasy, for example, can be distinguished from a subgenre in the field of history. In this sense, genres include explanations and expectations we have and strategies we use in constructing the possible meanings of a text. Genres constitute virtual systems of modes, such as fantasy, discursive prose, dramatic representation, folktales, dream symbolism, parodic satire—all of which contain gender expectations. Whether or not we subscribe to any explicit understanding of the interrelationship among genres (interrelationships such as those designed by Northrop Frye [1969] or Paul Hernadi [1972][20]— interdisciplinary taxonomies that include such terms as "religious poetry" and "secular drama"),[21] any analysis of our understanding of genre and gender will reveal presuppositions about the logical space between and among genric forms. Metaphoric process is operative whenever one insists on the equivalence of two genres, or of two conflicting notions of gender, each occupying distinctively different fields of meanings. When this forced identification warps both fields of meanings, we discover the emergence of a new genre. In this approach, the creation of the twentieth-century "new" novel appears in the superimposition of traditional narrative on indeterminate vignette, and the creation of the first-century "gospel" appears in the fusing of parable and biography. Likewise, a new gender can be said to emerge in "third sex" identities or a new way of being gendered in the life of an individual who has struggled with the problem of gender.

The foregoing model of genric process emphasizes the matter-of-fact function of both explanation and understanding in the interpretation of texts without sacrificing one in favor of the other.

When we use genric and gender considerations to explain a text, both taxonomies (texts considered in relation to one another and understood in terms of formal characteristics) and principles of production (texts considered in relation to acts of interpretation where texts are understood in terms of their compared and contrasted effects) come into play. Putting it another way, we might say that whereas genre and gender as taxonomies refer primarily to groups of texts understood in relation to one another, genre and gender as principles of production refer primarily to the processes of making intelligible wholes of texts and of making new genres.

Understanding genre and gender as explanation enables us also to locate their logical limits. The Freudian notion of "overdetermination" has been used to indicate the fundamental incommensurability that exists between dream texts and discursive modes of understanding. Overdeterminedness can be said to be reciprocally generated by the text and the strategies developed to understand both the text and the results of reading. The reciprocal overdetermination of the text and its strategies prevents the text from being determined or exhausted by any one of the strategies and keeps the interpretive process open to intuition, guess, change, and surprise (Trible 1978, 11).[22]

At the same time, the text with its multiple strategies and readings resists translation without remainder into other modes of thought. Genre and gender criticism make explicit the way the text encodes and guides all interpretations of itself. In this sense, the text can be said to demand always more appropriate readings of itself. For the logical limit of genre criticism and gender reflection is the recognition that the text both produces and is produced by a social world. In turn, the social world is potentially better for its ability not only to tolerate but to support many, rather than few, genres and more than one gender. Texts continue to call not only for explanation in particular but for hypotheses regarding genre and gender, hypotheses that enable readers to recognize texts for all they can be.

CHAPTER FIVE

States of the Arts: Gender and Genre Analysis

Our discussion will be adequate if it has as much clearness as the subject-matter admits of, for precision is not to be sought for alike in all discussions, any more than in all the products of the crafts.

Aristotle, Nichomachian Ethics *1094b*

Once their important implications have been understood, gender and genre, in lines borrowed from a popular musical, can be found to be "bustin' out all over." Chapter 4 argued that genre and gender as categories, without epistemological, historical, and hypothetical contexts, quickly become nominalist, or determinist, and considerable effort has been made to deny that categorization is the sole, even an indispensable part of genre. Nevertheless, once the praxis orientation of genre and gender is understood, categorization again becomes vital and productive to consider. Once seen as provisional and partial, genre and gender can readily be acknowledged as determinate as well, in the sense that they matter-of-factly designate some characteristics and functions rather than others.

In 1980 Clifford Geertz published "Blurred Genres," an essay that displayed the prominence genre had won across the disciplines. The title of his essay caught the sense of what had happened in the field of anthropology: how the breaking of boundaries could contribute to "the refiguration of social thought." Other radical examples of Geertz' blurred genres include, in his phrase,

philosophical inquiries looking like literary criticism . . . , scientific discussions looking like belles lettres *morceaux* . . . , baroque fanta-

123

sies presented as deadpan empirical observations . . . , histories that consist of equations and tables or law court testimony . . . , documentaries that read like true confessions . . . , parables posing as ethnographies . . . , theoretical treaties set out as travelogues . . . , ideological arguments cast as historiographical inquiries . . . , epistemological studies constructed like political tracts . . . , methodological polemics got up as personal memoirs. (Geertz 1980, 166)

Geertz's essay, revised and republished three years later, provided evidence that while genre may be in partial eclipse among some literary theorists—eclipsed by a fascination with exceptions rather than with rules—genre can be a vehicle for questioning and expanding boundaries of the contemporary academic disciplines, especially those that have peremptorily dismissed some crucial questions, such as that of gender.

In the meantime, issues of genre and gender were being raised in many corners of the academy—speech-act theory, semiotics, the sciences, history, anthropology, sociology, religious studies—and in critical theories such as feminist criticism, Marxist criticism, and psychoanalytic criticism. Old genres get reassessed in the light of gender analysis, and new genres spring up both within and beyond the bounds of literary criticism. Not least, the subjects of genre and gender are providing rationale for new interdisciplinary study.

Gender across the disciplines has had as checkered a history as has genre. Increasingly more scholars and thinkers, perhaps in every field, are sensitive to gender issues. Just as genre consciousness enables us to investigate the structures, patterns, and forms of objects that otherwise either are subsumed within larger issues or resist analysis entirely, so, too, gender consciousness alerts us to the effect of gender on almost every aspect of thought.

Indeed, the disciplines behave like genres: they create their own boundaries, their own language, their own symbols. The genric features of a discipline are so overriding that they create enormous differences among highly developed fields. Often the genric field is so large that both genre and gender considerations get lost within it. Algebraic and geometric statements do not "mean" in the same way: to "read" a statement it is necessary to know how to read its genre.

Today the use of genre and gender in and across disciplines

varies in the degree of theoretical self-consciousness employed, and this variety yields insight into the multiple ways that genre and gender considerations both effect and affect human understanding. Yet as we examine examples of genre and gender analysis across disciplines, we discover that too often either genre or gender is featured to the exclusion of the other. We begin with an extreme case, a debate in which gender analysis and genre analysis are at odds with each other.

WHAT HAPPENS WHEN GENDER AND GENRE INTERESTS COLLIDE

The distinction between gender and genre comes up in a debate in which Helen Vendler opposes Sandra Gilbert and Susan Gubar over the question of if and how gender issues are appropriately raised in relation to literary texts. One side insists on the necessity of doing a gender analysis of literary texts and the other side on the necessity of doing a genre analysis. Each side charges the other with slighting or omitting what the other insists upon. The debate is pertinent to this study, in which we have been assuming, not only that the question of genre was first raised with respect to literary texts and is derivative with respect to other kinds of texts, but that the more recently articulated question of gender can be unarguably applied to literary and other kinds of texts. In the Vendler versus Gubar and Gilbert debate we find a typical defense of the disciplines to raising issues of gender: namely, the implication that the question of gender does not belong (in this case) to the strictly literary meaning of literary texts. The opposite charge is that without gender analysis, literary meaning is blind to an intrinsic element of meaning. The charge and the defense, generalized, can be found across the disciplines.

The debate began with Vendler's review of seven books, the genre of which "used to be called 'feminist criticism' or 'feminist literary theory,' and is now sometimes called 'feminist cultural analysis' " (Vendler 1990, 19); Vendler includes one antifeminist book in the same genre. Vendler is of the opinion, as stated in her introductory remarks, that efforts to achieve equality for women have been successful in the "practical world" but have had "uneven results" in the "intellectual sphere." Except for history and sociology, where new information about women's lives has "explanatory power," Vendler knows of no clear gains from feminist criticism; yet she is able to find "possible benefits" as well as pitfalls in the texts she is reviewing (ibid.).

The problem, as she sees it, is that feminist critics of the 1960s and 1970s confused literary characters with real people. Thus, in their criticism of male authors for not being politically correct and not treating women characters more sympathetically, feminist critics were, first of all, anachronistic in that they overlooked the advances made by particular male authors for their respective times in their portrayal of women and, second, uneven in their criticism in that feminist critics failed to complain about the unsympathetic treatment of male characters by women authors. Vendler also takes issue with the claim of several feminist critics that there is or should be "a special female way of writing or 'women's language.' " Nor is she impressed with the French feminist appropriation of Barthes's distinction between "writerly" and "readerly" prose. Vendler abruptly dismisses the claim that readerly prose supports the masculinist status quo by its failure to provide "disruptive obstacles" to the assimilation of ideas and images with the rejoinder: "it ought to be self-evident that the disturbance quotient of any book cannot be simply equated with its stylistic quirks." She gave as an example of her point the work of Jane Austen, who, in Vender's opinion, is eminently readable and "at least as disturbing as Virginia Woolf" (ibid.).

However apt Vendler may be in her description of some feminist literary criticism, heightened sensitivity to gender issues she does not have. In their response, Gilbert and Gubar (1990) call attention to the unfortunate results of Vendler's assumption of sexual symmetry and her disturbingly untroubled view of the genius (theoretically female or male) who needs material conditions for writing but does not find them sufficient: "As for family history, gender definitions, political changes, ideological imperatives, cultural presuppositions, literary influences, audience expectations—these [in Vendler's view] have little or nothing to do with the transcendent (and virtually inexplicable) achievements of the 'solitary genius' " (Gilbert and Gubar 1990, 58–59). Gilbert and Gubar conclude that Vendler looks for sweetness (delight and ideological neutrality) in literary texts and relegates light (i.e., the light that comes from a gender analysis) to other kinds of texts; Gilbert and Gubar, on the other hand, expected to find both

126

sweetness (delight) and light (which comes from participation in the political/ideological fray) in literary texts.

In her rejoinder to Gilbert and Gubar's response, Vendler writes that she does not expect ideological neutrality in literary texts (Vendler 1990, 59). She charges that Gilbert and Gubar essentially strive for light in their criticism but miss the essential element of delight that makes literature what it is and not something else.

How are we to understand this debate? Is it the case that Vendler is secretly sexist in spite of her advocacy of gender equality? Or is it the case that Gilbert and Gubar have reduced literature to the cause of having or not having politically correct positions on gender equality? Neither of these charges does justice to the sophistication of either Vendler's or Gilbert and Gubar's work. Nor do the charges clarify what is at stake in their dispute.

Vendler assumes that literature *as literature* is different from the sociological, historical, psychological, and empirical elements of which it is constituted. She holds that, as a work of the imagination, literature is "overdetermined," that is, that it means more than the sociological, historical, or psychological information that can be found in it. By emphasizing this claim, Vender's literary analysis implicitly makes genre the exclusive criterion for the insight (sweetness) that comes from reading literature. In chapter 6 we explore this claim under the rubric of "overgenred" interpretation.

Gilbert and Gubar assume that literature as literature is not only *not* immune to the gender inequalities found throughout contemporary American and European culture but that literature provides a privileged account (because of its subtlety in comparison with other accounts of reality) of how those inequalities have been perpetuated primarily by male authors and resisted primarily by female authors. By emphasizing this claim, Gilbert and Gubar's literary analysis makes gender the exclusive criterion for the insight that can come from reading literature. Later we explore this claim under the rubric of "overgendered" interpretation.

It is also useful to understand the dispute in terms of Kristeva's three generations of feminist criticism, introduced in the last chapter, namely, the liberal, the transvaluational, and the horizonal. On this account, Vendler can be said to be primarily first-generational in her emphasis on equality but third-generational in her criticism of the possible effects of Gilbert and Gubar's work, namely, her concern that their exclusive focus on the inequities suffered by women and the need to transvalue many aspects of women's lives in the public realm may result in prolonging the battle between the sexes. Indeed, this possibility is borne out in the premise of the second volume of Gilbert and Gubar's *No Man's Land* (1989, xi): "the sexes battle because sex roles change, but, when the sexes battle, sex itself (that is, eroticism) changes." One could take this statement to mean either that they are making a historically descriptive statement or that they do not expect the battle to be avoided, even if they think it possible to do so. With respect to Kristeva's three generations of gender analysis, Gilbert and Gubar are primarily first- and second-generational in their focus on gender inequalities and their attempt to reevaluate certain aspects of women's experience. They describe *No Man's Land,* for example, as a study of men's and women's different efforts to *fantasize* about a privileged relationship to language, a *patrius sermo* or a mother's tongue (Gilbert and Gubar 1990, 58). This study of past efforts to transcend gender does seem to address Kristeva's third level of gender analysis. But the question is whether the premise of a "battle between the sexes," since it so decidedly locates gender issues outside the individual, precludes effective work on the third level. Perhaps Gilbert and Guber are doing primarily historical analysis after all, or perhaps their work is taking a new turn.

In "Cross-Dressing and Re-Dressing: Transvestism as Metaphor," the last chapter of volume 2 of *No Man's Land,* Gilbert and Gubar do engage women's writing on the third-generation level. Here they examine women writers' perception of an identity that transcends the gender roles assigned to them by society.[1] Gilbert and Gubar are at their best when they compare and contrast male and female authors' experimentation with gender-transgressive behavior. The difficulty of relating this part of their project to their premise may indicate that they have gone beyond the second level of gender analysis. (Unlike the rest of both volumes, for which each author drafted complete chapters, this chapter was written jointly.) Calling transvestism a metaphor also seems to indicate that something different is happening in this last chapter. In contrast, their debate with Vendler never reaches this third level of issues.

Some will be tempted to resolve the debate by siding with one or the other side. Another way of resolving the debate is to see the different positions as proceeding on different levels of Kristeva's paradigm. But what does each side contribute to our understanding of the relationship between genre and gender? Vendler reminds us that no matter how rich or informative a work might be, in the final analysis the excellence of the work is judged by its effectiveness for a variety of audiences. The classical word for this effectiveness is "sweetness"—for which Gilbert and Gubar take Vendler to task. But it little matters whether the word for effectiveness in the writing of something that lasts as a tribute to human spirit, inventiveness, and resistance is "sweetness," "touchstone," or "inspiration." Vendler's argument implies that genre is a correlative of this effectiveness because genre makes of any ephemeral saying a structured, recognizable something that takes the reader through an experience with predictable (though various) results.

Gilbert and Gubar explicitly treat the relationship between genre and gender, especially in volume 2 of *No Man's Land,* where, for example, they contrast Henry James's and Edith Wharton's use of the ghost story genre and T. S. Eliot's and Virginia Woolf's use of the elegy, explore the reasons for Willa Cather's choice of "genres written specifically by men" (ibid., 176), and study Gertrude Stein's use of the lesbian fairy tale in the *Autobiography.*[2] Here they are most effective in showing subtle differences between the use of contemporary genres by men and by women. But in the debate, they use the results of their investigation either to point out inequalities between men and women or to emphasize the need for a change in the ways that literature is legitimated and evaluated.

THE REFERENT OF GENDER AND GENRE CRITICISM

The Vendler/Gilbert-Gubar debate does force us to ask for the referent of the literary text. In historical and sociological analysis, the referent of the text is what can be known about individuals, groups of people, situations, or relations among various phenomena. In literary analysis, the referents of the text are the meanings that come to be known through the text. Using Paul Ricoeur's analysis of literary referent, we will presume that every text says something about something (Ricoeur 1976, 2–23). In literary analysis, the "something" about which the text speaks is not so much found in or behind the text as it is to be reconstructed in front of the text, that is, as the reader's affirmation of what emerges from the text in the process of reading it. For the reader to say something about the "something" of the text is to require other elements to be noticed besides the historical, sociological, and empirical referents, however important and vital the latter may be to the meaning of the text.

Ricoeur's theory of literary reference helps distinguish literary analysis from other kinds of analysis. His theory is modeled, first of all, on the difference between spoken and written discourse. The referents in spoken discourse are by and large unequivocal since they can be supplemented by gesture, tone of voice, pointing, and so forth. Moreover, in spoken discourse, if the referents are ambiguous or absent, the interlocutors can ask and be asked for clarification.

Analogously, we may say that the referents in sociological, historical, and scientific discourse are by and large unequivocal because they can be supplemented by prior intersubjective understandings (like the referents in spoken discourse). If the referents are ambiguous, the reader can usually find clarification in the discipline(s) in which the discourse purports to locate itself.[3] But what of existential meaning, of reality, of truth?

Constructing Reality by Reconstructing Texts

Besides inviting empirical questions, literary texts also invite reconstruction in terms of reality and truth. But unlike Augustine, who said that he understood time until he was asked what time is, most are content to leave reality and truth in the status of it-goes-without-saying. In his book on interpretation, *Plurality and Ambiguity,* however, David Tracy writes that reality is "what we name our best interpretation" and truth, "the reality we know through our best interpretations":

Reality is constituted, not created or simply found [as "something-already-out-there-now-real"], through the interpretations that have earned the right to be called relatively adequate or true. Reality is neither out there nor in here. Reality is constituted by the interaction between a text, whether book or world, and a questioning interpreter. The interaction called questioning can produce warranted assertions through relevant evidence. The interaction in scientific inquiry elicits reflections on the more basic interaction of language and understanding in its warranted assertions. (Tracy 1987, 48)

In this sense, we may say that the reconstruction of texts is a construction of reality. In terms of the hermeneutical spiral (see chapter 1, fig. 7), reality and truth are constituted by interpretations of texts—not least by interpretations of texts, gathered, questioned, pondered, and finally assessed in private and public discourse.

We turn now to examples of efforts to extend genre theory and gender analysis within and outside the field of literary criticism. A common element to be seen in all of these efforts is the way in which a text reconstructed (or interpreted) is a construal of reality. By focusing on genres that are privileged by respective disciplines, we see that disciplines can be thought of as fields of genres that legitimate competing senses of reality—ultimately of what becomes our reality. We proceed from examples of literary analysis of conventionally literary texts, to analysis of other kinds of texts, and finally to texts whose meaning depends on much more than their written component. Since this chapter is intended to illustrate the breadth of applicability of gender and genre analysis, the reader is encouraged to apply further what has been presented regarding gender and genre in previous chapters.

GENRE AND GENDER IN NEW LITERARY CRITICAL STUDIES

One of the most innovative literary critical theories of genre has been that of Mikhail Bakhtin's sociological poetics. As the term suggests, his treatment of genre is related to but differs significantly from that of both formalist and sociolinguistic theory. In Bakhtin's view, formalism isolates the work from "the reality of social discourse and the thematic mastering of reality [and instead makes] genre the fortuitous combination of chance devices" (Bakhtin and Medvedev 1978, 135). Nor does he think that sociolinguistic analysis (see "Genre in Sociolinguistics" below) alone can account for the multiple ways that human beings are conscious of and know reality. His is an eloquent refutation of the unqualified claims by some semiotic and linguistic analysts to the effect that language is all there is to human understanding. After acknowledging the "essential role" that language plays in the way human beings are conscious of and conceptualize reality, Bakhtin insists:

> Every significant genre is a complex system of means and methods for the conscious control and finalization of reality. . . . It is the forms of the utterance, not the forms of language, that play the most important role in consciousness and the comprehension of reality. . . . We think and conceptualize in utterances, complexes complete in themselves . . . [which] cannot be understood as a linguistic whole, and [whose] forms are not syntactic forms. . . . One might say that human consciousness possesses a series of inner genres for seeing and conceptualizing reality. *A given consciousness is richer or poorer in genres, depending on its ideological environment.* (ibid., 133–34, my emphasis)

Bakhtin is equally insistent that genre must be a first consideration in the interpretation of a work, rather than, as it was for the Formalists, the summary of all discrete elements. He holds that the "thematic unity of the work is inseparable from its primary orientation in its environment, inseparable, that is to say, from the circumstances of place and time" (ibid., 132). Genre is doubly bound: to the reality in which it is performed, heard, read, and to the aspects of reality it controls. Because each genre has different principles of selection, each controls different aspects of reality and brings the reader to conceptualize reality differently in terms of different genres.

Bakhtin's analysis, more than most others, makes explicit the participation by the reader in the ways that genres function. In carnivalesque genres, such as ritual spectacles, pageants, shows, parodies, and billingsgate, for example, laughter is the dominant principle of selection. Bakhtin argues that these genres constitute the borderline between art and life and expose the double aspect of the world: the official (the political and the ecclesiastical) world with its double. Carnivalesque genres belong to the marketplace; they repeat claims to eternal truths and established norms only to recast and replace them. In Bakhtin's work we find the strongest affirmation of genre and the most critical assessment of its function in understanding.

Literary History

One genre periodically affected by historical states of affairs is science fiction. In his introduction to *Science Fiction Dialogues* (1983) Gary Wolfe notices the increased attention to past science fiction predictions. The year 1984 was a harking back to George Orwell's famous book of that title; the twenty-fifth century will be scrutinized for events out of the Buck Rogers comic strip; and the year 2001 is likely, he thinks, to be equal to the anticipation of the year 1000, with its apocalyptic visions. Wolfe also notices a "blurring of boundaries," both with respect to "authors who do not ordinarily write science fiction and readers who do not ordinarily read it" (Wolfe 1983, 113). These groups increasingly include science fiction writers and readers. Within the university, science fiction is increasingly of interest to historians of ideas, thus establishing the interdisciplinary character of the genre.

Whereas both of the foregoing analyses of genre lack explicit gender analysis, Jane Spencer's *The Rise of the Woman Novelist: From Aphra Behn to Jane Austen* treats the emergence of the novel and the emergence of professional women writers as "two remarkable and interconnected literary events" (Spencer 1986, vii). But in literary history, until recently the first event was heavily "documented and debated while the second was largely ignored" (ibid.). In terms of critical response, Spencer notices that eighteenth-century critics had a low opinion of the genre novel but were obsessed with its connection to women writers. Modern critics, on the other hand, have a relatively high opinion of the genre, but they tend to belittle the contributions of women writers in it. Spencer carefully documents the "changes in ideology of womanhood" from the late seventeenth into the eighteenth centuries and shows how women novelists responded in different ways to the changes: by protest, conformity, or escape.

Spencer's study is based on economic and class analysis. Whereas Virginia Woolf's question in the collection of her essays and reviews *Women and Writing,* "Why did women begin writing in the eighteenth century?" went unanswered, Spencer can observe that formal education was spreading to the middle classes, therefore creating a larger reading public. Many women wrote novels simply because they were paid for them. Spencer notices that eighteenth-century women authors reflect that century's greater diversity among occupations in the public realm for women—a diversity that had been lost since the Middle Ages and Tudor England to early forms of capitalism. In short, the rise of the novel provided ideological and financial encouragement for the growth of women's writing. The literary form enshrined domestic, moral, and sentimental values thought of as feminine, and allowed women a special literary authority (ibid., 22). Spencer also notices a new genre antecedent to the novel: women writers' self-portraits, which were semiautobiographical and provided an opportunity to a woman writer for "projecting herself in fantasy and trying to justify herself to the world" (ibid., 41).

However close the connection between the burgeoning of women writers and the emergence of the genre novel, Ellen Moers reminds us in *Literary Women* that long before the eighteenth century some women were writing and that women authors can be found for every historical form and style (Moers 1963, 45). Ovid, for example, coined the word *heroides* to refer to "loving heroines," and the name is thought to refer to those who wrote as well as to those given a voice by him. Nevertheless, it is not accidental that women writers were attracted to the novel since, according to Moers, for writers it is the "least concentrated form of art and can be taken up or put down more easily than the play or the poem." It is also a genre that is a good fit for what women culturally have been trained to do; that is, "being surrounded by people, she has been trained to use her mind in observation and in analysis of character" (ibid.). One might add that merely observing people closely can be a form of self-protection, whereas writing about them is to enter the realm of public discourse.

In a related study, *Sensibility: An Introduction,* Janet Todd shows how the term *sensibility* had positive connotations from 1740 to 1770 but negative connotations thereafter. Her hypothesis is that sentimental writing was downgraded "due to the connection with the rise of women writers and readers" (Todd 1986, 8). Todd also fills in some of the background to the emergence of women writers and the novel. She records that women actors came onstage for the first time in England in Restoration drama. She also lists the kinds of seventeenth-century protonovel that were the precursors of the eighteenth-century novel: rogue histories, whore biographies, marvelous travel tales, scandal chronicles, and romantic novellas. In her view, the novel was an amalgam primarily of two kinds of protonovel: the scandal narrative and the cautionary tale.

Sometimes literary history is rewritten with a radical reevaluation of a single text. Such is the case with Jane P. Tompkins's essay "Sentimental Power: *Uncle Tom's Cabin* and the Politics of Literary History" (1985, 81–104). Tomkins recalls that Harriet Beecher Stowe's book was the first American novel to sell more than a million copies. More than its economic success, however, was its function as the "*summa theologica* of nineteenth-century America's religion of domesticity, a brilliant redaction of the culture's favorite story about itself: the story of salvation through motherly love" (ibid., 83). Tompkins does not ask the literary establishment to dethrone Hawthorne, Melville, Poe, Emerson, Thoreau, and Whitman—all of whom wrote in the same period as Stowe—but only to recognize that *Uncle Tom's Cabin* as a sentimental novel works successfully in ways different from those of other works canonized as masterpieces. Tompkins uses the code of the sentimental novel to show the conjunction of political, religious, and literary artistry in Stowe's novel, thus making it possible to read it as a classic in its own right.

An old genre that has had its boundaries stretched by feminist criticism is the ghost story. Allen Gardner Smith has shown how Edith Wharton, aside from her major fiction, habitually employed the genre ghost story to experiment with what was invisible and outside the areas of consensus. Her ghost stories, by her own admission, function more by mystery than by apparition. Indeed, the striking feature of her ghost stories is her interest in "the haunting *by absence* in everyday life rather than by presence in an extraordinary one" (Smith 1980, 150). Smith takes these stories to illustrate Wharton's "complexity of approach to such issues as the unease of women in male roles, the mistrust of women and the distortions of the master/servant, employer/employee situations, in which the unspoken, suppressed issues of status and suborned affection return in terror or the attribution of occult powers, and the servant/employee is perceived as a witch or spiritualist with access to psychic forces denied to the ostensibly superior woman" (ibid., 152). In Smith's interpretation, Wharton

135

seems particularly intent upon revising the conventional notion of woman as having a static and essential nature and presenting a new notion of woman as having a dynamic and existential existence. We notice that Smith's interpretation is at odds with that of Gilbert and Gubar (See "What Happens When Gender and Genre Interests Collide" above). Whereas Smith emphasizes the horror of the suppressed, Gilbert and Gubar show that the need for new roles and rules, as evoked by Wharton, was "more real" by virtue of the ingenious ways she used to leave them "unsaid" (Gilbert and Gubar 1989, vol. 2, 159–68).

Genres of Minority Literature

One way of reading the genres of minority literature is to emphasize their relationship with traditions of protest and commitment in indigenous societies. In his "Protest and Commitment in Black American and African Literatures," N. Adebayo gathers supporting evidence for the claim that "black literatures derive very closely from social phenomena and are very closely bound with particular moments in the history of black societies" (Adebayo 1985, 98). Adebayo asks how the genres change when some political rights are won, and responds that black writers write differently when they bear the burden of commitment than when they are in the forefront of reeducation and regeneration. He gives evidence that suggests that the difference is reflected in the number and kind of genres they develop.

William S. Simmons (1986, 98) holds that "beliefs, memories, and legends of Native American literature are more cultural than they are historical." He cites cases of the giant bird and the floating island that brought the first Europeans as instances in which the "forms respond to, and help interpret historical events and orient the believer's action in these events." Simmons emphasizes that "the event itself, in this case the early coming of Europeans, is impressed into a cultural stereotype, and the amount of history that can be reconstructed is negligible" (ibid.). Simmons's interpretation is based on a presumed dichotomy between history and fiction and therefore affords the reader only events to be reinterpreted rather than a view of what it is possible to know through fiction.

Cultural Studies

Considerable new attention is being given to popular genres and formulaic genres. The study of popular genres results from a kind of democritization of literature, in reaction to those who would confine literature to a classic canon. The study of formulaic genres often goes hand in hand with the development of interest in popular genres. In his *Interpretation and Genre: The Role of Generic Perception in the Study of Narrative Forms* (1986) Thomas Kent argues that the best literature is a combination and deformation of several "pure" genres, none of which gives decisive form to the literary text. Pure genres, in his view, are automatized; that is, they are predictable and are constituted by a finite number of elements in a small number of possible different arrangements. Kent uses Russian Formalism and Prague Structuralism to analyze the patterns of elements in the American genre "dime novel." He studies the corpus of Herman Melville and shows that the early works were almost invariably representatives of pure genres, whereas Melville's later masterpieces, *Moby Dick* and *The Confidence Man,* each comprise at least five pure genres. Finally, Kent studies Mark Twain's *Tom Sawyer* and *Huckleberry Finn* to show how each is an instance of deforming and recombining pure genres.

In "The Medieval Pastourelle as a Satirical Genre" W. T. H. Jackson claims that the medieval genre pastourelle reflects "the true relationship between the classes during the period of the courtly lyric, a relationship in which the peasant girl was regarded as fair game by any wandering knight and one far removed from the spiritual ecstasy and torment of the *Minnesang*" (Jackson 1985, 68–69). Jackson describes the early form of the pastourelle as simple and brutal; the later form, in which the knight could be mocked or consoled for loss of a courtly lover, achieved the same status as that held by courtly poetry. Courtly love poetry, in turn, was influenced by the classical conventions of pastoral poetry; for example, clerics came to be included among the courtly lovers. Jackson notices that courtly love poetry was excluded at first from accepted types of courtly poetry. Some 150 poems are extant; they are late and conventional. Jackson does not comment on the gendered patterns of the relationships in the genre.

In her study of medieval women's song Ria Lemaire shows how a gender analysis challenges the claim, implicit in Jackson's work, that "the first true love-poetry in the vernacular languages was . . . created by men" (Lemaire 1986, 733). Among a corpus of five hundred medieval Galician-Portuguese love songs, called the "cantigas de amigo," Lemaire shows how the earliest songs (one hundred or so), improvisations sung by two dialoging women soloists with a refrain, provided a basis for the later songs (four hundred or so), written imitations of the women's songs and attributed to men. Lemaire's study restores women as rightful authors to a genre, only a part of which represented women exclusively as passive objects of love. Lemaire articulates two levels of denial in the humanities of the existence of a tradition of women's love songs: "women have been explained away as active subjects, who formulated their own desires and took initiatives, on equal terms with men, to satisfy them, i.e., the woman as represented subject of the women's songs has been mutilated by later interpretations; [and] women have been explained away as representing subjects, as singing and composing poets, as *homo sapiens*" (ibid.). Six changes that take place in the transition from the women's songs to the men's courtly love poetry are documented by Lemaire:

1. The word *coita*, which originally means anxious, active desire, including joy and pain, comes to mean the sorrow of love, or passive, unilateral suffering.
2. Whereas the present and future tenses of the verb ("I will go," "I will sit down," etc.) dominate in the women's songs, the future tense all but disappears in the later poetry.
3. The two verbs that are most frequently used by women singers, "to go" and "to make haste," vanish in the later poetry.
4. The subject of the action shifts from "he whom I love" to "he who loves me."
5. All but one of the seven synonyms for "handsome" attributed by the confident singer to herself disappear, and the remaining synonym is used less frequently.
6. In the later poetry, women no longer take sexual initiative, and mythic nature symbols, used to describe their "erotic phantasies," disappear (ibid., 731).

Lemaire thus provides a text that preceded courtly love poetry, a genre that according to Denis de Rougement's well-known study

Love in the Western World (1956), has shaped the Western tradition's ideas, not only of love as separation, sorrow, and death, but also of gender.

In *The Lay of the Land: Metaphor as Experience and History in American Life and Letters* Annette Kolodny further describes the shift in the genre of the late sixteenth-century English pastoral (see Jackson above) to the seventeenth-century American pastoral as a process of "gendering the land":

> Eden, Paradise, the Golden Age, and the idyllic garden, in short, all the backdrops for European literary pastoral, were subsumed in the image of an America promising material ease without labor or hardship . . . ; and all this was possible because, at the deepest psychological level, the move to America was experienced [in terms of] its single dominating metaphor: regression from the cares of adult life and a return to the primal warmth of womb or breast in a feminine landscape. (Kolodny 1975, 6)

Kolodny rehearses what happened when, by the nineteenth century, it became obvious that a man's relation with the land was neither easy nor innocent. The ambiguity of the image was finally abandoned in favor of a regression to the maternal. Writers like Washington Irving, James Fenimore Cooper, and William Gilmore Simms understood that "the bold exercise of masculine power . . . [was] inextricably connected to the vocabulary of a feminine landscape" and began to experiment with solitary figures "living out a highly eroticized and intimate relationship with a landscape at once suggestively sexual, but overwhelmingly maternal" (ibid., 134). Kolodny's study documents intricate links between genre and gender and illustrates how utopias constitute what Gary Saul Morson calls an "intra-generic dialogue" on the status of women (Morson 1981, 79–81).

EXTENDING GENRE TO NONLITERARY TEXTS

Nonfiction and Non-Western Genres

In literary criticism, genre theory is also at work in the analysis of new genres. Gerard Genette edited a collection of studies entitled *Palimpsestes: La literatur au second degre* (1982), in which authors explored such genres as dedications, musical titles, and prefaces. Cult movies, prose expositions, spy fiction, soap operas, and women's romances have generated vital discussions both despite and because of their previous exclusion from the parameters of literary criticism. In his *The Post Card: From Socrates to Freud and Beyond* (1987) Jacques Derrida treats the unconventional genre of postcard as a sustained conceit. In "The Problem of Speech Genres" (1986) Mikhail Bakhtin calls into question the literary "corner" on genres. Standard military commands, the formality of business documents—these and others, he thought, deserved genric analysis. As we saw in chapter 2, Barbara Herrnstein Smith (1978) was one of the first to be interested in genres of the marketplace—such as greeting-card messages and paid political announcements—which in New Criticism were excluded from literary consideration or were marginalized in relation to it.

Morphological critics are also newly interested in nonfiction genres. Klaus Weissenberger (whose earlier work in morphological criticism was discussed in chapter 2) has edited a collection of essays on nonfiction genres, *Prosakunst ohne Erzahlen: Die Gattungen der nicht-fiktionalen Kunstprosa* (1985). Weissenberger sees his investigation of nonfiction genres not as a reaction to either the traditional genres of lyric, epic, and tragic or the purely practical forms of public discourse, but rather as a sequel to the interest of morphological criticism in the entirety of each genre understood from the complementarity of model cases and individual genre representations or from genre function and speech forms. The collection's authors confront styles of life with genre styles, poetic intention with poetic realization. They locate a major victory in the "emancipation of the authorial I" and the failure of the attempt to absolutize art in solipsism. Those nonfiction genres read morphologically by Weissenberger and his colleagues are aphorism, autobiography, biography, letter, dialogue, essay, fragment, sermon, travel literature, and journal.

The translation of non-Western texts, especially those of minority peoples, also raises the issue of genre, for Western readers are unfamiliar with non-Western genres and have neither the benefit nor the bane of classical mediations of them. The transfer of texts from one medium to another is also at base a question of genre. In 1989, for example, during the planning of the first European religious meeting of the International Peace and Environmental

Life Conference in Basel, German bishops opposed the televised ecumenical service on Pentecost Sunday on the grounds that some people might not fulfill their weekly obligation to "celebrate" Mass. In this instance, although the text of the Mass would have been literally unchanged, the change in medium posed a problem for viewer reception, similar to the problems that occur in some instances of reader reception.

Political Analysis

In his 1989 article "Refolution: The Springtime of Two Nations" Timothy Garto Ash reports on a new genre of opposition anecdote in Warsaw, a genre called "corridor stories." The stories tell of fantasized encounters between oppositionists and their former persecutors during the two months of the Round Table, the negotiations between the Communist government and the trade union Solidarity that led to Solidarity's attaining legal status in April 1989. One (true) example: Dawid Warszawski, the pseudonymous editor of a leading underground journal, *KOS,* conducted a video interview with the interior minister, General Kiszczak, head of the police apparatus responsible for seven years of struggle with the underground. The general politely observed that he had much enjoyed reading Mr. Warszawski's articles over the years. The editor, now using his real name, Konstanty Gebert, responded by asking the general to give an interview to *KOS*—an offense for which the general should then, presumably, punish himself. The general hesitates for a moment. "Do you offer a large coffee?" he says. Since the genre "corridor story" is a variety of joke, it fulfills a political mediation between oppressors and formerly oppressed people that is both dramatically poignant and politically constructive because it shows the former oppressor handling his mock indictment with a modicum of dignity (Ash 1989, 3).

EXTENDING GENRE FROM LITERARY TO OTHER FIELDS

Speech-Act Theory

Speech-act theory, as originally developed by J. L. Austin and John Searle (1962), is paradigmatic of the attempts to construe reality in terms of speech genres derived from within the field of literary analysis. The premise of the speech-act theory of literary discourse is that literature is not a special language or even a special use of language. Speech-act theorists such as Mary Louise Pratt claim instead that an unbroken continuity exists between ordinary language and literary texts. They then proceed to explain that continuity on the basis of presumptions that must be made about the ability of ordinary language to communicate. One presumption is that a speaker addresses an audience with a narrative utterance for the purpose of "display." Assuming that the utterance is "tellable," the speaker will be successful so long as she observes the "cooperative principle[s] and maxims specified for such utterances"—maxims such as knowing the story, providing the necessary relevant information, and evaluating adequately. Success means "making our audience-ship worth it" (Pratt 1977, 205). The claim of continuity between literary and ordinary language limits the applicability of speech-act theory to relatively simple genres with straightforward expectations. For example, in an ode, the presumption is that someone has died and that the apostrophe of the poem is addressed to the dead person. In Truman Capote's *In Cold Blood* (1966), a nonfiction "novel," the presumption is that the occurrence of reported events is given precedence over the imagination with which they are narrated.

As one might expect, speech-act theory works best with narrative forms that most closely parallel everyday speech. On the basis of this fundamental analogy, the theory provides a helpful typology for deciphering the unmarked narrative voice:

1. The framing voice may be the same as the author's voice telling about someone else's experience (e.g., third-person narrative or epic).
2. The framing voice may be given a name and reflect the personal experience of the author (e.g., first-person narrative).
3. The framing voice may be a vehicle for someone other than the author (e.g., in Dariel Defoe's *Moll Flanders* the framing voice is that of the editor; in Emily Brontë's *Wuthering Heights* the framing voice is the fictional speaker's narration of Bessie's narration of Bessie's experience, which, in turn, contains Bessie's narration of Catherine's experience).

For complex genres that work against naive or immediate perception, speech-act theorists identify texts that cannot be decoded according to everyday language usage by relying on the concept of genric deviance. For all texts, rules for writing and reading determine "what does not count for deviance and . . . how we decode what is not deviant" (Pratt 1977, 206). These rules prescribe that a "reader will assume the text is itself definitive, accurate, complete, stylistically appropriate, free of gross accidental errors, and 'worth it,' [provided the reader is not] invited to think otherwise" (ibid.). Deviance flouts expectations set for us by rules for writing; unless flouted, those expectations are the same as those for a "real-world narrative display text." Some real-world texts, such as joking and teasing, also flout conventional speech-act expectations: for example, saying to a friend who has just broken a vase, "That's all right—it's just my most valuable possession." Whereas the deviancy of everyday language is often marked by tone, facial expression, or admission ("I'm just teasing"), deviancy or the breaking of genric rules in literature is often unmarked and must be detected by identifying the narrative voice.

Some literary critics carry the notion of deviancy further when applying speech act theory to literary criticism. Speech-act theory sees deviancy in the contemporary novel as a "linguistic subversiveness . . . a tendency to increase the limitations on the fictional speaker's ability to fulfill his communicative purpose." Thus, speech-act theory explains that Robbe-Grillet's *In the Labyrinth* has a narrator unable to "solve his sequencing problems even if he wanted to, for he doesn't know the order of things in the first place." And Nabokov's *Pale Fire* has a narrator who is "hopelessly insane" (ibid., 211).

One application of speech-act analysis is to be found in *The Jury Summation as Speech Genre* (1988), in which Bettyruth Walter uses an ethnographic approach to analyze the summation, or counsel's closing speech to a jury. She holds the concepts of speech act, speech event, persuasion, and a standard differentiation among genre to be interrelated:

[They] form a structure with the speech act serving as minimal unit, and the genre as the maximum unit, each higher term incorporating the ones below. Therefore, the speech act is a constituent factor of the speech event summation, which is used for the function of persuading a jury when a summation is spoken by a lawyer during a trial within the social setting of a courtroom. . . . The summation as genre is a communication form recognized by lawyers and many non-lawyers alike within American culture, and is identified by the labels of "summation," "closing speech," or "closing argument." It involves preliminary activities of preparation, occurs as a speech event within the trial courtroom setting, and has an aftereffect on the juror audience. Its stated primary function is to persuade. (Walter 1988, 6)

In spite of such concise identification, Walter maintains that the setting is largely determinative of whether or not any given closing speech is in fact a jury summation. If someone were to stand up at a party and speak the traditional "Ladies and gentlemen of the jury . . . ," the genre would not pertain. According to Walter, the main purpose of the address would then be to amuse, because the setting is not a courtroom. Walter also lists "small genres of speech" that may be found within the larger form of the jury summation: "apologies, compliments, descriptions, enumerations, insults, jokes, politeness formulae (e.g., thanks to jurors), requests, rhetorical questions, sarcastic comments, suggestions, urgings" (ibid., 129). Surprisingly, none of these "small genres" is indispensable to the summation genre, even though, when present, they can be said to constitute the genre.

In the end, however, the notion of genre in speech-act theory is limited to the analogy between speaker and narrator, which, however valid, tends to disallow, deflect, or discourage other more formalist approaches to understanding the text. As a result, the application of genre in speech-act theory is narrower than its application in Russian Formalism, for example. By limiting the explanation of genre to the analogy of the speaking subject, speech-act theory also limits the scope of the genre. Whatever the advantages of examining texts in relation to a speaker, real or analogous, it remains vital for some purposes to compare and contrast texts in terms of other formal characteristics.

Critical theory, as developed by Jürgen Habermas (1979) and others, also brings to bear an exigence largely overlooked by speech-act theory. In speech-act theory one *presumes* that "the speaker is trustworthy, the discourse accurate, complete and stylistically appropriate unless led to think otherwise." In critical theory the verification of the possibility of systematic distortion makes it necessary to posit the presumed speech conditions, not as the ordinary state of affairs, but as *ideal* speech conditions— conditions hardly, if ever, actually fulfilled. Habermas makes a further distinction he finds lacking in speech-act theory, between the interactive and the cognitive aspects of a statement. Warnings and pieces of advice, for example, can be analyzed in terms of either aspect: "the right to issue certain warnings and advice depends on whether the presupposed norms to which they refer are valid or not (and, at a next stage, ought or ought not to be valid)" (Habermas 1979, 56). Speech-act theory tends to be naive about the nature and extent of the analogy on which the theory is based: there would seem to be a greater complexity between the speaker and the figure executed in language than is taken into account. Of the four aspects of a theory of genre—speaker, audience, text, and world—to be taken into consideration, speech-act theory is exemplary on the first two, is less capable with respect to the text, and, as does most linguistic theory, tends to ignore the world beyond acknowledging that every speaker has one. Speech-act theory is therefore only partially and even then unevenly successful in providing a basis for understanding genre.

Genre in Sociolinguistics

The need to retrieve the social dimension of genre has been a common feature of all criticism formulated in opposition to either Russian or Anglo-American Formalism (see "The New Criticism" in chapter 2). A more recent development is that of sociolinguistics, as used, for example, by William Labov, using the disciplines of sociology and linguistics.

Let us compare sociolinguistics with sociological poetics, the term coined by Mikhail Bakhtin (1978) for his combined literary and social analysis. In Bakhtin's approach, genre requires that the text be studied in two ways: (1) how the work is oriented toward the listener and perceiver—its "duration of real space and real time"—and (2) how the work casts a horizon thematically and stylistically. Genres, in Bakhtin's view, are necessary frames— "controls" for making sense of *parole* (see chapter 6) and for shaping reality. Nevertheless, each genre is capable of framing only "certain definite aspects of reality" (Bakhtin and Medvedev 1978, 129–36, esp. 131).

In contrast, sociolinguistics study genre as a form of expression endemic to a particular group or culture. They may study variations of dialect in relation to the dominant grammar, to the social organization or to the culture of those who speak the dialect, and in relation to the social problems—usually pertaining to education—

immediately involved because of differences between the dominant grammar and the dialect. William Labov's (1972) analysis of "ritual insults" provides a good example of the application of genre by sociolinguistics. In his study of English vernacular among inner-city black youths from eight to nineteen years of age, he observes that discourse is outside, or at best at the periphery, of the concerns of linguists. Sociolinguists, however, go beyond the linguistic boundaries of the sentence and consider such elements of social knowledge as the selection of speakers, the identification of persons and places, and the social competences that make it possible for members of a group to engage in communication. But first, in order to distinguish what is said from what is done, Labov sets forth "invariant relations between the linguistic units and actions intended or interpreted" (Labov 1972, 304). He records numerous examples of ritual insults (called by group members variously "sounding," "woofing," or "cutting") and banter, sometimes in the form of trick responses, such as the following:

A. How tall are you?
B. Five foot seven.
A. I didn't think shit piled that high.

Labov distinguishes personal insults from ritual insults—the latter are played off one another in the group as a sort of contest with recognized winners and losers—by documenting the way ritual insults are received by other members of the group, including the one against whom the insult is directed. He also formulates four properties of ritual sounding in relation to Erving Goffman's rules for ritual games:

1. A sound opens a *field,* which is meant to be sustained. A sound is presented with the expectation that another sound will be offered in response, and that this second sound may be built formally upon the first. The player who presents an initial sound is thus offering others the opportunity to display their ingenuity at his expense.
2. Besides the initial two players, a third-person role is necessary.
3. Any third person can become a player, especially if there is a failure by one of the two players then engaged.
4. Considerable symbolic distance is maintained and serves to insulate the event from other kinds of verbal interaction. (Ibid., 343–44)

Labov concludes that members of the group develop a high level of syntactic, semantic, and rhetorical competence in their use of the ritual genre sounding, a competence that exceeds anything they learn or produce in a classroom setting.

Labov's only mention gender issues is found in his discussion of the degree to which male youths think females are capable of "sounding." In his monumental study *The Signifying Monkey: A Theory of Afro-American Literary Study* (1988), Henry Louis Gates attributes to Labov a high sensitivity in his study of black language usage. Gates nevertheless notices the racist implications of sociolinguistic interpretation of sounding insofar as the analysis is done completely apart from the larger phenomenon of "signifying" in Afro-American communities. Gates illustrates that sounding historically is a reflexive speech figure and a double-voiced utterance that also articulates a theory of literature in the black tradition. Just as the use of slang provides little or no insight into classical literature, however, the use of sounding by urban teenagers does not represent conventional literate activity. Gates also provides evidence that women are as adept at signifying as men.

In a critical application of sociolinguistic theory Jack Zipes (1983) cites Fredric Jameson and Roland Barthes as affirming that literary fairy tales were written as part of a "social process, as a kind of intervention in a continuous discourse, debate, and conflict about power and social relations." In his *Fairy Tales and the Art of Subversion: The Classical Genre for Children and the Process of Civilization* Zipes argues that fairy tales are neither universal nor ageless; indeed, the nonhistory of the fairy tale genre is one argument for its transcendence of cultural boundaries. In some sense, fairy tales are therapeutic. Writers appropriated the oral genre of the folk tale and "converted it into a type of literary discourse about mores, values, and manners so that children would become civilized according to the social code of that time. . . . The writers *acted* ideologically by presenting their notions regarding social conditions and conflicts, and they *interacted* with each other and with past writers and storytellers of folklore in a public sense" (Zipes 1983, 1). This process led to institutionalized symbolic discourse. Zipes locates the original oral tale socially somewhere between governesses and children. "Blue books" were later sold by peddlers to peasants and the lower classes. As soon as there was courtly approval, the oral tale became related to the genre of the conversation of the time. As such, the oral tale was "noncompulsive" in the sense that the audience was "spontaneous in the reception and exchange of remarks" (ibid., 3).

A central theme of oral tales of the precapitalist era was that might makes right: "He who has power can exercise his will, right wrongs, become ennobled, amass money and land, win women as prizes and social prestige." Peasants were attracted to these tales, Zipes believes, because of "conditions that were so overwhelming that they demanded symbolic abstraction": starvation of children, rape, corporal punishment, ruthless exploitation (ibid., 8). Zipes builds on the analysis of Heide Gottner-Abendroth in *Die Gottin und ihr Heros* and, with her, thinks it highly probable that the matriarchal worldview and motifs of the original folk tales underwent successive stages of patriarchalization. "By the time the oral folk tales, originally stamped by matriarchal mythology, circulated in the Middle Ages, they had been transformed in different ways: the goddess became a witch, evil fairy, or stepmother; the active, young princess was changed into an active hero; matrilineal marriage and family ties became patrilineal; the essence of the symbols, based on matriarchal rites, was depleted and made benign; the pattern of action which concerned maturation and integration was gradually recast to stress domination and wealth" (ibid., 7). Here again we have a powerful example of an explicit link between gender and genre.

In one of the more self-critical uses of genre in sociolinguistics, Herbert W. Simons and Aram A. Aghazarian argue for the "blurring of distinctions" among the literary, the rhetorical, and the political (Simons and Aghazarian 1986, 8). In their study of form and genre in political discourse they acknowledge, nevertheless, that the rhetorical and the political are more bound to situational factors than is the literary. Political genres are more reliable and lend themselves more readily to genric analysis. Political genres also have greater "practical force" and "prescriptive power" than literary genres. Genric conventions are also more likely to be satirized, deliberately transgressed, or ignored in literary discourse, although individual elements will occasionally be perverted in political discourse as well.

Simons and Aghazarian use one of the best-known genres of American political discourse, the presidential inaugural address, to show the strengths and limits of genre analysis. Some contributors to their volume of essays examine cultural forms already named as genres, such as the presidential address, the "sales pitch," the eulogy, and the editorial. One author, following Kenneth Burke, addresses what he calls "forms-in-the-large," showing how one text, such as Martin Luther King's letter from Birmingham Jail, might be read as black rhetoric, Southern rhetoric, protest rhetoric, ministerial rhetoric, religious rhetoric, apologia, and public letter writing. The latter idea is related to my own notion of genre testing and gender testing (see chapter 7), in which individual texts are queried in terms of different genres to determine what sets of intersections in the network of genres best illuminate each text's design and its rhetorical effects.[4]

Film Criticism

In film criticism since the 1950s, genre theory has been in competition with auteur theory. Today, however, genre theory has won dominance as the more credible explanation for the effects of certain kinds of films on specific audiences. Especially interesting is the application of the term *genre* only to commercial feature films that, through repetition and variation, tell familiar stories with familiar characters in familiar situations (Grant 1986, xi). All other films are considered by film critics to be "art films," a category treated either as unrelated to the other genres or often not as a genre at all. But in Barry Grant's simile, genre films are the iceberg, hidden beneath the small visible tip of art films.

Genre theory in film criticism came to the fore as a result of a sequence of reflections on films that began with the early theorist Robert Warshow's distinction between the "real" city, which produces criminals, and the "imaginary city" of the gangster film genre, which produces gangsters (as quoted in ibid., xii). Genres from that time on have been used as labels to inform audiences. Originally, genres were linked to auteur theory and were a means of making explicit the ideology—such as romanticism, naturalism, or realism—in a director's code. Most recently, genre thus conceived has become the locus of investigation and deconstruction by other ideologies, for example, Marxism, semiology, and structuralism. Genres in film criticism are usually explained either by a common intention (to horrify, to entertain, etc.) or by a set of principal characteristics (cowboys, waitresses, bank robberies, chase scenes, etc.). The theoretical difficulties of relying on either of these two descriptions are overcome by "lean[ing] on a common cultural consensus as to what constitutes a [body of films] and then go[ing] on to analyze it in detail" (Tudor 1986, 5). In this sense, "genre is what we collectively believe it to be" (ibid.).

Film criticism, perhaps more than other uses of genre theory, emphasizes the dependence of genres on specific cultures. Even though an audience has to be exposed to a number of films using the same conventions before the conventions can be expected to carry meaning, the "visual conventions provide a framework" within which a plot can be constructed and understood (Buscombe 1986, 15). The plot establishes a framework that can be effective; the framework controls the kind of plot that can successfully develop. This use of genre in film genre criticism (as distinct from its use in film reviews) is largely limited to the formulaic. *High Noon,* for example, one of the most highly regarded films of its decade, has been described in film genre theory not as unique but as something of an accidental deviation from the Western genre: "So, too, if you are going to make a Western, you will tend not to consider certain themes or subjects, (unless, as in *High Noon* . . . you are consciously trying to adapt the form to your purpose in an arbitrary way)" (Buscombe 1986, ibid).

As helpful as genre theory has been in film studies, it seems limited by its unwillingness to go beyond "pure" genres as the only object of investigation. Such unwillingness generally goes contrary to the intrinsic value placed on uniqueness (see chapter 4) on the one hand, but is consistent, on the other hand, with the argument that, to interpret anything, one has to have a framework.[5]

Some uses of genre theory in film studies are reflective and critical. In Alexander Coleman's "Cutting a Film and Making *Ficciones*" (1985), film itself is treated as a genre in order to redefine a literary genre. Coleman claims that since 1945 the genre novel has been "contaminated," that is, has been subjected to a "positive interference," by other arts, modes, and genres. Novels—for examples, Coleman cites those of Mario Vargas Llosa, Gabriel García Márquez, Jorge Luis Borges, Machado de Assis, Macedonio Fernandez, Ramón Pérez de Ayala, Miguel de Unamuno, and Carlos Fuentes—are no longer forms of "simplistic social realism" (Coleman 1985, 98). In Coleman's view, Borges especially, among these authors, "confounds and mixes up" all genres, thus implying "not a slice of life, but a slice of the imagination" (ibid., 99). Coleman sees film as the only appropriate genre in which to interpret Borges's work: Borges saw many films and wrote "stories and poems which in many ways can be read as if the blank page were a screen, crowded with apparently chaotic images and appearances, laid out with grand chronological freedom, in a total fluidity of time." In addition, Borges spoke of his "cinematographic novels, made up of significant moments, nothing more." Coleman feels that "film gave to Borges a teleology for his fictions, a way of summarizing the world and the cosmos in a series of refracted and disconnected images, yet unified in the viewer's and the reader's imagination." In this sense, Borges's fictions are "akin to poetry, an art which is the declared enemy of the genre known as the novel, the mimetic impulse." Borges's art, therefore, can best be explored as a cinematic "montage," a kaleidioscope of "juxtaposed planes" (ibid., 100).

Here film, having developed its own theory of genre, comes back to literature to challenge the adequacy of literary critical categories for the work of some contemporary writers.

The Natural Sciences

The natural sciences offer a good example of how fields themselves can be thought of as constituting genres. In highly developed fields—chemistry, biology, physics—genre is so overriding that it creates enormous differences in the language and symbolism of each field. Indeed, the fields as genres are so large that the notion of genre tends to get lost.

Aside from the affinity between *genre* and *genus* in biology (discussed in chapter 4), scientific discourse uses the term *genre* only occasionally. William B. Ashworth, Jr.'s *Theories of the Earth, 1644–1830: The History of a Genre* (1984) isolates a genre of works that accompanied the birth and early development of the science of geology. This genre was born out of a realization that the earth itself (as distinct from the people, animals, plants, and objects on it) had a history. The genre numbered several hundred texts published within two centuries and is characterized principally by the subject of alternative hypotheses to the Mosaic conception of the earth. "Theories of the earth" were written by philosophers, theologians, geographers, collectors of rocks and fossils, astronomers, and chemists. The genre gave impetus to the birth of the science of geology, the development of which ironically caused the demise of the genre.

A somewhat more reflexive use of genre in science is the discovery that scientific articles before 1940 included an element of self-deprecatory narrative in which the author told of the difficulties incurred in arriving at a conclusion, together with qualifications regarding the circumstances under which the conclusion was not likely to hold true. Gradually the narrative element disappeared altogether, and today's genre of scientific report diminishes to the point of excluding as well any negative conclusions or contrary evidence. This is one of the rare instances of the use of genre in self-criticism in the sciences.[6]

The gender analysis of science has been a difficult but rewarding enterprise since the early 1980s. In her *Reflections on Gender and Science,* Evelyn Fox Keller argues that the notions of women, men, and science have been socially constructed in relation to one another and that "the historic conjunction of science and masculinity [is dependent on] the equally historic disjunction between science and femininity" (Keller 1984, 4). Keller traces some of what could be called genric decisions to their origins in gender differentiation. Plato, for example, divided the logical from the physical and imaged the logical in a "distillate" of male sexuality. Bacon changed the self-understanding of science to a "chaste and lawful marriage between Mind [male] and Nature [female]" (ibid., 30–31). Barbara McClintock offers a new model for what science involves: she proposes an identification with the object of investigation to preserve the integrity of both scientist and nature. Keller's critical gender study exposes the ideological dimension of science as a "male preserve" and thus opens the way for contemporary sciences to address systematically, perhaps for the first time, the gender bias that has been constructed into the very genre of science.

Drama

In his *Theory of the Modern Drama* (1987) Peter Szondi argues that Hegel historicized the concept "form" and "genre." After Hegel, Szondi claims, there are three viable alternatives: (1) One can claim that the three primary categories (tragic, comic, lyric) of traditional poetics have "lost their raison d'etre along with their systematic character." This was Benedetto Croce's position when he "exiled them from aesthetics." (2) One can go back to timeless conceptions. An example is Staiger's anchoring of genre in modes of being and in three "ecstasies of time" (Szondi 1987, 3). (3) One can view genre as a dialectic between the statements made by form and content. Szondi uses the third alternative in his attempt "to explain the different forms of recent works for the stage as efforts to resolve" contradictions between form and content by seeing technical demands of the drama as "reflections of existential demands." According to Szondi, drama began in Elizabethan England, "the result of a bold intellectual effort made by a newly self-conscious being who, after the collapse of the medieval worldview, sought to create an artistic reality within which he could fix and mirror himself on the basis of interpersonal relationships alone." Szondi sees drama as the sphere of the "between"— in this genre there is no "before or after" of "freedom and obligation, will and decision" (ibid., 7). In many of Samuel Beckett's plays, for example, the main (and frequently only) character speaks to the elements as if they were characters.

In Joe Park Poe's *Genre and Meaning in Sophocles' "Ajax"* (1987), tragedy is seen as "beginning to change its character" already in the extant plays of Aeschylus. By the middle of the fifth century B.C.E., tragedy had changed considerably, especially in the eyes of the audience. From the plays it can be seen that "both Sophocles and Euripides felt more free to confront their audiences with moral and existential imponderables; . . . to reanalyze and reinterpret myth in conformity with their perceptions of human nature and quotidian reality" (Poe 1987, 12–13). Poe might have added that, for Euripides, the existential imponderables included gender perspectives, which he explored, for example, in the *Medea* and *The Trojan Women*.

With the "blurring" of genres mentioned in the introduction comes a need to relate genres previously unacquainted or even opposed to one another. We must speak equally of a blurring of genders to respond to the neglect of one gender because of the exclusiveness of the other or the rigid and arbitrary stereotyping that continues. By now it should be clear how indispensable genric and gender considerations are to rhetorical analysis and how rhetorical analysis in turn calls for a multidisciplinary treatment of both.

It is also clear that it is not adequate merely to transfer methods from one discipline to another as recipes to be followed. Such a transfer is rarely critical and is even at best incapable of producing anything more than isolated illuminations of a text. Adapting from Jauss, we may say that such a critic will author "only cookbooks, catechisms, party speeches, travel brochures, and similar documents" (Jauss 1978, 143). Given the conflicting nature of methods, it is necessary for the successful use of any one of them for the critic to understand what is the horizon of expectation of a particular kind of interpretation.

What can be shown is that Geertz's plea for more inclusivity in his own discipline, anthropology, has been heard. The proof can be seen in the results: far more interesting hypotheses and a field that now embraces genres and questions, for example, from the field of religious studies. No matter that this original borrowing has almost been forgotten in the more recent lending by anthropology to religious studies. Most remarkably, the "blurring" of genres has meant that the one-great-idea syndrome no longer defines any field (except, perhaps, sociobiology).

Besides the blurring of the boundaries of fields and the borrowing of genres between and among disciplines, there is the necessary process of arbitrating among the genres whose status has been damaged by gender bias. Deconstructionist criticism has discredited that tradition of philosophy which pretended that it alone was above the fray and play of genres. And the demystification of philosophy with respect to genre has been accompanied by an exposure of its willing or unwilling association with bias against gender, that is, its association of "intellectual merit with certain kinds of argumentative discourse and subject matter." Jane Tompkins calls this bias a "long tradition of academic parochialism" that has operated by means of gendered oppositions: "light 'feminine' novels versus tough-minded intellectual treatises; domestic 'chattiness' versus serious thinking" (Tompkins 1985, 83). Such biases are deep-seated and often inhabit thought designed to make other points: Heidegger's ([1927] 1978) notion of *Gerade,* or distractions of the everyday, for example, is all too easily related to the derogation of women's speech as "talking about nothing." It is true that *Gerade* is a specific subgenre of conversation, but without a genric distinction among different types of conversation how is the reader to know the limits to Heidegger's exclusion of *Gerade* from "authentic" speech?

It behooves us to be careful about the understandings of genre and gender through which we choose to interpret texts. The world we reconstruct by means of them will be our own.

CHAPTER SIX

The Well-Read Reader? The Genric and Gendered Reader

The power of [an assumption] is to be found not in its influence on any particular argument . . . but in its framing of the very terms of argument, in its definition of the tacit aims and goals.
Evelyn Fox Keller, Reflections on Gender and Science *(1985, 167)*

Critical attention to the role of the reader in the constitution of "meaning" culminates in a reformulation of the hermeneutical circle—one that makes explicit the role of genre and gender in the constitution of the text as a "whole." In this chapter we press the concept of reader with more specific questions: "What kinds of readers exercise discernible effects on genre and gender definitions? Is there a sense in which texts can be said to select their readers? If genres frame readers as well as texts, what rights do readers exercise against being "framed" by books with which they disagree? Here we will rely on approaches designed to make the reader's role explicit first in relation to genre and then in relation to gender.

"READER" AS CURRENTLY CONCEIVED

Typical references to the general concept of reader range from Alastair Fowler's historical-critical observation that during certain historical periods readers have ignored genre, to his study of diverse audiences who affect and are affected by the development of a genre (Fowler 1982, 1971). In her introduction to a collection of essays by major theorists on the role of reader in the text, Susan Suleiman calls attention to a new general emphasis on audience or reader in interpretation that has developed since the mid-1970s

(Suleiman 1980, 2–45). She mentions a long list of critics in whose work the shift in emphasis can be documented: Wayne Booth and E. D. Hirsch as pioneers, Jonathan Culler, Stanley Fish, J. Hillis Miller, Walter Ong, Paul de Man, Roland Barthes, Gérard Genette, Jacques Derrida, Tzvetan Todorov, Wolfgang Iser, and H. R. Jauss. She could have mentioned as well those feminist critics for whom the reader is by definition a central issue, critics such as Barbara Johnson, Gayetri Spivak, Elaine Showalter, Sandra Gilbert, Susan Gubar, Mieke Bal, Pat Jobling, Mary Daly, Carolyn Heilbrun, Annette Kolodny, Jane Spencer, Janet Todd, and Ellen Moers. Suleiman notes the affinity between genre studies, especially in applied speech-act analysis, and the new emphasis on reader. On the same front, Mikhail Bakhtin (1973) opens an area fraught with both promise and difficulty in his notes on the relations between speech genres and emotions.[1] Others, such as Eugene Kintgen (1983), have tried to go beyond the study of speech genres to an empirical analysis of text genres by replacing the definition of reader with the act of reading.[2] Because readers and acts of reading can now be included in judgments about texts, the emphasis on reader makes it possible to link genre and gender studies in ways not previously feasible.

In this chapter we explore, as a theoretical basis for making the gendered reader explicit in genre theory, some general principles both to encourage and to set boundaries for the claims about gender and genre in empirical studies. The kind of risk we take is to steer between a dominantly empirical approach with only ephemeral footings in theory and a primarily ideational approach with little relation to historical genres. The results of this study are apt to "blur" conventional thought about genres arrived at historically and descriptively.

The contemporary conception of reader reverses the usual direction of analogies for reading as being like something else; in Francis Bacon's ([1597] 1986) analogy, for example, books were like food and reading was like eating. The concept of genric reader suggests that since we know how to read, we have a basis for knowing in other ways as well, because reading includes a primary form of interpreting. For postmodern thinkers it is more insightful to think of X as like reading, instead of reading as being like X. Indeed, the deconstructionists go one step further in encouraging us to think of writing as "overwhelming" and "effacing" language in the sense that writing "comprehends" language in a way that it does not comprehend itself.[3] The new concept of genric reader enables us to experience reading as itself overdetermined and determining other ways of knowing, in the sense that most knowing apart from reading depends on the analogy of what it means to read.

In addition, we can distinguish the classical conception of reader, which is best correlated with traditional texts, from a contemporary conception of reader, which can be correlated with both contemporary and traditional texts. Implicit in this project is the assumption that contemporary texts are different from traditional texts and that the responsibilities involved in reading both contemporary and traditional texts are peculiarly contemporary. The concept of genric reader is contemporary rather than classical in the sense that the concept was made possible by the development of general interpretation theory in the nineteenth century and its refinement into what Susan Suleiman calls "positive" and "negative" hermeneutics in the twentieth century (Suleiman and Crosman 1980, 16–17). Wilhelm Dilthey's work represents positive hermeneutics in its ambition to overcome the romanticist, subjectivist bias of interpretation and to provide the possibility of achieving what Dilthey called "a universally valid interpretation [which would be] the basis of a historical certainty" (Dilthey [1870] 1968, 18). Negative hermeneutics, in contrast, retains the ambition to discover or invent the general principles of interpretation, but negative hermeneutics regards the goal of a universally valid interpretation as being unrealizable in practice. Nevertheless, the concept of a "universally valid interpretation" functions not only as an unrealizable goal but also as a norm that makes possible a range of partially impartial judgments and a range of evaluations of actual interpretations.

According to negative hermeneutics, the contemporary reader is ideally responsive to the intertextuality of the world—aware not only of texts as individual texts but also of the relations among them. One might argue, for example, that an individual text is individual by virtue of the multiplicity of texts that exist and that call for its differentiation. The plurality of texts functions in a manner analogous to *langue* in the field of linguistics: to treat an individual text is to play "Boswell" to some "Johnson," that is, to read the *parole* of an idiosyncratic life construct in terms of and against the implicit *langue* of other life constructs. The resulting affirmations and negations of both the understanding of a single text and of the implicit totality of texts constitute the normative process, which is simultaneously relatively stable and also in flux. In this sense, the multiplicity of texts *and* of readers is the condition for the possibility of reading and understanding any one text. Genric readers are readers overtaken in the spaces among texts, and they can be expected to be surprised to discover their own reader competence over and over again, or lack of it. This same reader competence, far from being merely an individual skill, is the sine qua non of understanding in general.

Genre and gender testing presuppose a reader consciously critical of the process. The most self-conscious reader is of course likely to be aware of the aspects of the reading that are not under conscious control. We treat first of all these less than controllable aspects of reading under the rubric of "genric competence." Next we explore the senses in which there is a reader *in* the text. Our conclusion is that to be a well-read reader—both of and in the text—it is necessary to be a "genric and gendered reader."

GENRIC AND GENDER COMPETENCE

Genric competence is a term designed to bring to consciousness a capability that, after it is possessed, functions more or less spontaneously and unreflectively. We are aware of this capability only when we observe that another lacks it or possesses it to a significantly greater degree than we ourselves do. As the capacity for vital experience, the concept of genric competence shares some of the difficulties we have with other concepts, for example, the tendency to take it for granted. Consider the concept of gravity. Before Newton, people realized that bodies fell to the earth and gave various explanations for such occurrences, but not until Newton's formulation was there an explanation commensurate with the demand for intelligibility of certain invariances in the experience of and the phenomenon of "falling." Similarly, readers have perceived that different kinds of texts give rise to different kinds of expectations. They have offered multiple explanations for the similarities among texts and for the ways similar texts function. But only by applying the concept of genric competence can we achieve an explanation compatible with the demand that the relationships between readers' experiences and textual forms be intelligible.

Genric competence is perhaps best understood in relation to Noam Chomsky's (1965) notion of linguistic competence in his general theory of linguistics. Linguistic competence is "the speaker-listener's knowledge of . . . language" (Chomsky 1965, 4).[4] Linguistic competence designates the potential of human beings to understand presently existing expressions and to construct new possible expressions in the future, given that such expressions are structured according to specifiable grammatical principles (Chomsky, 1968, 84). By analogy, we may say that genric competence designates a potential of human beings for understanding presently existing and future possible texts, given that such texts are structured according to specifiable genric principles.

These basic definitions pertain only initially to the "native" languages and texts of speakers and hearers, writers and readers. The notion of competence does not preclude the case in which speakers, hearers, writers, and readers gain linguistic or genric competence outside their "native" language. Nor does the idea of competence preclude the more complicated instance of reading texts in translation. The possibility of surpassing the language and texts of one's native culture is a vexed issue because of the privilege given to the historical dimension of genre. Moreover, in Chomsky's work the surpassing of the boundaries of individual languages raises the controversial possibility of a theory of language that could be applied universally. In the issue of genre the same, even more controversial, possibility becomes manifest. There is also a sense in which language speaks in human beings as much as human beings choose the words they speak, and there is a parallel sense in which genres overtake human beings as much as human beings choose the genres they understand. We will not attempt to solve these problems here. The further questions cannot be ignored, however, because of the assumption that neither linguistic nor genric competence is limited to the culture of the original audience of the text.

Before continuing with the analogy between linguistic and genric competence, we must distinguish between competence and performance. According to Chomsky (1965), competence refers to the speaker-listener's knowledge of the language in the ideal sense: Competence presupposes a "homogeneous speech community" and a perfect knowledge of the language. Performance refers to "the actual use of language in concrete situations" (Chomsky 1965, 3–4). This distinction allows Chomsky to equate competence with grammar: "A grammar of a language purports to be a description of the ideal speaker-hearer's intrinsic competence" (ibid., 4). Strictly speaking, Chomsky (1968) says, "if the grammar is . . . perfectly explicit—in other words, if it does not rely on the intelligence of the understanding of the [speaker-listener] but rather provides an explicit analysis of [the speaker-listener's] contribution—we may call it a *generative grammar*" (ibid., 5). Performance, on the other hand, includes such conditions as "memory limitations, distractions, shifts of attention and interest, and errors (random or characteristic)," which occur in the application of the knowledge of language to speech-listening situations. It may seem from this distinction that it could be possible to dispense with the aspect of performance and to treat grammar (or in the case of genre and gender, anatomies of genre and gender) as a distinct phenomenon. One may do so only at the risk of forgetting that competence is known only through reflection on performance. In other words, competence is a derivative concept dependent on performance. Conversely, since "performance does not *directly* reflect competence" (ibid., 4, my emphasis), performance and competence must be understood in relation to each other.

The concept of linguistic competence makes it possible for us to understand a familiar phenomenon: on the side of the speaker-listener, the ability to handle language in such a way as to generate and to understand sentences, and on the side of the system of language, the principled diversity of spoken expressions. By contrast, the concept of genric competence makes explicit two factors that are largely ignored in learning theory, unfocused in postmodern criticism, and frequently treated as an "it-goes-without-saying": on the side of the writer-reader, the ability to read a text, and on the side of literature, the principled diversity of texts. Again, whereas the marvel of speech acquisition is repeated every time a child learns to speak, the marvel of genre acquisition is largely a hidden process. Moreover, because the process is hidden, except in specifically genric inquiry, it is usually left to chance and is deprived of both support and criticism.

The role of genre in relation to any text is more complex than the role of linguistic principles in relation to single sentences. Indeed, in actual performance genric competence encompasses linguistic competence. Notwithstanding this complexity, issues of genre draw less attention than issues of grammar. The phenomenon of genric innovation, for example, is less studied than the phenomenon of linguistic innovation. Until recently, genric studies have been primarily an affair of historical and sociological, as distinct from hermeneutical and philosophical, interest. Since historical and sociological inquiry is often conducted by means of categories already historically defined, genre in these studies tends to be treated as a mere principle of categorization. Genric innovation, for example, tends to be confined within the documented shift from one historical genre to another, and the phenomenon of new genric competence tends to be ignored. Genric competence extends beyond the horizon of the text to the horizon of the reader as well. For this reason, understanding a text is never a simple matter of discovering its "original" genre. Because genres produce, as well as identify, meanings, genric analysis at its best is always in the service of a hypothesis.

But before reaching the level of a deliberate hypothesis, genric competence involves more than the recognition of specifiable conventions and forms. We do not begin by knowing all the conventions of literature, nor do texts "fit" simply into genres. We have hunches, compose hypotheses, make imaginative guesses as informed minds already at work in an area of inquiry—hypotheses that are found to illuminate new data and used to find confirmation in experimental trials. Because the foregoing considerations are both numerous and complex, it is doubtful that they can be illustrated by a single example. I have chosen, therefore, to illustrate three different ways in which genric competence becomes explicit through genre testing: genre testing as multiple hypotheses, as modification, and as innovation. In each example, the reader draws from an immense archival memory, which includes large "modes of cognition," such as narrative, philosophical argument, history (as particularized, for example, in chronologies, journals, and treatises), and science (as particularized in laboratory reports, journal articles, and data files); the "major" genres, such as drama, the epic, and the lyric; "subgenres," such as tragedy, comedy, and dialogue; and components of all of these, such as conversation, aphorism, and anacoluthon. The reader's ability to work among, between, and beyond these "levels" of categorizations discloses some of the complexity of genric competence in relation to the productive function of genre.

By now we would expect that gender testing is not something separate from genre testing. Maggie Humm describes the gendered reader as one who can "deal with difference without constituting an opposition" (Humm 1986, 14). Gendered readers have three kinds of competence, according to Humm. First, they are alert to the "maleness" of traditional texts, including an awareness of the narrator's gender perspective. They take into consideration the role of women and men as consumers of predominantly male-produced texts. Gendered readers supplement this tradition with texts by women and women's oral culture. Second, gendered readers are skilled in new methods of reading—Humm cites "those techniques of signification [such] as the mirroring of mothers and daughters, or role playing and transvestism" in which the language becomes literary. Third, gendered readers are skilled in forming what Josiah Royce (1900) called new "communities of interpretation," or what Humm describes as "new communities of writers and readers supported by a language spoken for and by" both women and men. An equal amount of effort is probably required of male and female readers to become gendered readers, since what needs to be changed has to do with habits of language, tradition, and signifying, rather than with biology.[5]

Genre and Gender Testing as Multiple Hypotheses

Heather Dubrow graphically illustrates how different genric hypotheses change our expectations and interpretations of the same text. In her book *Genre* she asks the reader to consider the following passage from a hypothetical book:

> The clock on the mantelpiece said ten thirty, but someone had suggested recently that the clock was wrong. As the figure of the dead woman lay on the bed in the front room, a no less silent figure glided from the house. The only sounds to be heard were the ticking of that clock and the loud wailing of an infant. (Dubrow 1982, 1)

Dubrow argues that two radically different readings of this paragraph result from our assumptions about its genre. If we read the passage as detective fiction, we are likely to assume that the dead woman has been murdered, and we will notice the time on the clock as evidence to corroborate or to challenge what we will later learn about the activities of the murder suspects. We are apt to see the doubt about the time as part of the detective game or riddle to be solved. We will ask for empirical reasons to explain the clock's being inaccurate, for instance, that it might have been tampered with. With a chill we regard the "no less silent figure" as possibly the victim's murderer, and we begin to look for other clues to identify the victim, the murderer, and the motive for the crime.

If, on the other hand, we read the passage as part of a bildungsroman, we will tend to see the baby as the central subject and the "silent figure" as the midwife or the grieving father because the bildungsroman features the fortunes and development of a hero from birth to death. The clock we are apt to interpret symbolically, perhaps as an allusion to the disruption of ordinary time in a world about to be changed. At the same time we become alert for other references and ideas about time. Natural causes, rather than foul play, are likely to be invoked in the death of the woman we assume to be the mother.

This example makes explicit the hypothetical aspect of genre insofar as the reader is shown to be capable of testing alternative readings of the text *as* different genres. Reading is always *reading as,* but this fact of interpretation becomes manifest only in the capacity for reading the introductory paragraph in two genres, both of which "make sense" of the text. In principle, genre testing can be done for different reasons: one might test different genres in order to detect the original genre of the text, for example, or to compare and contrast one understanding of the text with another.

Not all genric considerations pivot on such clear choices as in the foregoing example. In recent New Testament studies of the text of 1 John, for example, we find different interpretations that hinge on at least four possible choices of genre:

1. A letter
2. A "comment" patterned on the fourth gospel
3. A "paper" in the modern sense
4. An "enchiridion" (handbook or manual)

In his review of different studies of 1 John, Fernando Segovia states that the text poses a distinctive problem of genre:

> Whereas the designation of 2 and 3 John as "letters" has never been seriously questioned, given their basic agreement with epistolary conventions of the first century CE, the search for the exact genre of 1 John has remained a topic of considerable debate in the literature. The absence of all such epistolary conventions within it, above all the lack of both a prescription and a postscript, has caused many to question its traditional designation as a "letter" and to look instead for other possible options. (Segovia 1987, 132)

Segovia shows how the issue of genre is emphasized in all but one of the six authors whose work he reviews, and how each interpretation is consequential upon the genric assumptions of each of the six authors, whether or not genre is emphasized.

Two of the genric designations ("paper" and "enchiridion") are not contemporary with the original audience of the text being studied. Segovia is ambivalent about the noncontemporaneity between the genric designations and the texts. Although he does not object to the designations being noncontemporaneous, he concludes that "alternative designations of genre, such as that of 'enchiridion' or 'paper,' should be grounded in and argued on the basis of similar writings roughly contemporaneous with 1 John; otherwise, such designations prove to be of little heuristic value in the end" (ibid., 133). Moreover, he feels that the choices of genre other than "letter" (whether "comment" on the gospel, "enchiridion," or "paper") are "by no means radically different from earlier proposals made under different appellations." He acknowledges the suggestion that 1 John is a "comment" patterned on the fourth gospel to be the most "novel" of the group under review, but judges that the genre of "comment" resembles an earlier explication of the text as an "epilogue" to the gospel. Here Segovia reaches toward novelty, as distinct from contemporaneity with historical context, as a decisive factor in his evaluation. His choice of genre appears to turn on both novelty and the power that the genric designation has for illuminating the text, rather than on the genre's contemporaneity with the text.

This example provides two clear instances ("paper" and "enchiridion") of the ancient context of the text being "augumented" by the contemporary context of the reader. We notice, in addition, that Segovia is not so much concerned with the correct identification of genre, but rather with how each genre controls the meanings of the text. His readings of the text in terms of several genres, drawn from both the ancient and the contemporary world, yields a broader and more critical understanding of the text than can be achieved with a single genre.

Genre and Gender Testing as Modification

Thus far we have used genric competence in a positive sense, namely, to designate a reading skill that promotes understanding. The word *competence* also has a negative sense, implying mediocrity or, more precisely, that a person possesses basic skills but is not capable of innovation. With respect to genre, the corresponding negative sense of competence implies a willingness to be satisfied with readings that are limited to genres that may have become redundant or irrelevant. To keep the positive sense of competence, a reader must recognize the need for and emergence of new genres as well as be able to understand those which are established.

Rosemary Ruether (1983) has illustrated the way in which new elements can be substituted in old genres to call into question the reified interpretations of traditional stories—interpretations that today are called sexist because they ignore the roles these stories, as written and as read, have played in reinforcing the domination of males over females. To replace the midrash of a God whose primary characteristic is male dominance, she tells a new story in the same genre. Her book *Sexism and God-Talk* begins with "The Kenosis of the Father: A Midrash in Three Acts," which presents a God who renounces his own patriarchal authoritarianism, recalls that he has "known other ways of being God," and extends them to others: "to slaves, to Gentiles, perhaps even to women" (Ruether 1983, 3).[6] This example, which is situated in the context of a systematic theology, illustrates the transposition of the genre of midrash—historically concerned with androcentric interpretation of specific biblical texts—into a new generic skin of religious etiology. The result is an effective reinterpretation of the original text, the meaning of which is called into question repeatedly but more starkly by Ruether's alternative narrative.

This example shows two kinds of competence: (1) the ability to retain many of the features of a genre (here, the genre midrash) and (2) the capacity for substituting other selected features so that an old genre is retrieved for contemporary appropriation. Genres are retrieved for many reasons, and Stanley Kauffmann gives another instance of the need for genric modification in one of his columns in *The New Republic*. Kauffmann defines a "genre film" as one that "wants the viewer to place it in a certain line of films, to remember its antecedents, and to admire it for either its fidelity to its forebears or its innovations or both" (Kauffmann 1987, 24–25). But when any genre is perceived as "too infantile a form" of what the audience believes, the genre must be made more "complicated" if it is to continue being effective.

One might point to *A Day in the Life of America* as an example of such complication. In this film, the genre mafia movie is complicated, first of all, by making the subject Jewish instead of Italian and the context neighborhood instead of family. Furthermore, readers with a competence in reading genres of ancient Judaism might find themselves playing the genre mafia against the genre narrative covenant. This mixture complicates the genre mafia movie by creating a new context for the classic elements of gangsterism and romance.

Genre and Gender Testing as Innovation

One other kind of genre testing is needed: finding a genre where one does not already exist. Whenever a group of texts is perceived not to belong to existing genres, it is potentially a new genre. The newly discovered texts must be found to have properties in common, properties that may be found in other genres, but not in the same combination or degree. As a group, the newly discovered texts must be sufficiently different from the texts of existing genres for the innovation to be recognized. If a new genre is not created for the texts in question, all but one or a few will cease to be objects of interest, and these few will continue to be marginal to existing genres. Another possibility is that newfound texts challenge the established cultural mores or the principles on which existing genres are built and come to constitute a forbidden genre. Pornographic literature, literature that fails to be "politically correct," or until recently, science fiction, are examples of forbidden genres.

In the 1960s a group of fictional texts by authors such as Nathalie Sarraute, Alain Robbe-Grillet, and Samuel Beckett were recognized as departing significantly from the genre of traditional novel. Several schools of criticism, including that of New Criticism, tried, but for the most part were unsuccessful in their attempts, to include these works of fiction in existing genres. Robbe-Grillet himself wrote a *For a New Novel* (1965), which although it lacked a theoretical basis, provided a useful description of what was eventually accepted as the genre of the "new" novel. Chapter 7 includes a detailed analysis of the new genre of the "new" novel.

THE READER REREAD

Besides being consumers of and audiences for texts, readers are also constructed by texts. This is to say that, although a text theoretically is open to anyone who can read, there are devices within books that attract certain readers to some books rather than to others. We shall use the term *genric reader* to refer to the reader as constructed by texts and to emphasize the role of genre in setting up expectations in readers. The genric reader, in other words, is not only a reader theoretically capable *of* reading every text: the genric reader is also the reader inscribed *in* specific kinds of texts. The question then becomes, How do genric expectations function in the construction of a genric, or "well-read," reader?

First of all, consider the statements of an author who deliberately cultivates certain kinds of readers. In *Postscript to "The Name of the Rose"* (1984), Umberto Eco explains how he wrote his novel *The Name of the Rose* (1983). He confides that his friends and editors found the first hundred pages difficult and demanding and suggested that he remove them. Eco refused, believing, as he says, that a reader who did not read those pages "would never manage to read the whole book." Eco insisted that the first hundred pages are, he says, like a "penance" or an "initiation . . . so much the worse for [readers who do not like them. They] can stay at the foot of the hill" (Eco 1984, 37). Eco uses one unfamiliar genric term, "penance," and one familiar, "initiation." The choice of term perhaps reflects the choice with which the reader is confronted: into what kind of reader will she allow herself to be made.

Eco is startlingly deliberate about choosing the readers of his book. In his *Postscript* he muses, "What does it mean, to imagine a reader able to overcome the penitential obstacle of the first hundred pages? It means, precisely, writing a hundred pages for the purpose of constructing a reader suitable for what comes afterward." Just what kind of "reader" did he want to construct?, we might ask, and he would answer, "One who, once the initiation was past, would become . . . the prey of the text and would . . . [want] nothing but what the text was offering" (ibid., 38). In other words, Eco saw his text as predatory and his successful readers as hooked.

How shall we understand Eco's *Postscript?* Is he really designing to trap readers in his book? Are we witnessing a confidential disclosure that Eco—and perhaps all authors—have designs on readers? If Eco's designs turn out to be successful—as they have, judging from the enthusiastic reception of the book—would we not say that Eco's readers have been well read by him? If we bring gender considerations to bear on Eco's choice of analogy, we do not ignore its predominant masculinity in its image of man as hunter, as trapper, as seducer.

The idea that books trap their readers is well known, of course, in a commonsense way. We say, for example, that a certain book was so good that we "couldn't put it down." Sometimes authors cast their nets broadly to catch every reader. Others, like Eco, are more selective and set out to snare only a specific kind of reader. The phenomenon of selective readership as described by Eco raises the issue of authorial and reader intention in a new and interesting way. The phenomenon also makes us ask, are authors created by authors or by readers?

For example, what guarantees that any reader has not misread the title of this chapter? One could say that the title is an initiation or a penitential test with which the author set out to select and then trap readers. Let us presume further that the author has counted on those readers' *mis*understanding to be the matter-of-fact occasion for their coming to a new understanding—much as Schleiermacher thought that all understanding begins with misunderstanding.[7] Perhaps they think that the term *genric* means only categorization. Perhaps they think that the term *reader* refers only to actual readers. Perhaps they think the term *gendered* refers only to biological males and females. Indeed, there are no guarantees for declaring a misreading; the only warrants are the evidence available in the text as that evidence is accumulated, appropriated, and if necessary, argued by different readers.

If genre competence designates the reader's capacity for understanding texts in terms of the multiple genres through which they are structured, gender competence designates the reader's capacity for understanding texts in terms of the different ways that gender can be construed. There are at least three levels of competence.

A first level of gender competence is primarily noncritical. These readers are unaware that gender is an issue in interpreting a text. Or they believe that biological or stereotypical factoring of human beings into male and female is sufficient. These readers readily accept the designation of texts "for men" or "for women" and are content to remain within those constraints.

A second level of gender competence characterizes readers who recognize that gender is historically and culturally defined, as well as biologically inclined. Yet they tend to substitute other kinds of certainty about gender categories for biological determinism. In *The Book of J,* we recall from chapter 3, Harold Bloom offers several reasons why the Yahwist may have been a woman, among them: (1) the Yahwist, unlike all of the other authorial voices of the Torah, does not speak normatively, and (2) the Yahwist does not have any male heroes (Bloom 1990, 32). Although he is aware of the dangers of essentialism, Bloom argues for a gendered authorship on the basis of presumed differences between men and women, namely, that women can be expected to oppose power and that women will not have male heroes. Another example can be found in Louis Spitzer's (1954) argument that *Letters to a Portuguese Nun* had to have been written by a man because a woman would have had neither the skill nor the ability to distance herself from the experience in order to write as well as the author of the *Letters.* Still another example is that of readers who understand that a "double critical standard" is operative in both literary and mass-culture studies. They are sympathetic to reports such as that of Tania Modleski that one cannot find any writings on popular feminine narratives to match the aggrandized titles of certain classic studies of popular male genres ("The Gangster as Tragic Hero") or the inflated claims made for, say, the detective novel. . . . At a time when courses on popular culture have become semirespectable curricular offerings in the universities, one is hard put to find listed on the syllabi a single novel, film, or television program which makes its appeal primarily to women. As Virginia Woolf observed some time ago, "Speaking crudely, football and sport are 'important'; the worship of fashion, the buying of clothes 'trivial.' And these values are inevitably transferred from life to fiction." (Modleski 1982, 11)

More recently, however, feminist critics have identified and begun to study works that are "aimed predominantly or exclusively at a female audience"—works such as Harlequin novels, Gothic romances, and soap operas (ibid, 31). Readers at the second level of gender competence resist stereotypes at least minimally by acknowledging that they exist.

A third level of gender competence is illustrated by those readers who are both discriminating in their resistance against gender stereotypes and persistent in the face of overt opposition. Examples include the three Marias who, in 1982, published *The New Portuguese Letters* and were jailed for their clever and outspoken parody of contemporary marital stereotypes. One would be likely to find other examples among those who do not conform to the gender expectations of their time. Such seems to be the situation, clearer undoubtedly in retrospect than in her time, of Jean Guyon, a seventeenth-century mystic who persisted in writing spiritual treatises for publication in spite of their being denounced largely because she was a woman.

In literature we often find explicit signs of the genric reader in the presence of a character who is occupied with reading in an analogous sense: for example, Ambrose, whom Augustine observed reading only with his eyes, and not with voice and tongue, and who is the analogue for Augustine's reading and writing of his own life in the *Confessions* (c. 400, 6.3.3); Binx Bolling, the "moviegoer" in Walker Percy's (1961) novel of that title; or Grace Strasser-Mendana, who early in Joan Didion's *A Book of Common Prayer* (1977) shifts from reading human beings as an anthropologist, to reading them more demonstrably as a microbiologist, to reading them finally in a way that is informed by but something different from either reading. There is the further implication that reader analogues are more apt to be fragmented selves in contemporary than in traditional fiction.

FRAMING READERS

In the context of interpretation theory, what does it mean to be a reader? Let us first of all turn to a contemporary theorist who has schematized a number of current issues regarding the role of "reader" in the interpretation of texts. In a programmatic article, "Theses on the Transition from the Aesthetics of Literary Works to a Theory of Aesthetic Experience (1978)," Hans-Robert Jauss explains that he wants to convert literary criticism from a study of texts considered to be autonomous into a study of the experience of reading texts. Jauss distinguishes between the explicit reader and the implied reader. Explicit readers are actual readers, in their concrete psychological and physical reality. Jauss describes the explicit reader as a "historically, socially, and biographically distinct reader . . . an ever-changing subject" (Jauss 1978, 142). The explicit reader is more difficult to understand than the implicit reader not only because of the multiple subjective factors involved in the ongoing integration that dynamic selfhood implies, but also because there are, in the explicit reader, social dependencies that tend to conceal themselves in the act of reading.

Social dependencies prolong specific genre preferences. One of the most pervasive dependencies has to do with the notion of *enlightenment* as it pertains to the evaluation of the genres of myth and scientific prose. According to Max Horkheimer and Theodor Adorno, enlightenment is not confined to the seventeenth-century scientific prose; it is a mode of thought that "recognizes itself even in myths" (Horkheimer and Adorno 1972, 6). Indeed, they claim, "mythology itself set off the unending process of enlightenment in which ever and again . . . every specific theoretic view succumbs to the destructive criticism that it is only a belief" (ibid., 11). In the seventeenth-century Enlightenment view, rational thought and myth are seen as incompatible with each other, and myth is translated into what is thinkable in terms of familiar concepts. In Ulrich von Wilamowitz-Moellendorf's reading (1931) of the *Odyssey*, cited by Horkheimer and Adorno as an

172

example of enlightenment thinking, the voyage from Troy to Ithaca indicates the way taken through the myths by the self. The self in the *Odyssey* is always physically weaker than the powers of nature. Nature is understood as the prehistoric world, a space whose measure the self must take and whose old demons must be forced back into their caves and caverns. Nevertheless, the victory by the "enlightened" self is only partial: in the epic, adventures are made to occur in places that have foreign names, and barter is interchangeable with sacrifice. But Enlightenment fails because the prehistoric is not conquered but only temporarily held in check by the ordering imagination (ibid., 52–53n). The irrational forces remain. As the poet T. S. Eliot wrote, they are

> Like . . . the ragged rock in the restless waters,
> Waves wash over it, fogs conceal it;
> On a halcyon day it is merely a monument,
> In navigable weather it is always a seamark
> To lay a course by: but in the sombre season
> Or the sudden fury, is what it always was. (T. S. Eliot, *Four Quarters* 2:116–23)

Thanks to critiques of the Enlightenment, present-day readers are able to objectify "Enlightenment readers" and to a certain extent understand them as explicit readers.

Another example of the explicit reader occurs in Ian Watt's study of Defoe, Richardson, and Fielding, which highlights the changing social conditions and ideology of the eighteenth-century English middle-class public (Watt 1951, 51). Watt finds the eighteenth-century novels both a consequence and a direct expression of the values and aspirations of eighteenth-century readers. The individualism and concern with sentiment by a new class of readers is appropriately captured in the epistolary genre, which, along with its predominant themes of courtship and marriage, provided language and an occasion for readers to talk publicly of their private experiences.

In contrast with the explicit or actual reader, the *implied reader* means "the necessary requirements of the act of reading *as indicated in the text*" (Jauss 1978, 142, my emphasis). Jauss took the implied reader's role to be the "condition for the possibility of effects"—the condition "which pre-orients, but does not pre-determine, the actualization of meaning" (ibid.). Within the context of a literary aesthetics, the implied reader takes "methodological preference" over the explicit reader. In short, to ask questions about the explicit reader takes one into the codes of a biographical, historical-sociologically determined reader, and of a specific *Lebenswelt*. To ask questions about the implied reader takes one into the "codes of the historically determined reader as indicated in the text," as discerned from the structures of the text.

What does this distinction between explicit and implied reader mean in practical terms? On the one hand, the distinction helps us to overcome the bias in favor of what Jauss called "the substantialist conception of a work" (ibid., 138), a conception that invites the ideal of a reader who is solitary, literally one who is lost in contemplation. The substantialist conception also invites the ideal of a text that is autonomous, its autonomy defined by "criteria such as perfection, form as complete entity, reconciliation of the parts into an organic whole, correspondence between form and content, and unity between the general and particular." In the substantialist conception, the ideal reader "would be the classical philologist who reduces the meaning of the text through an objective revelation, given once and for all, and who, as an interpreter, must disappear" (ibid.). To make the distinction between explicit and implied reader is already to call into question the substantialist conception of the text.

Jauss's concept of the implied reader in turn demystifies the single, or what we might call the hypothetically nongenric, text. Jauss claims that if we have read a single text, for example a detective novel, we cannot say that we know "what the pleasure of the reader of detective novels is" (ibid., 144). That is, however competent in following the story, the explicit reader of only one text is incapable of responding to the "code" of the implied reader inscribed in the text. Without an explicit horizon of expectations, a reader can anticipate neither the process of the story nor any departure from that genrically determined process.

Jauss insists on the priority of the reader's experience over the individual text. The effect of this priority is to reverse the priority of works over the experience of works prevalent in the tradition. As we have seen in chapter 2, however, the priority of the text is sustained in formalist literary criticism by the idea of a self-contained, unique work of art. According to Jauss, the unique work of art is a fetish whose origin is hidden in the past, a fetish that appeals to a bourgeois mentality. To replace the mystification intrinsic to the idea of the uniqueness of the work of art, Jauss emphasizes that the pleasure that attends the aesthetic consciousness is incomplete unless the reader perceives variations from one text to another, in other words, unless the reader understands texts genrically.

As an example, Jauss argues that much of medieval literature has been misunderstood because the classical ideal of a self-contained, unique text has been uncritically imposed. The *Song of Roland,* Jauss points out, has been subjected to the question of unity of form in "thousands of essays during the past hundred years" until Eugene Vinaver showed that "the quarrel about unity was without foundation . . . but was rather the unrecognized consequence of an applied aesthetics that every French positivist carries with him from his classical training." Similarly with the question of "corrupt variants" of a lost original version, Jauss thought that the question is better posed as that of "continuation within an imitation" (ibid., 145). This same principle is enunciated in John Dominic Crossan's book *In Fragments* (1983). In his early work, Crossan, a New Testament scholar, was preoccupied with determining what were the original sayings of Jesus. In this later work, however, his focus is on what he calls "inevitable interpretations and ineluctable responses" to original texts. In his earlier work he would have regarded these "ineluctable responses" as merely "divergent versions," even corruptions, of the text (Crossan 1983, xii).

For a related argument on the need for a genric understanding of the reader, let us turn to another literary critic whose work has for a number of years focused on the rhetorical effects of the text. In his classic study *The Rhetoric of Fiction* (1961) Wayne Booth makes a distinction between the actual author and the implied author. By the term *implied author,* Booth proposes that, quite apart from the "sincerity" or "seriousness" of an author, what we read is the "ideal, literary, created [genred] version of the real [author]" (Booth 1961, 75). He supports Jessamyn West's idea that "sometimes 'only by writing the story [does] the novelist . . . discover . . . [the story's] writer.' " The author is accessible to a reader's understanding only through such mediated choices as style, tone, and technique. Booth's distinction precludes any immediate access to the author. Booth summarizes the difference between the actual and the implied author as follows: "Regardless of how sincere an author may try to be, [any author's] different works will imply different versions, different ideal combinations of norms" (ibid., 71). The sincerity of the author, in other words, does not preclude several discrete, even conflicting versions of the implied author. Here we might recall, for example, the radically different characters named Helen created by Euripides in his tragedies and comedies (Gerhart 1991).

It is tempting to say that Booth's implied reader is the complement of Jauss's implied reader, and of course, to a certain extent the correlation holds. But there are certain discrepancies crucial for our theory of genre. First of all, we notice that, in spite of his general affirmation that "the author . . . makes [a] reader as [one] makes [a] second self, and the most successful reading is one in which the created selves, author and reader, can find complete agreement" (Booth 1961, 138), Booth's explicit reference to the "reader" is conveyed in his distinction between actual reader and mock reader, a distinction not parallel to his understanding of author. "Mock reader," a term Booth borrows from Walter Gibson, refers to the "discovery on reflection that we have allowed ourselves to become a 'mock reader' whom we *cannot* respect, that the beliefs which we were temporarily manipulated into accepting cannot be defended in the light of day" (ibid., 139). Booth's mock reader and Jauss's implied reader both pertain to a reader postulated by the text as distinct from actual readers.

Yet the mock reader has a curious relationship with the actual reader. For Booth, the mock reader is postulated by "books that depend on 'beliefs' or 'attitudes' . . . which we cannot adopt even hypothetically as our own" (ibid., 138).[8] Here, the mock reader is rejected by the actual reader *after* the book has been read, that is, after the actual reader has been caught up in the play and roles of the inscribed reader in the text. The mock reader turns out to be a special kind of implied reader. By means of the distinction it becomes clear that actual readers never perfectly coincide with the implied reader. In the case of the mock reader, the actual reader refuses to become what the text expects her to become. But it is dubious that the mock reader—that is, the reader she has become while reading—can ever be so simply rejected. The very act of reading—the act of being "temporarily manipulated into accepting what cannot be defended in the light of day"—has taken place and is henceforth an event that must be reckoned with. We are assisted in this matter of understanding the reader's dilemma (and that of the author as first reader) by phenomenology and psychoanalysis, both of which affirm our expectation that the intentions of authors or readers are neither so simple nor so transparent as they were in the classical faculty theory. Above all, both models demand that objects of attention be included in the analysis. In phenomenology, consciousness is always conscious of something. In psychoanalysis, consciousness is an affair of constructing meaning out of apparent objects of desire. In both models, the attempt to be sincere is surpassed by the desire to be authentic. In neither model would the concept of mock reader (a reader, that is, who having put on the mask and having played the role of the reader, subsequently denies the implications of that act) be coherent.

For our purposes, both models can be understood as disclosing the possibility of a new concept of reader in relation to genre. For it is genre that triggers the reader's realization that she is perhaps being fooled. By means of a certain style of writing, the reader becomes aware that she is being "framed" or perhaps even the target of a "con job" and aware further that she does not want to buy into that particular hypothetical world proffered by the text. Nevertheless, similar to the buyer who must go through and beyond the advertiser's zeal to sell her product, the reader has to become experienced in the business of accepting and rejecting her own mock readers. Sophistication comes from a wealth of experience and critical reflection.

The Well-Read Reader

In contemporary theory, genres are best construed not so much as techniques but as hypothetical constructs of both the author's and the reader's alternative selves and worlds projected through the text as read. The alternative selves and worlds are, of course, both repetitive, in the sense that they can be perceived more than once and by more than one person, and unique, in the sense that the lexical signs converge with other signs and that the citing of signs is always limited by the attentiveness of the hearer. The alternative worlds and selves are at once determinative, in that they set certain horizons of expectations, and open-ended, in that horizons are objectified and can be sublated, after we have passed beyond them, into others. Finally, the alternative worlds and selves are simultaneously temporal, by having the character of events informed by history, and transhistorical, by being preserved through and by means of discrete traces, records, and monuments.

One implication of the concept of genric reader for interpretation theory is that it is helpful to move from a renunciation analogy (wherein one must repudiate the undesirable experience of having been duped by the author into wearing a mask, which afterward one rejects) to another kind of analogy in which the possibility of being duped is desirable. One such analogy is that of inoculation: if texts trap readers into being implied readers, the best remedy for interminable entrapment is inoculation. What does it mean to be inoculated? It means that we host a germ under special circumstances for the purpose of developing antibodies. The analogy suggests that we read many books conceived as the same or similar genres in order to be capable of appreciating and discriminating among them. On another level, it means reading many books conceived in dissimilar genres in order to experience radically different ways of representing human action in relation to our actual selves and actual worlds. On a third level, it means testing the same books with different genres in order to understand the texts and our own grounds for evaluation. Genre criticism is equivalent to genre testing, and genre testing is the act of making explicit one's horizon of expectations in the role of implied reader.

Nor is the implied reader limited to actual readers as individuals. The concept genric reader implies that genre testing is ideally performed implicitly or explicitly in the context of a community of interpreters. The acquisition of meaning is no longer understood on a derivation model but instead on a constitution model; that is, meanings are not extracted from within or behind the text, but constructed in front of, in accordance with, and sometimes even against the text.

Finally, the concept genric reader, in a revised deconstructionist sense, promotes confident readers, ones who can understand themselves as engaging in the play of truth by way of delusion. The orthodox deconstructionist position, we recall, is to presume a fundamental undecidability with respect to genre: every genre exists merely to be destroyed by the individual text. Without denying that genres are not ends in themselves, that some texts have a more uneasy relationship to existing genres than others, and that some texts invite the construction of new genres, we have decided that the "basic undecidability" doctrine is far too limited in applicability and wanting in explanatory power. As Derrida himself said about Poe's "Purloined Letter," there is something indestructible about the letter, and it "resides in that which elevates toward the ideality of a meaning" (as cited in Johnson 1980, 115, 123). As representative of all literature in this sense, the letter is a "final word which is, when all is said, at the origin or at the end (proper course, destination) a word which is not feigned, a meaning which through all the imaginable fictional complications, does not mislead or else truly misleads, still teaching us the truth of decoy" (ibid., xii). But whose voice is it who teaches us this truth? If the implied reader is a decoy for the truth of decoy, is there any guaranteed hearing of the truth of the text?

No, in fact there is no guaranteed normative reading, just as in classical religious traditions it was held that one could never be absolutely certain of one's salvation. But that reading is apt to be best which is constructed by an explicit reader jousting with the structures of decoy in the text in the company of fellow interpreters, past and present. This reader reconstructs and in turn is reconstituted before the text. The reconstituted reader is thereby assimilated to that arch of interpretation, always already in the process of being constituted a world of ultimate meaning. The reader has become a genric reader.

The "Overgenred" and "Overgendered" Reader

In arguing for both genre and gender testing, we have been assuming some kind of necessary relationship between them. Some would object to gender testing as a form of genre testing on the grounds that gender interests are "purely" ideological. We introduce the criticism here and attempt to resolve it in chapter 7.

One form of the criticism states that gender testing cannot help being partial to either women or men. But this criticism is to overlook the partiality that has existed without gender testing—partiality that gender testing is designed to mediate. One example of such mediation over the question of differences between women's and men's voices—in this instance as they appear in literary discourse—can be found in Peggy Kamuf's essay "Writing Like a Woman" (1980). Kamuf reviews the three-century-old controversy over the author of *The Portuguese Letters,* a text published in 1669. The text, whose historical author is unknown but which was claimed to have been "found" by its editor, is a series of five letters, described by the first publisher as having been written by a Portuguese nun to a French officer who had an affair with her and then returned to France. Part of the argument rests on a gender differentiation built on the distinction between nature and verisimilitude. Several prominent (male) critics down to the 1950s have argued that the text could not have been written by the nun because as a woman she would not have had the competence to master the literary artifices so manifestly a part of the text. Their assumption was that a woman's voice is natural, whereas a man's literary accomplishments are the result of acquired taste and skills. Supposing the text had been written by a woman, we should, according to this view, attribute the final form of the text (whether or not it had an original form of letters) to a male editor in order to account for its literary excellence. A second assumption is that it is not likely to have been written by a nun. Here the issue focuses on the possibility of verisimilitude: a woman who has taken the vows of religion is likely to have had neither access to the experience described in the text nor to the necessary literary training to write about it.[9]

Kamuf thinks that both arguments are wrong-headed because they presume some entity that can be identified as a woman's voice. Presenting counterexamples of males who had written "like a woman," Kamuf shifts the argument away from possibility to what would be involved in "writing *like* a woman." In other words, she changes the misleading and misplaced question of what is metaphysically possible for women to the question of the ways women are represented in any given historical-cultural setting. She concludes, on the basis of text and gender analysis, that it is more reasonable to think that *The Portuguese Letters* were written by a woman than by a man:

> The *Portuguese Letters,* then: written by a "man," by a "woman," as "fiction," as "authentic letters"? We may of course still want to

provide some answers to these questions, but such empiricism cannot be counted on to lead us outside the circle of its own pre-ordained tautologies of what is woman's writing, man's writing, fictional, or authentic. If, on the other hand, the theory and practice of writing *as a woman* . . . are to be in any measure critical levers with which to displace the imponderable weight of patriarchy, then it is only to the extent that we bear down at the most vulnerable point, that interval where essence risks seeping out into pretense. For "as a woman" is also a simile, a comparison which associates two terms through resemblance and which can diminish but never abolish their difference. Only with this simile the effect is the contrary: "a woman writing as a woman"—the repetition of the "identical" term splits that identity, making room for a slight shift, spacing out the differential meaning which has always been at work in the single term. And the repetition has no reason to stop there. (Kamuf 1980, 298)

Kamuf's point is that, given a patriarchal culture where man's writing is normative, writing *as a woman* can never be purely and simply based on nature or verisimilitude.

The issue of differentiating between men's and women's voices is not merely a historical question, as can be seen in a more recent version of the debate. In her study of failures in oral communication between women and men, *You Just Don't Understand: Women and Men in Conversation* (1990), Debra Tannen observes that it has been commonplace to regard the everyday speech of women as different from that of males.[10] Males are frequently heard to complain that "women don't say anything when they talk" or "their talk isn't *about* anything." To notice that women do not mean what they say is already an acknowledgment that some genres of women's discourse have no space or status within public discourse. To claim that women talk about nothing is to imply that their genres do not have referents in the world of public meanings.

As described by Tannen, the issue is one of a difference of gender and of reference. We have already seen, in Ricoeur's distinction between spoken and written language, that the reference in spoken language can usually be clarified by the speaker at the request of the interlocutor. The problem that Tannen treats however, is not only a matter for clarification: she herself refers to it as an issue of style. *Style,* however, would seem to be too idiosyncratic a term for identifying what is essentially an epistemological problem. Tannen also describes the problem as one of framing, which in our terms is explicitly a species of genre. The kind of speech that has come to be called "male" language (i.e., "report talk") is used as a means of preserving men's "independence and to negotiate and maintain status in a hierarchical social order" (Tannen 1990, 77). In contrast, that which has come to be called "female language" (i.e., "rapport talk") is used by women to "signal support, to confirm solidarity or to indicate they are following the conversation" (ibid.). The problem of framing is the problem of genre.

Tannen argues that the reason why "report talk" has been associated with males is that men expect (and are expected by the culture) to dominate women, even when the intention to dominate may not be present. In the face of such dominance, either actual or expected, women as a matter of habit come to use "rapport language" as a means of self-preservation, as a means of communicating with those expected to dominate when conversation is not possible, as an alternative means of attempting to dominate. Women use these means since the culturally approved means are of too high a risk for them to employ or because "report language" has not been available for them to learn in their acculturation as females in our culture. Achieving commensurability between the languages (genres) of report and rapport is most explicitly, but not merely, an issue of competence. Tannen does not address the further question, namely, whether "report language" and "rapport language" are gender-differentiated only in the relations of women and men. We might expect to find similar differences among other groups defined by race or class.

Tannen's investigation presumes that if men and women understood each other's different styles—that is, if they acquired the competence to understand the genre of "report language" and "rapport language"—a mutual rapprochement would be possible. Using Kristeva's (1981) three-generation typology, Tannen's work is primarily a work of the second generation; that is, it transvalues a speech genre traditionally denigrated by its distance from another speech genre become normative in a culture. One could imagine the study becoming third-generational if the investigators were to attempt to overhear both genres in their own speech and then to attend to the tension between the genres in their own experience. Indeed, Tannen calls for an overcoming of the "battle between the sexes"—a description of gender relationships that characterizes the unstated or explicit premise in many gender analyses of language.

In these two gender analyses of language, the first (by Kamuf) focuses on a past problem, the urgency of which has declined in part by the sheer numbers of women writers whose "voices" complicate the problem of defining "a woman's voice." Kamuf also redefines the problem from knowing the essence of "a woman's voice," which would be biologically determined, to an analysis of strategies by which an author could "write like a woman" in a given historical-cultural context. The second gender analysis (by Tannen) focuses on the need to interpret the oral genres of "women's speech" and "men's speech."

In both cases, nevertheless, the question is less about the capability of women regarding the use of literary artifice or of object-oriented language than it is about the transvaluation of values presumed to be inherent in writing and speaking that is understood as being rooted distinctively in women's experience. In other words, the gender question is the issue of the means for making public space for some kinds of writing that have not been valued in the past. On a more complex level (or at the level of Kristeva's third generation), the gender question makes explicit the tension between the so-called masculine values and so-called feminine values in the consciousness of anyone who has to make choices in these matters. It is at this point that efforts to reconstruct the meaning of opposition become crucial. Kristeva resists the tendency to reduce difference to opposition, exclusion, and hierarchic arrangement. To notice difference is to be invited to find a discourse in which difference-on-the-way-to-opposition becomes one difference among many differences, all of which constitute a changing situation. The sex/gender dichotomy, for example, in Kristeva's approach, becomes "a highly context-specific concept,"[11] one that must be examined in detail to discern what is happening and how best to overcome the dichotomy.

Gender testing pertains to the representation of women and men, as distinct from their immediate existence. For this reason, gender testing is best conducted as a part of genre testing. Gender interests, taken alone, can easily remain at the level of ideology. When a gender label is applied ideologically, it is done so without exception, without attention to details, and without regard for interpretive possibilities. Genre and gender labels are applicable to any phenomenon: calling a Jew a woman in what is intended to be a double insult; calling a novel a potboiler to ban it from serious literature. When ideological labels are applied, no defense can be made, because the one who proscribes a particular genre or view of gender appears to be doing something constructive, like saving the world.

What can we say of a gendered reading that is not genred? Such a reading is likely to be conducted at the first- and second-generational levels of gender awareness. That is, the goal of a gendered reading that is not genred is to achieve equality of treatment (that is, it will discover instances of inequality in the situations of men and women, instances that depend directly or indirectly on gender assumptions) or the transvaluation of traditionally defined values (that is, it will critique values that are the result of exclusively male privileges and enhance values that have been lost as a result of such privileging). Overgendered readings are valuable insofar as they illuminate aspects of texts that need attention. Their major contribution is increased information: they enable us to see the pervasive ways in which gender stereotypes have structured not only the everyday but also the worlds of imagination in the past and the present. The shortcoming of a gendered reading that is not genred is that it is incapable of discerning exceptionally great works, which—if they are truly great—can be expected in some way to resist as well as express gender stereotypes. Even when it is applied to a recognized classic, a gendered reading that ignores genre issues could just as well have been done on a period piece. In choosing not to address the question of why the text is authentically great, gendered readings can be said to be "overgendered," that is, to become doctrinaire because they overlook or ignore the differences among genres.

What can we say of a genred reading that is not gendered? Such a reading is likely to be restricted to traditional and ideological expectations regarding genre and to be dismissive of the deconstructive approach to genre. The goal of a genred reading that is not gendered is to account for the effectiveness of specific texts. The shortcoming of such a reading is that it is unable to disclose how the diversity of human achievements have been framed as gender attributes. The genred but ungendered reading also fails to recognize or resist the destructiveness of the ways in which gender assumptions have informed genre classifications. It is also likely to be blind to the self-interest that motivates what a reader identifies in the text and oblivious to the ways in which even great texts systematically distort our perception of the "other" sex and perpetuate gender exclusivity. Finally, the genred, ungendered reading is not one that allows the reader to appropriate gender conflict within the self. For these reasons, it is appropriate to call a genred reading that is not gendered "overgenred." Those who do "overgenred" readings largely overrate their ability to make distinctions solely by means of formal logic and fail to discern when it is necessary to revise their expectations as shaped by traditional genres. Genred readings that are relatively untouched by explicit gender considerations are also unaware of the ways in which conversion from sexism is likely to be different for males and females.

But gender testing done in conjunction with genre testing is a reliable hermeneutical tool for using and surpassing ideological labels. Genre and gender testing then becomes a method for rescuing reason. As a strategy for change, it changes the frames.

CHAPTER SEVEN

Genre Testing and Gender Testing: Some Case Studies

"When you meet a human being," he says, they say, first of all, "the first distinction you make is 'male or female?' and you are accustomed to making the distinction with unhesitating certainty" . . . How? . . . Silence, then, on the subject of that extreme assurance which keeps you from being mistaken at first sight *about the sex of the person you run across. The important point, it seems, is for you to be firmly convinced, without possible hesitation, that you cannot be in error, that there is no ambiguity possible.*
Luce Irigaray, Speculum of the Other Woman *(1985, 13–14)*

A phrase comes along. What will be its fate, to what end will it be subordinated, within what genre of discourse will it take its place? No phrase is the first. This does not only mean that others precede it, but also that the modes of linking implied in the preceding phrases—possible modes of linking therefore—are ready to take the phrase into account and to inscribe it into the pursuit of certain stakes, to actualize themselves by means of it. In this sense, a phrase that comes along is put into play within a conflict between genres of discourse.
Jean-Francois Lyotard, The Differend: Phrases in Dispute *(1988, 136)*

In this chapter readers encounter two kinds of texts. The first comprises those texts for which genre and gender appear not to be issues, because the texts appear to be easily understood in terms of conventional genres, such as mystery, romance, tragedy, and complaint. For these texts, genre and gender testing opens the possibility of interpretations alternative to the accepted meanings of the text. The second kind comprises those texts that resist being understood in terms of known genres. These texts urge the reader toward genre modification or genre innovation and toward gender transformation as well. Time and again we shall see that gender and genre are made most evident when their conventional forms are transgressed either by the reader or by the text. Hence the following examples.

TESTING WITH MULTIPLE HYPOTHESES

In the process of genre testing a text that at first glance appears to belong to only one genre, it is always surprising to find many genres coming to light. Henry James's familiar novella *The Turn of the Screw* is a good candidate for this aspect of genre testing. Framed by a cozy scene of storytelling around the fire by resort guests on a Christmas eve, the text appears so conventional that its genre is taken for granted by most readers, even if they fail actually to designate a genre. But consider the differences in genre and the implications for gender in the following interpretations of James' well-known text, interpretations here reformulated as hypotheses:

1. Suppose *TTOTS* is a subtle detective story in which the governess, Miles, Miss Jessel, and Peter Quint have all been victims of the most clever and desperate Mrs. Grose, the housekeeper.
2. Suppose *TTOTS* is a case study in pathology in which two children, under circumstances where there is no one to realize the situation, are put, for bringing up, in the care of an insane governess.
3. Suppose *TTOTS* is a story of unrequited love in which the governess, dreaming of romance with the master, begins to have hallucinations because of sexual neurosis.
4. Suppose *TTOTS* is a demon-ghost story of horrifying corruption.
5. Suppose *TTOTS* is a masked autobiography in which the governess is James's portrait of his sister, Alice, who had a mental breakdown and who could not be written about directly because James did not dare to express his true feelings about her.
6. Suppose *TTOTS* is a religious essay about the spiritual struggles of a heroine, the governess.
7. Suppose *TTOTS* is a potboiler hoax that Douglas makes up and passes off as someone else's story just to add a turn of the screw.
8. Suppose *TTOTS* is a biography of a woman who falls in love with ten-year-old Miles, identifying him with the master, and who hugs Miles to death because she cannot tolerate her picture of his sexuality, which is homosexual.

Cases have been made for James's novella being each of these genres in critical essays published over several years.[1] None of them, as far as I know, have been tested for gender implications. Is any one of the hypotheses better than the others? Wayne Booth (1979) argues that reading *The Turn of the Screw* as a ghost story (no. 4 above) best accounts for what actually happens in the story. This hypothesis also fulfills two criteria for a good interpretation: accounting for all or most of the important elements in the story noticed by readers, and appealing to readers at a high level of persuasion. The text may be explored productively in the light of other hypotheses as well, but interpretation no. 4, Booth thought, is the best claim on which a highly persuasive argument can be built. If we disagree with Booth's judgment about the most appropriate genre for interpreting the text, we would have to reread the text and bring other evidence forward to argue in terms of a different genre.

The status of the hypothesis is something more than E. D. Hirsch's (1967) heuristic genres and something less than his intrinsic genres. For Hirsch, genre as heuristic is discarded as soon as the text is understood. In the context of genre and gender testing, genres are conceptual tools by which a reader addresses the text as a whole and proposes supporting evidence. Genre and gender testing allows the presuppositions and interests of the reader to become explicit and therefore to be questioned by the text and by other readers. Period pieces are quickly exhausted in the testing process. Tours de force please by the novelty with which they are perceived to respond to gender and genre inquiry. But we would expect that classics, by contrast, would prove to be resilient to gender and genre testing, inviting many hypotheses, yielding insights to several, and very likely being exhausted by none.

Let us pursue conflicting interpretations in greater depth in the case of two films, *The Stunt Man* (1980) and *The Land of the Disappearing Buddha: Japan* (1977). To set the stage, three results from recent film research provide empirical substantiation that the process of genre and gender testing is familiar at some level to the general public.

First of all, results of film research indicates that filmgoing audiences in the United States can distinguish some thirty different genres of film, including the western, thriller, detective story, murder mystery, light comedy, family drama, romance, ghost story, cowboy yarn, and so on. One reason for this ability to distinguish is, of course, the use that film advertising makes of categories (Austin and Gordon 1987, 20). Although film advertising ordinarily avoids explicit gender categories, certain genres (such as tearjerkers or action adventure movies) are advertised in ways that are presumed to appeal to women and men, respectively. Film research does not address the issue of whether and how genres change, the status of female- or male-oriented genres in box office receipts, nor the interrelatedness of genre preferences in any given epoch.

Second, in addition to basic genres, filmmakers refer to what is technically known as the art film, a genre that, as we noticed in chapter 5, is defined negatively by film researchers. An art film is defined by researchers as one that is *not* confined to any one of the familiar genres: an art film surpasses, frustrates, falls short of, or breaks the boundaries of familiar genres (Grant 1986, xi). This difference between basic genres and the genre of art film discloses an important insight, namely, that one must have a knowledge of genres to know when they have been surpassed. The uncertainty of the sense in which a particular genre has been surpassed discloses the need for genre and gender testing. Here, too, we see that genre and gender frames are most likely to be perceived by an audience when they are transgressed.

Third, film researchers find that filmgoers like or dislike films more on the basis of whether or not the filmgoers' expectations were fulfilled with respect to genre than on the basis of their preferring the genre itself or sometimes even their appraisal of the quality of the film. That the same expectation is operative with respect to gender in the related genre of drama has been documented to be true as early as the fourth century B.C.E. (see chapter 2). The single most important factor affecting viewer response is whether or not the film meets announced or anticipated genre designations. If viewers expect a film to be of the genre romance, for example, most will dislike the film if it is perceived to be something other than a romance. In other words, an excellent murder mystery can be expected to be well liked by viewers who expect to see a murder mystery, irrespective of whether or not they like murder mysteries in general. But viewers of the same film who beforehand expect to see a adventure film will probably dislike it (Austin and Gordon 1987, 15–16).

From this research we may conclude that, for many viewers, films do "belong" to genres, that genres are built on premises about gender, and that critical viewing means reading in terms of genre and gender, that is, codes or formulas by which cultural expectations are constructed. To interpret a film without paying attention to its genre(s) and its gender implications is to risk missing the relationship of the individual elements to the whole film. Failure to notice the genre and gender implications of a film obstructs critical reflection on the multiple ways in which human beings construe their worlds.

A film like *The Stunt Man* effectively illustrates the role of gender and genre in constructing a viewer's world. The film opens with a young Vietnam War veteran (Cameron) escaping on foot from law officers and nearly being run down by a stunt man, who drowns as his car plunges off a bridge. Cameron takes the job of the drowned man and is attracted to the leading lady (Nina) of the movie company. The director (Eli) is at times viewed as protecting Cameron and at other times as exploiting him in a mad attempt to make a winning film. When Cameron attempts to escape during the final filming session, his car (with Nina supposedly in the trunk) also plunges off the same bridge from which the first stunt man was killed, but Cameron survives to find Nina alive and with the other actors cheering his performance. The film continuously manipulates viewer expectation from the very first scene when Eli (off-camera) pronounces: "That's just your point of view."

Throughout the film, the viewers' experience of at least two genres is highly conscious. The conflict and constant shifting between the genres of the confidence game—any swindle in which the crook after gaining the confidence of the victim, robs the victim by simultaneously cheating in a game and appropriating something entrusted for investment—and what Richard Gollim (1989) has identified as psychodramatic conversion forces viewers to do genre testing throughout. The viewer is assisted by musical background: circus music signals the genre of confidence game, here complicated by the knowledge that it is *just* a movie and cynical statements by the director about the effects of previous war movies on their audiences. Dramatic music signals the genre of psychodrama, engaging viewers in the personal fate of Cameron. These transitions are integrated with shifts in visual language (camera angles, movement, and position) and lighting (glaringly bright for the confidence game and appropriately shadowy for psychodrama).

190

What are the limits of the genres confidence game and psychodrama? What important elements of the film does each leave out, obscure, or distort? This explicitly genric question opens the film to seeing more than we ordinarily see through the interpretive lenses of psychodrama or confidence game. For example, psychodrama focuses on only one character, that of Cameron. But the genre wavers between completely ignoring the fate of a second major character, Nina (the question she asks, "What will happen to me?," is not likely to arise when we test the film as psychodrama), and reducing her to a mere sex object, as is the case in Richard Gollim's (1989) interpretation of the film as a psychodrama: "These [purgational ordeals] end with the young man reborn into sanity and trust, confident of his skills, assertive of his market value, and rewarded by the love of a good woman, *or at least by the promise of good sex with a caring woman*" (my emphasis).

The inability of the genre psychodrama to account for all the significant details in the film signals the need to move either to another genre test or to challenge the status given to that particular genre. In other words, is psychodrama the best or largest frame for reading this film? One can, I would argue, make a better case for the film as a confidence game than as a psychodrama. This case depends largely on the interpretation of two key scenes. What are we to make of the unique superimposition of Nina's face in the same frame with Cameron's as he, for the first time, thinks of disobeying the script and springing for his freedom? Is this frame best read as a romantic overlay of their lives as they are soon to be liberated from Eli the tyrant (psychodrama), or does it mark a momentary assimilation of Nina totally into Cameron's fantasy of her (confidence game)? Interpreted in the context of the whole film, I think the latter reading is more sound. And what are we to make of Eli's last words, muffled by the credits at the very end (a privileged position in any text), "Sam, cross the little bastard in the first act," a line that says to the audience that the film is about to be (re-?)made without Cameron?

The Land of the Disappearing Buddha: Japan poses a different problem. The film explores four contemporary faiths in Japan: Zen (with an emphasis on meditation), Shinto (a form of nature and spirit worship), Soka (a society for the creation of values), and Pure Land (a form which opens to the masses a faith formerly

191

restricted to monks and the educated). It is a documentary presentation conducted by a narrator who has just arrived from a study of forms of Buddhism indigenous to Sri Lanka.

This film seems to be constructed as only one major genre, that of a documentary—here, a traveler's interview of people in their own setting. Buddhism, we are told by the narrator, is one of more than one hundred religions that have sprung up in Japan. Our strategy for interpretation here is to compare and contrast a reading done in terms of a documentary with a reading done in terms of a confidence game, not for the purpose of reducing one reading to the other but to understand it in the light of the other. The wager is that the complexity of the documentary genre will become visible and productive of more understanding by means of the comparison.

What do documentaries do? On one level, they give us information of what the Buddhist believes through many of the narrator's impressions. At the same time they give us a point of view, here specifically, on the risk of asking questions in the first place. One limitation of the documentary genre is its claim to present information simultaneously as a fact and as a judgment idiosyncratic to the interviewer. Another limit is its inability to raise general issues, such as, in this instance, the question of religion as distinct from questions about one of the religions—here, about Japanese Buddhism. Finally, the documentary does not readily invite testing by several genres.

The capacity of a genre, such as the documentary film, to lend itself to testing by multiple genres is increased, however, by comparing one representative film with another. Following is one possible line of inquiry for comparing *The Land of the Disappearing Buddha: Japan* with *The Stunt Man*. Both films are male-oriented: in both films together there are only three women, and of them, only Nina speaks more than one sentence. Similarly, both films are informed with values of the military. One contrast is between an interventionist god (in the character of Eli) and the Buddha, whom, it is said, nobody knows. Another contrast is the experience of having one's interpretation repeatedly fail in *The Stunt Man*, on the one hand, and having no confirmation of any interpretation in *The Land of the Disappearing Buddha: Japan* on the other. As the narrator in the documentary says, "Who is the Buddha? You, me, this stick, nothing, dead teacher, myth, uniqueness of things, empty circle, compassion, shake of the head. There is nothing you can point to and say that is the Buddha." A third contrast is in the explicit possibility that *The Stunt Man* is a confidence game and the lack of evidence that the Disappearing Buddha may be a "put-on" by the narrator. We know that *The Stunt Man* is a confidence game because we see Cameron, Nina, and Eli together alive after the shooting of the scene during which Cameron is killed. In *The Land of the Disappearing Buddha: Japan,* we are not given opposing views of scenes that make unfamiliar claims. For example, the significance of the shot of Buddhist monks praying in a trancelike state is left unclear.

The Land of the Disappearing Buddha: Japan satisfies some curiosity about Eastern religions. In a sense, it is voyeuristic because although it has some allusions to Western religions, it serves only to tantalize rather than to show structural similarities between the two kinds of religion. In the documentary we have a guide doing the work for the viewers, a guide who asks questions while the passengers watch through a window. The passengers on a tour bus see only what the guide wants them to see.

In *The Stunt Man,* the viewers are fooled over and over again, and yet they seem willing for it to go on forever. The viewers are unable to rise above a status where they can always be fooled again. In *The Land of the Disappearing Buddha: Japan* there is also the danger that one is being fooled, since it is said that learning more, studying more, is no guarantee that one may not still miss experiencing enlightenment. *The Stunt Man* can be taken to make a minimal affirmation: it is better to be fooled by what may turn out to be a confidence game than to lose what is best for one's self and world. Similarly, *The Land of the Disappearing Buddha: Japan* may be taken to make a minimal religious affirmation conceived as the wisdom of Pascal's wager: belief in the Buddha may be false or true, but it is better to seek enlightenment as though what the Buddha teaches were true.

The Stunt Man and *The Land of the Disappearing Buddha: Japan* are examples of the first kind of text referred to at the beginning of the chapter, namely, those for which genre and gender are scarcely issues because the films appear to be easily understood in terms of conventional genres—in this case, psychodrama, confidence game, documentary. In the process of our genre testing, no one genre appears to exhaust the possibilities of meaning. At the same time, we are able to make a better argument for one interpretation of *The Stunt Man* than the other by testing for gender as well.

Without reflection on the effects of genres and gender implications used as interpretive frames, viewers play a role in *The Stunt Man* equivalent to the crowd on the beach who swoon and cheer on cue. In *The Land of the Disappearing Buddha: Japan* viewers become transparent observers whose questions are asked by the interviewer. In both films, genre and gender analysis builds on the need to be alert to achieve a partially and provisionally true understanding.

TESTING TEXTS THAT RESIST BEING CLASSIFIED AS A CONVENTIONAL GENRE: THE "NEW" NOVEL

The critical reader comes to a text with some genric and gender expectations already in hand. These expectations are structured by culture, tradition, and personal experience. For contemporary readers, they include established and emerging genres and suppositions about the meanings and influence of gender on literary expression. Michael McKeon argues that the novel in the twentieth century has become par excellence "the *modern* genre," especially in its authority to answer questions pertaining to "truth" and "virtue" (McKeon 1987, 11). McKeon claims that "the persistence of the traditional categories is . . . an optical illusion, since the categories themselves [literary categories, such as "romance" or "elegy," and social categories, such as "bourgeoisie"], and the crucial 'traditionality' that determines our sense of their persistence, are conceptual products of the same centuries in which 'the novel' and 'the middle class' come into being." In McKeon's view, the novel is "a deceptively monolithic category that encloses a complex historical process" (ibid., 19).[2] The significance of McKeon's argument is that any study of contemporary genres must take into account the primacy of the novel for contemporary readers.

The two texts I have chosen to illustrate the emergence of a new genre reflect the primacy of the novel as described by McKeon, but at the same time resist being classified with the traditional novel. Both because and in spite of the designation "new" novel in this inquiry, I shall argue that, with respect to a significant number of texts, the genre is better understood as genre innovation than as genre modification. From a conventional point of view, the "new" novel is a traditional name with a difference. In an ideological position, the title "new" novel intensifies the opposition—a fight for inclusion and exclusion—between a potentially new genre and traditional genres. In deconstructionist usage, "new" novel denotes a self-contradictory tautology.

Focusing on the emergence of the "new" novel corresponds to our experience with a significant number of texts, namely, that the novel has changed in the twentieth century—in the first half with the "experimental" novels of Joyce and Woolf and in the second half with "new" and postmodern novels. Most contemporary readers can be expected to define a novel in one or more of the following ways. One reader might see it as a relatively long narrative with plot, characters, rising action, and denouement (conventional view); another reader, as a relatively long narrative with an arbitrarily imposed ending reflecting bourgeois aspirations (ideological view); and a third reader, as a relatively long narrative whose internal networks of meaning call one another into question (deconstructive view).

Some of the questions suggested by Kristeva's three phases or generations of the women's movement provide a general outline for gender analysis that corresponds roughly to the three views of genre above. For example:

1. How are females and males represented in the "new" novel? Is the prevalence of either justified?
2. To what extent are female and male stereotypes operative in "new" novels? To what extent are gender stereotypes challenged or broken?
3. To what extent do the meanings and values represented in the "new" novel as gendered pose choices to be made by the reader? Is the deconstructionist notion of a fragmented self represented as well by a fragmented gender?

The Conventional View: A Historical-Critical Overview of the "New" Novel

Most histories of the novel link the rise of the traditional novel to the rise of the bourgeoisie in England and on the continent in the eighteenth and nineteenth centuries. Ian Watt, for example, finds the aspirations and development of a middle class, the growth of individualism, and the philosophical innovations of the seventeenth century major factors in the emergence of what we now call the traditional novel (Watt 1957, 12–61).

The French "new" novel originally defined itself over and against traditional novels. When the "new" novel began to receive major critical attention in the 1950s, it posed, for many critics, a threat to the continuity of the traditional novel. At that time the "new" novel referred principally to the group of French novels and texts that initiated the contemporary discussion. The conventional approach to this potentially new genre was to look to literary history for its origins. However, the "new" novel was perceived as bypassing the "experimental" forms created by Virginia Woolf and James Joyce, which had finally been accepted as serious literature.

A long tradition of English and French criticism treated the "antinovel" and "new" novel as equivalent terms. As early as 1627 there appeared a romance entitled *Le berger extravagant,* referring to "impertinences" of the novel and of poetry in its subtitle. The author's preface states clearly the central concern of the "new" novel ever since: the claim that antiliterature has more access to authentic reality than the romance or novel:

> Au reste je me moqueray de ceux qui diront qu'en blasmant les Romans, j'ay fait un autre Roman. Je respondray qu'il n'y a rien icy de fabuleux, & qu' outre que mon Berger represente en beaucoup d'endroits de certains personnages qui ont fait des extrauagances semblables aux siennes, il ne luy arrive point d'auantures qui ne foient veritablement dans les autres Autheurs: tellement que par un miracle estrange, de plusieurs fables remasées, j'ay fait une Histoire veritable. (Sorel 1627, n.p.)

In the translator's "Remarks to the Reader" in the English translation, *The Extravagant Shepherd* (1654), we find this same concern for reality and truth elaborated as an imperative to go beyond meanings sanctioned only by "Reverence" and "Authority":

> Poetry (which is the Representation of the Life of man) . . . being a chymical extraction of all that the action of man can present, or the mind of man think, and requiring not only great happiness of Thought, but also a noble restraint of Judgment. . . . The Generality of mankinde are wholly led away with their first thoughts, and are guided

by Authority and Tradition, rather than satisfied with the scrutiny of their own reason. (Sorel 1654, n.p.)

Tradition (represented elsewhere in the translator's remarks by Homer and Aristotle) is neither extolled nor blamed. Whether tradition is more or less true from any given vantage point is not in question. The issue is whether or not poets and philosophers are themselves authentic: whether or not they are truly poets and philosophers depends upon the extent to which they rely on "the scrutiny of their own reason" and practice a "noble restraint of Judgment." The "discovery of new Worlds" by poets and philosophers depends on their fidelity to Reason and requires finally that they go beyond "first thoughts" by means of the self-critical process of judgment.[3]

The location of authority, whether in the tradition or in the author's own reasoning, was the issue when, three centuries later, Jean-Paul Sartre saw the antinovelists' quest for authentic reality as an intensification of the antinovel's (as distinct from its author's) self-reflection. From a conventional perspective, this change brought about a significant modification of the genre novel. Sartre describes this distinctive characteristic in his preface to Nathalie Sarraute's *Portraite d'un inconnu* (1956):

> One of the more singular characteristics of our literary epoch is the appearance, here and there, of deep-rooted and primarily negative works which can be called anti-novels. I rank in this category the works of Nabokov, those of Evelyn Waugh, and, in a certain sense, *The Counterfeiters*. It is not a matter of their making an attempt against the novelistic genre as such. . . . The anti-novels keep the appearance and the contours of the novel. They are works of imagination which present us with fictive personages and relate to us their history. But it is [in the anti-novel] more in order to deceive: it is a matter of contesting the novel itself, of destroying it under our eyes in the instance which seems to construct it, to write the novel of a novel which is not made, which is not capable of being made. . . . These strange and difficult-to-classify works do not witness to the weakness of the novelistic genre; they note only that we are living in an epoch of reflection and that the novel is charted to reflect on itself. (Sartre 1956, 7)[4]

In this Preface, the "new" novel found a powerful and somewhat unexpected ally in Sartre with his defense of its quite explicit intention to reflect on reflection itself. In his now definitive essay, Sartre was even willing to exonerate the "new" novel from its indifference to humanistic concerns on the grounds that it testifies to a concern for authenticity, even though as fiction the "new" novel confines itself to purposeful inauthenticity.

Taking Sartre's view of the "new" novel as conventional, we can identify it as a strong hermeneutics of belief, one in which being partial is either ignored or assumed to be good and correspondent to reality. The conventionalist is satisfied with finding one genre or frame for the novel. The frame itself is untroubled in its relationship to reality.

The Ideological View: Robbe-Grillet's Description of the "New" Novel

The term *"new" novel* was given new authority in *Toward a New Novel* (1965), a collection of critical essays by Alain Robbe-Grillet. At the time Robbe-Grillet was the foremost proponent of the "new" novel, having established himself as a controversial figure with three "new" novels, several screenplays, and essays defending the genre against its critics. In one of his best-known essays from that collection, "On Several Obsolete Notions," he lists four elements that have been decisively changed in the "new" novel: character, story, form, and commitment (Robbe-Grillet 1965, 27). Whereas the traditional novel was committed to character development, the "new" novel has no character, no titled— not even named or propertied—human being, according to Robbe-Grillet. Instead, the "new" novel has a "banal he," the subject of verbs. The story in the "new" novel does not have an auspicious beginning nor a predictable ending; instead, like random walk, the story in the "new" novel goes in any direction: the story, in other words, tells itself. The form of the "new" novel does not conform to literary standards; it is neither avant-garde nor conventional: form follows from the act of writing. The author of the "new" novel, not politically committed to any cause, is committed only to the writing, wherever it may lead.

Robbe-Grillet's proposal for a new genre in the form of the "new" novel continues to be raised as a question of genre in his different kinds of imaginative fiction. A cursory view of Robbe-Grillet's novels discloses his manipulation of conventional genres—the detective story (*The Erasers*), the love-triangle romance (*Jealousy*), the adventure story (*In the Labyrinth* and *Project for a Revolution in New York*). Unlike the "traditional" novels of Austen, Balzac, or James, where either *what* happens or what *happens* sustains and fulfills readers' expectations, the action of Robbe-Grillet's novels is suspended between meaninglessness and a superabundance of clues. Readers of *The Voyeur* ([1955] 1958), for example, may naively expect it to be a novel from its length, title, and the context in which the book is advertised. But as a "new" novel, it departs radically from conventional expectations regarding the novel.

To move to the ideological approach is to move to a theory that is an interpretative framework, one that is explicit about one set of readers' expectations. The correlative of ideology is what Paul Ricoeur called a hermeneutics of suspicion—a suspicion that the way the world is, is not what it ought to be, an interpretation based on doubt and a negation of classism, racism, and sexism wherever these forms of oppression may be thought to exist. Because ideology critique is closely linked with political action, its application involves a double bind. On the one hand, the determinate designation or category that identifies the oppression is elaborate and explicit. On the other hand, the general principles on which any attempt to change the oppressive situation (e.g., sexism) must be based remain implicit and are apt to be affirmed only as slogans or goals that "go without saying."

In an application of the ideological approach to the "new" novel, at least two potential ideologies come to light: the position that is being critiqued and the position from which the critique is made. Robbe-Grillet, for example, critiques the conventional novel for the latter's espousal of bourgeois values: private property, tradition, literary fashionableness. At the same time, the source of the critique also appears to be potentially ideological: some form of quietism, Marxist espousal of a classless society, or idealization of the act of writing. Juxtaposed as ideologies, the two different positions expose the potential weakness of the ideological approach to genre. For might the two positions overwhelm genre in the attempt to test the text for politically correct ideas?

How might we rescue genre in a critique of ideology? We notice that whereas the hermeneutics of belief is satisfied with a partial view attempting to be truth, the hermeneutics of suspicion wagers that reality is systematically and unconsciously distorted in an ideological perspective. It is possible, however, to bring an ideology partially to consciousness; doing so results in a shock of recognition that all our judgments have been co-opted. Contrary to the reactionary point of view, all is not lost in ideological critique. Indeed, according to Ricoeur, a comparison of the function of ideology and the perspective of the social construction of reality shows the positive features of ideology and its usefulness within bounds. In his essay "Science and Ideology" Ricoeur outlines five ways in which ideology is useful, perhaps even indispensable to a society:

1. In reviving and reactualizing, through convention and rationalization, the act that founds a society
2. In motivating, justifying, and projecting the necessary actions that carry a society along
3. In idealizing the self-representation of a group to its members
4. In codifying belief by means of sharply etched self-representations that can be grasped by every member of a group
5. In prolonging the achievements of the founding act by legitimating the typical and discouraging novelty for its own sake.

In Ricoeur's analysis, these can be positive functions of ideology. Negative aspects arise only on the basis of positive functions and have to do with dissimulation for the purpose of domination and distortion by reversing social life processes.

In the ideological approach to the "new" novel, a dialectic between bourgeois values and a particular kind of originality come to light. So long as they remain only ideological, the two sides of the dialectic are both bound by and opposed to each other. A hermeneutics of suspicion makes it possible for the two sides to recognize that each is defined by its opposition to the other, thus opening the way to a mediation or alternative strategies. The ideological approach also enables us to distinguish between the experimental novel of the 1920s and the "new" novel: the effect of the experimental novel is to suggest alternative ways of representing reality, whereas that of the "new" novel is to question the possibility of affirming anything intelligible about reality.

Unlike other schools of criticism analyzed in chapter 2 (e.g., the New Criticism, morphological criticism, structuralism), which have gravitated toward one genre or a few genres to present that applicability of their theories, ideological critics find forms of oppression in many genres and potentially in all genres. Their constraint is rather in the kinds of oppression they are willing to examine. In practice, the ideological critic is likely to bring to bear only one frame. The difficulty with the ideological approach is that any reading that cannot be guaranteed to yield a condemnation of what has been determined to be the case prior to the reading of any given text is likely to be resisted.

The relationship between the frame and reality is troubled, however: the critic has a sense of being "framed" even as she "frames" by means of genric considerations.

The Deconstructionist View: Thiher's Study of Postmodern Fiction

The "new" novel shares many of the characteristics of the "postmodern" novel. In his *Words in Reflection: Modern Language Theory and Postmodern Fiction* (1984), Allen Thiher treats the "new" novel as a subset of postmodern fiction in terms of the latter's relationship with contemporary language theory. Thiher notices, first of all, a parallel shift in the novel and in contemporary philosophy: a shift from the primacy of the visual, as originally expressed in the Horatian doctrine *ut pictura poesis*, to the problematic status of the visual, as expressed both in the "postmodern" novel and in recent philosophical thought about language (Thiher 1984, 3). Unlike the traditional writer, whose ambition is to present a successful vision or image, the postmodern writer is more likely to forego revelation of any kind in favor of foregrounding the very language that revelation employs. Thiher argues his thesis by recalling in detail the work of Martin Heidegger, Ferdinand Saussure, Ludwig Wittgenstein, and Jacques Derrida on language and then comparing and contrasting the work of fiction writers on the ways their work reflects either the primacy of the visual or the tenets and doubts of contemporary language philosophy. Thiher uses Woolf's *To the Lighthouse*, Joyce's *Ulysses*, and Flaubert's *Madame Bovary* as representative of the primacy of the visual and the writings of Robbe-Grillet, Beckett, Nabokov, John Barth, Julio Cortázar, and others as emphasizing the inseparability of language from experience.

Thiher explores four issues—representation, voices, play, and reference—that a postmodern novel can be expected to raise. On the issue of representation, Thiher regards Sartre's *Nausea* as marking "the beginning of our postmodern paradoxes" (ibid., 93). As read by Thiher, *Nausea* probes the relation between the autonomy of language and the instability of the phenomenal world. Thiher sees Faulkner's *Absalom, Absalom!* as "founded on a larger history that seems to lie outside [the characters'] capacity to say it" (ibid., 121). Again, we see that the deconstructionist approach is self-referential. It presumes a fragmented and fragmenting self and highlights the difficulty and partiality of framing.

On the issue of voice, Thiher shows that the voices of *Absalom, Absalom!* however self-sufficient they seem to their characters, are limited and shaped by a fullness and a totality that is absent and inaccessible. Borges's short story "Pierre Menard, Author of the *Quijote,*" which hypothesizes what it would mean to reproduce, as a twentieth-century novel, Cervantes's seventeenth-century *Don Quixote,* is another example of writing that discloses a historical consciousness that appears to be straightforward but is actually fraught with ambiguity.

On the issue of game, according to Thiher, Menard's fiction "would have, one can imagine (and even verify), quite different meanings for whoever might play the game of explaining these meanings. This second version would be the same, but different, deriving its meaning from the totality of nineteenth-century [sic] language games that surround it, as well as from a kind of intertextual play with the 'original' novel" (ibid., 160). A game has rules, in other words, which the player, in this case the reader, agrees to follow, at the same time as the player is aware of playing the game. Understood as game, Borges's story provides an apt analogy to genre testing. Like the psychological test that affords the possibility of a viewer's seeing at different times either an old woman or a young lady (but never both at the same time), the reader of Borges's story must choose between a seventeenth-century or a twentieth-century *Quixote*. Both are arbitrary but not necessarily ambiguous.

On the issue of referent, Thiher describes several ways in which the postmodern novel can be distinguished from the traditional and modern novel. In Joyce's *Ulysses,* Thiher's example of a modern novel, a "mythic dimension grounds these fragments [events of a single day] in some atemporal space that escapes from history" even as it depends on historical meanings (ibid., 218). By contrast, Claude Simon's postmodern novel *Histoire* lacks a narrator's unified consciousness and any external principle of order. In Simon's novel, history as an assumed way of imposing meaning on events has been replaced by fictions whose disjuncture, one from another, in turn thwart any attempt to bring order into experience. Thiher's distinction between disjointed fictions and coherent meaning corresponds to the deconstructionist and the traditionalist use of history, respectively. In Thiher's other examples of postmodern novels, for example, Günter Grass's *The Tin Drum* and Gabriel García Márquez's *One Hundred Years of Solitude,* other kinds of stylistic disjunctures call attention to a disreputable history that has been forgotten, repressed, and which is no longer capable of being recalled consciously, but nevertheless lurks, as a kind of subconscious, "sub-plicit" in the unconventional images, figures, and events of the novel. In these novels, history is represented both as a cover-up, that is, as alternative fictions substituted for true accounts of events that really occurred, and as something covered up, that is, an account of events that are no longer accessible to consciousness. In the deconstructionist act, there is no demand to achieve another kind of history or to seek alternative forms. This distinction echoes the one we have made between the ideological and the traditional uses of history.

For all his doubts and affirmations of the linguistic theorists' and the postmodern novelists' use and abuse of history, Thiher nevertheless shows the historicality of the relationship between genre theory and genres. He describes the deconstructionist skepticism regarding the possibility of history, regarding it as an important option to ponder but not necessary to adopt. Nevertheless, the deconstructionist approach cares little or nothing about the world outside the text. Instead, deconstructionism is mesmerized by fluctuations in meaning in the text.

On the basis of Thiher's observations as a critical reader of the postmodern novel, we can formulate a working hypothesis in the deconstructionist mode for the "new" novel, as a representation of one type of postmodern novel. Presume the "new" novel to be a fictional writing of significant length that, by making explicit the arbitrariness of writing, calls into question the reliability of narrative voice and the matter-of-fact occurrence of narrated events and actions. In its deconstructive self-reflexivity, the "new" novel is its own frame. The relationship between this frame and reality, however, is relative and arbitrary. All frames are suspect: one game plan is replaceable by another.

GENRE AND GENDER TESTING THE "NEW" NOVEL

Robbe-Grillet's The Voyeur

One of the earliest of the "new" novels, Robbe-Grillet's *The Voyeur* ([1955] 1958) suspends one of the effects of the genre detective story: namely, that of purposeful action. The first reaction of many readers to *The Voyeur* is to suspect that it is a psychological case study. Indeed, some critics have given a psychological diagnostic name—"homicidal maniac"—to the central "character" of *The Voyeur*. But the nonoccurrence of the homicide is presented as being just as likely as its occurrence. The *possible* occurrence or *possible* nonoccurrence of the event is echoed throughout the book in descriptions that contradict one another and whipsaw the reader from one judgment to another. The original French title (*Le Voyeur*) and its English translation (*The Voyeur*) both denote someone who observes and obtains sexual gratification without being observed. But the title can also serve as an analogue for the narrator and the reader of the story insofar as they see the whole story and receive pleasure from trying to figure it out. To persistent sexual stereotypes continuing from the traditional novel is added the irony that the reader never explicitly "sees" the crime and is not able to answer factual questions raised by the story. Unlike a case study, what is meant by "fact" is open to question throughout the book. In several passages, the question is made explicit by the use of metalanguage (language about language). "It was stupid, under such conditions," says the narrator at one point, "to refer to the 'fact' that the girl had taken a path at the crossroads" (Robbe-Grillet 1958, 96). And again (ibid., 120): "He emphasized the word 'five' to show that it should be taken in the opposite sense. Furthermore, like most islanders, he used 'hope' instead of 'imagine'—which in the present case seemed more likely to mean 'fear.' " Questions become explicit as well in Robbe-Grillet's use of metathought, or thought about thought, as the narrator provides hypotheses (ibid., 94, 105) for his own itinerary for selling watches on the island.

The first paragraph of the novel is a single sentence, "It was as if no one had heard" ("C'était comme si personne n'avait entendu"). This *as if* structure is spun out judiciously: the crowd is "motionless," reactionless, petrified, uniform. "No one had heard." No one, that is, except the "he" who observes the crowd, he who "*had* heard the story before" (ibid., 3, my emphasis) ("On lui avait souvent raconté cette histoire"). In fact, he had heard it often. But instead of beginning to narrate the (a?) story, the narrator seduces the reader into constructing a (the?) story out of free-floating objects, geometric measurements, and random associations as "he," now named Mathias, searches for "a point of reference" (ibid., 8).

Soon Mathias "chooses" ("Mathias essaya de prendre un repère") a particular mark on the dock wall as reference point, forcing himself to "keep his eyes in the same place for several seconds" although he is not "quite sure he was looking at the same mark—other irregularities in the stone looked just as much like— or unlike" (ibid., 9) ("Quand it revit, trois secondes plus tard, l'emplacement qu'il s'était efforcé de ne pas quitter des yeux, il ne fut plus tout à fait sur d'y reconnaitre le dessin repéré"). Mathias's search for a reference point is analogous to the reader's repeated attempts to get a bearing in the story. A story begins to be limned, nevertheless, although as much by relinquishing as by grasping associations and details. In particular, by having to follow Mathias's peculiar vacillations of thought, the reader retains a sense that this story could have been, indeed at any point could be, another story just as well. The multiple duplication of scenes (for example, the drawing of a gull, a movie poster, bicycle gears), the "hole" (i.e., the absence of any central event or criminal action in the face of mounting evidence for one) all invite the reader to speculate on the origin of sufficient reason to affirm a happening. But the suggestion of a crime of violence by an adult male against a female youth is fairly clear. Nevertheless, the reconstruction of signifiers in the story demands that the reader go beyond the genre erotic murder mystery as the principle informing the novel. Whereas erotic murder mystery accounts for some actions in the text, it does not account for the "it-could-have-been-another-story" aspect that presides over the novel, perhaps the litmus test for a "new" novel.

This aspect becomes clear in an analysis of the structure of the novel. Although the novel has three parts, the parts are practically indistinguishable because the actions are frequently repetitious, fragmentary, and synesthetic. Most telling of all is the difficulty in knowing how to "read" the most basic elements of the text. This difficulty is not, as in reading conventional novels, a matter of distinguishing among several levels of meaning. The difficulty is rather one of being unable to establish the story line or the ending. Returning to a "new" novel to clarify the action lends greater ambiguity to the elements of the text.

Beckett's Stories and Texts for Nothing

As a second example, we turn to a text constructed in such a way that the diminution of characterization and action, together with intensity of questions, repeatedly brings the reader to the brink of a philosophical and narrative void. Even the title of Samuel Beckett's *Stories and Texts for Nothing* ([1958] 1967) (*Nouvelles et textes pour rien*) places the reader at the intersection of the everyday and the ontological. What does it mean to be "for nothing"? the reader is forced to ask. The unusual structure of the book causes the reader to stop and reflect on its genre. It is not usual for the title of the book to state its genre first; moreover, in the case of this book there are two genres stated, "stories" and "texts." The three "stories" followed by thirteen "texts" can be read as being narrated by the same voice, although some readers have difficulty affirming continuity on a first reading. Nevertheless, the voice—musing, describing, philosophizing, lamenting, ceasing, and initiating—is the most constant element in this halting narrative.

The first of the three stories, "The Expelled," begins with the narrator's being thrown out of the house of his birth and landing at the bottom of a stairs. The description of the narrator establishes his gender as male, but unlike the narrator of *The Voyeur* not aggressively so. The number of steps is a problem: he does not know where to begin nor where to end counting. He arrives at three different figures:

> It is true that if I were to find, in my mind, where it is certainly to be found, one of these figures, I would find it and it alone, without being

able to deduce from it the other two. And even were I to recover two, I would not know the third. No, I would have to find all three, in my mind, in order to know all three. Memories are killing. So you must not think of certain things, of those that are dear to you, or rather you must think of them, for if you don't there is the danger of finding them, in your mind, little by little. That is to say, you must think of them for a while, a good while, every day several times a day, until they sink forever in the mud. That's an order. (Beckett 1967, 9)

Il est vrai qu'en retrouvant, dans la mémoire, où il se trouve certainement, un seul de ces chiffres, je ne retrouverais que lui, sans pouvoir en déduire les deux autres. Et même si j'en récupérais deux, je ne saurais pas le troisième. Non, il faudrait les retrouver tous le trois, dans la mémoire, pour pouvoir les connaître, tous le trois. C'est tuant, les souvenirs. Alors il ne faut pas penser à certaines choses, à celles qui vous tiennent à coeur, ou plutot il faut y penser, car à ne pas y penser on risque de les retrouver, dans la mémoire, petit à petit. C'est-à-dire qu'il faut y penser pendant un moment, un bon moment, tous les jours et plusieurs fois par jour, jusqu'à ce que la boue les recouvre, d'une couche infranchissable. C'est un ordre.

The difficulty of counting steps decisively—which one would expect to be an elementary, unequivocally objective task—is emblematic of the indeterminacy of making sense of the stories and texts taken together.

In Beckett, two limits are continuously invoked: the nothingness from which human consciousness comes and the end to which it is going. All the rest is story. The end of "The End," the third story, reads:

The memory came faint and cold of the story I might have told, a story in the likeness of my life, I mean without the courage to end or the strength to go on. (Ibid., 72)

Je songeai faiblement et sans regret au récit que j'avais failli faire, récit à l'image de ma vie, je veux dire sans le courage de finir ni la force de continuer.

That there is a possibility of an alternative story the narrator *might* have told may be read in two mutually exclusive ways. It may be read as a commentary on the radical indistinguishability of writing that is more conscious of itself than of an impossible "objective" world. Alternatively, and more in keeping with the genre "new" novel, the possibility of an alternative story emphasizes the literary discreteness of the three stories that are told. The three "stories," which comprise only some of the narrator's acknowledged possibilities, are unlike a conventional story with a discernible beginning, middle, and end. The three "stories," by contrast, underscore the shortcomings of story conventions for representing certain aspects of contemporary life, in which one may be "without the courage to end or the strength to go on."

In each of the thirteen four- to five-page "texts" that follow, the narrator reflects on metaphysical questions, asked by a narrative voice conscious of being-toward-death. The questions are posed not so much for final answers but as occasions for reflections about going on:

> Where would I go, if I could go, who would I be, if I could be, what would I say, if I had a voice, who says this, saying it's me? . . . yes, there are moments, like this moment, when I seem almost restored to the feasible. Then it goes, all goes, and I'm far again, with a far story again, I wait for me afar for my story to begin, to end, and again this voice cannot be mine. That's where I'd go, if I could go, that's who I'd be, if I could be. (Ibid., 91, 94)

> Où irais-je, si je pouvais aller, que serais-je, si je pouvais être, que dirais-je, si j'avais une voix, qui parle ainsi, se disant moi? . . . Oui, il est des moments comme en ce moment, comme ce soir, où j'ai presque l'air restitué au faisable. Puis ça passe, tout passe, je suis de nouveau loin, j'ai encore une lointaine histoire, je m'attends au loin pour que mon histoire commence, pour qu'elle s'achève, et de nouveau cette voix ne peut être la mienne. C'est là où j'irais, si je pouvais aller, celui-là que je serais, si je pouvais être.

The going on and the sense of being over against nothingness are encompassed in a necessary final question (interestingly enough, punctuated as a statement):

> Is it possible, is that the possible thing at last, the extinction of this black nothing and its impossible shades, the end of the farce of making and the silencing of silence, it wonders, that voice which is silence, or it's me, there's no telling, it's all the same dream, the same silence, it and him, him and me, and all our train, and all theirs, and all theirs,

but whose, whose dream, whose silence, old questions, last questions, ours who are dream and silence. (Ibid., 139)

Est-ce possible, est-ce là enfin la chose possible, que s'éteigne ce noir rien aux ombres impossibles, là enfin la chose faisable, que l'infaisable finisse et se taise le silence, elle se le demande, cette voix qui est silence, ou moi, comment savoir, de mon moi de trois lettres, ce sont là des songes, des silences qui se valent, elle et moi, elle et lui, moi et lui, et tous les notres, et tous les leurs, et tous les leurs, mais de qui, songes de qui, silences de qui, vieilles questions, dernières questions, de nous qui sommes songe et silence.

In spite of the convoluted and interrupted prose, it is striking that the subject of the sentence is the extinction of nothing in all of its "shades" and the verb is to question the possibility of the extinction. But that question is itself a statement, as if to affirm that "the question is the only answer to our dreams and silences regarding last questions." The denouement of Beckett's texts consists typically in some kind of strategy for withholding classical philosophical answers. These texts by Beckett do not readily lend themselves to other genres for testing—a clue that it may best be understood as a "new" novel. The "new" novel is not the only new form of the genre novel, but it has many of the characteristics of postmodern fiction.

TESTING TEXTS AT THE MARGINS OF THE TRADITIONAL NOVEL AND THE "NEW" NOVEL: GENRE MODIFICATION

We turn now to three texts that have undergone genre modification but not to the extent of calling for a new genre. The works of Joan Didion, John Barth, and Fernando Alegría, each in distinctive ways, stretch the conventions of the traditional novel. Distinguishing them from the "new" novel augments our understanding of the "newness" of the "new" novel.

Didion's A Book of Common Prayer

Joan Didion's *A Book of Common Prayer,* brings into question the status of literature in relation to empirical reality. This is seen most explicitly in her later books, such as *Salvador* (1983) and *Democracy* (1984), where the author self-consciously presents herself as first-person narrator and where the political situation is currently that of the author's, as well as the narrator's. The seemingly eventless world of the private everyday is revealed both to mask and manifest the public political world. One frequent strategy, even in the earlier books, is to question the ordinary sufficiency of language. In *A Book of Common Prayer*, for example, Grace, the narrator, reports the death of another character as follows:

> It is a little more than a year now since Charlotte Douglas's death and almost two years since her arrival in Boca Grande.
> Charlotte Douglas's death.
> Charlotte Douglas's murder.
> Neither word works.
> Charlotte Douglas's previous engagement. (Didion 1977, 52)

In this passage Grace's search for the most accurate word replicates the reader's search for clues to understand what happened to Charlotte. From the beginning of the novel, moreover, definition is attached to fields of meanings. Grace, dying of cancer, begins by staking her identity on the differences between Charlotte and herself. An anthropologist who has "stopped believing that observable activity defined anthropos," Grace has taken up biochemistry, "a discipline in which demonstrable answers are commonplace and 'personality' absent" (ibid., 4).

Grace needs more than demonstrable answers to communicate with Charlotte's daughter. The following passage overtly calls attention to the questionability of everyday language through the character of Marin.

> When Marin Bogart asked me without much interest what her mother had "done" in Boca Grande, There was very little I could think to say. . . .
> "She did some work in a clinic," I said.
> "Charity," Marin Bogart said.
> The indictment lay between us for a while. . . .
> "And after that she worked in a birth control clinic."
> "Classic," Marin Bogart said. "Absolutely classic."
> "How exactly it is 'classic.' "
> "Birth control is *the* most flagrant example of how the ruling class practices genocide."

"Maybe not *the* most flagrant," I said.

A lost daughter in a dirty room in Buffalo with dishes in the sink and an M-3 on the bed.

A daughter who never had much use for words but had finally learned to string them together so that they sounded almost like sentences.

A daughter who chose to believe that her mother had died on the wrong side of a "people's revolution." (Ibid., 216–17)

Putting words and expressions in quotation marks has the effect of calling their choice into question. This metalinguistic element, which in Didion's later novels develops into a self-reflexive language commenting on the actual writing of the story, here focuses on the reality of words as words. The text invites testing also as biography, nonfiction novel, or the genre hybrids of "faction" and docudrama.

Even in this early Didion novel, the narrator's voice is that of a feature journalist. But Grace, who prides herself for listening and seeing more than others, concedes that she has not been an impartial witness: she now knows that people see what they are willing to see, that she herself was not immune to self-deception and the temptation to discount significant information. The novel casts doubt on the basis for reporting on other human beings, given that the basis for one's own observation is selective. Grace knows how to "make models for life itself, DNA, helices double and single and squared," but her attempt to make a model of Charlotte Douglas's "character" is like the "shimmer of an oil slick" (ibid., 218). Doubt is reinforced by the continual questioning of ordinary everyday language like "character," "decision," and even the verb "to do." Doubt is further maintained by the combination of two genres, fiction and feature journalism. Whereas in the nonfiction world, feature news reports are published and believed, in the novel they strive for, but do not achieve, credibility. Charlotte's feature article, for example, was never completed.

Barth's Lost in the Funhouse

A second variation of the traditional novel genre, John Barth's *Lost in the Funhouse* (1969) is a series of stories whose narrative progression invites us to consider it first of all either as a "new" novel or as a collection of short stories. Reading it as a novel, though—demanding more constructive thought from the reader—accounts for more of the details than reading it as an eclectic collection of stories.

Initially an unidentified persona poses philosophical questions in archaic diction: "Is the journey my invention? Do the night, the sea, exist at all, I ask myself, apart from my experience of them? . . . Why need believers hold that all the drownéd rise to be judged at journey's end, and nonbelievers that drowning is final without exception?" (Barth 1969, 3, 7). These and other eschatological questions are not given answers. But the questions function as if in a riddle, and once the reader guesses that they come from the mouth of a spermatozoon, the riddle is satisfactorily, if hyperbolically, answered.

The narrative voice presumably "grows up" from being a lucky spermatozoon into the narrator of subsequent stories, such as "Ambrose, His Mark," a story of naming. This authorial voice, "metalinguistic" in the sense that language is the subject of its commentary, is introduced in "Autobiography," a story of a tape-recorded story told by the story. Here, metalinguistic self-reflection makes explicit the precariousness of the lifeline of a story. It begins (with interrupted typography), "You who   listen give me life in a manner of speaking" (ibid., 33), and ends in a *double entendre:* "Nonsense, I'll mutter to the end, one word after another, string the rascals out, mad or not, heard or not, my last words will be my last words" (ibid., 37). The absurdity of a story telling its own technical tale jars the imagination: "I see I see myself as a halt narrative: first person, tiresome. . . . Surrogate for the substantive; contentless form, interestless principle; blind eye blinking at nothing. Who am I. A little *crise d'identité* for you. I must compose myself" (ibid., 33).

But the most audacious feat of self-reflection is still to come. Gradually, the metalinguistic, and increasingly literary-critical, voice gains ascendency over the commonsense narrative events. "Echo," for example, opens with a deliberate adoption of a mythic allusion: "one does well to speak in the third person, the seer advises, in the manner of Theban Tiresias" (ibid., 95). But the self-reflective storyteller plaintively interrupts the narrative at several points:

I can't go on.
Go on.
Is there anyone to hear here?
Who are you?
You.
I?
Aye.
Then let me see me! (Ibid., 97)

The drama of self-reflection here surpasses the story line of the narrative.

In the last story, the "Anonymiad," the narrator is a minstrel-author. On the heels of accepting a much-coveted title, he writes a story about attempting to outline his story and to continue it at the same time, thus producing a metafiction, that is, fiction reflecting upon itself:

> Part Three, consequently, will find the young couple moved to new lodgings in the palace itself, more affluent and less happy. Annoyance at what he knows would be her reaction has kept the minstrel from confiding to his friend the condition of his Acting Chief Minstrelship; his now-nearly-constant attendance on the   No use, this isn't working either, we're halfway through, the end's in sight; I'll never get to where I am. (Ibid., 177)

Forced by a rival love to leave Mycenae, the minstrel is stranded on an island for eight years. Isolated, and feeling like Prometheus pinned to the rock, he contemplates ending it all until he remembers that "a man sings better to himself if he can imagine someone's listening" (ibid., 186). Because memory is still a problem he invents parchment, paper, and a "frame tale" entraining, at different times, from one to seven narratives, each removed from the initial narrator by the technically correct number of quotation marks. Exchanging song for written speech, the narrator begins to glory in isolation and learns "to abandon myth and pattern my fabrications on actual people and events: Menelaus, Helen, the Trojan War. It was as if there were this minstrel and this milkmaid, et cetera; one could I believe draw a whole philosophy from that if" (ibid., 186). With this unabashed use of metathought, the minstrel nevertheless begins to run out of "world and material—though not of ambition" (ibid., 187).

The title story, "Lost in the Funhouse," is placed in the middle of the text. The self-consciousness of the now adolescent Ambrose is balanced by a self-conscious narrative, which represents growing up into a world of stories. Simultaneously, the narrator's (Ambrose's) "life" can be seen in Barth to give rise to more narratives. The reader vicariously experiences the ways in which these stories both shape life and are linked with stories of other times and places. Several of the story titles are marginally genric: for example, "Halt Fiction" and "Anonymiad." The stories invite testing as riddles, epics, and literature of fantasy.

Lost in the Funhouse, particularly the "Menelaiad" and the Anonymiad," is a good example of what Barth himself has called the "literature of exhaustion." Michael Hinden comments that this kind of fiction is based on a "notion of ultimacy turned against itself by means of style that is self-exhausting and yet comically triumphant. [*Lost in the Funhouse*] reveals a dazzling display of modernist techniques even while it examines the depletion of certain forms of modernist expression and the unbearable self-consciousness of intellectual life" (Hinden 1973, 108). Although Hinden's reading is persuasive, one may also observe that the total plot of *Lost in the Funhouse*—the birth, growth, and development of a narrative voice—also invites being tested as a bildungsroman, which traditionally traces the life as a single character through potentially dangerous episodes into adulthood. Reading *Lost in the Funhouse* as a bildungsroman overcomes the final effect of the parts parodied and renews the strength of exhausted, depleted, and paralyzed forms. *Lost in the Funhouse* incorporates a medley of techniques—puns, novel points of view, variations of typography, contemporized myths and parody—and relieves the self-consciousness of intellectual life. Reading *Lost in the Funhouse* alternatively as both parody and bildungsroman makes it possible to experience the text alternatively as an intellectual and aesthetic dead end and as resistance to the meaninglessness of depleted forms.

Alegría's Chilean Spring

In a final representation of a modified form of novel, Fernando Alegría's *Chilean Spring* (1980), the metalinguistic element both subverts the linear narrative and is in turn subverted by the assumed realism of photography and the presumed simplicity of truth. The subject of the novel is a Chilean photographer who has covered President Salvador Allende for a feature story just before the latter's death in the 1972 military takeover. The photographer's life is a story within the story: his notebook and letters, which have been given to the narrator friend by the photographer's mother, constitute the novel as "The Gospel According to Cristián." The text is ostensibly about the state of Chile preceding and during the revolution: "Ercilla, the epic poet, called us a 'fertile chosen province.' He calls us a 'province' and he added 'chosen'! This is the formula that has best defined us throughout history. We live inwardly cultivating the particular" (Alegría 1980, 93).

Flashbacks of Christián with his wife, Luz Maria, his brother Marcelo, his two children, and his mother and father reveal, however, that his own life, as well as that of his country, is undergoing a revolution:

> People like me who lived off images, off visions, were suddenly asked to consider the word "conscience." And I reacted sadly but forcefully. Conscience meant heartbreak, being uprooted again, fear of a new void, but it also meant maturing, ripening. Since they shook our tree and we fell to ready soil, we won the strength and persistence of our secret need. We decided, then, to fight. . . .
> I think about the word "terror." I compare it to this spring which has suddenly erupted in branches of lights, in foggy mornings and in parasols of almond and peach, cherry and plum trees. . . . What's left for me? A modest grief which I drown little by little, day by day, so that I can believe that spring has also come from me and flies out of my hands seeking those people who look at me in surprise, recognize me, and . . . start saying goodby to me. (Ibid., 148)

By cutting short the facile and unappropriated solution, *Chilean Spring,* in contrast to both "politically committed" literature written about the revolution and traditional narrative with its "well-wrought" beginnings, actions, and ends, calls into question the positivism inherent in the traditional dichotomy of fiction versus reality.[5] Yet it does have a reference point in relation to reality and lends itself to a narration that has, to use Frank Kermode's term in contrast with the "new" novel, "a sense of an ending." This text invites testing also as a memoir or a poetic reverie.

These three novels modify the traditional novel in similar ways:

Didion by her emphasis on the inconclusiveness of the most insignificant human event, Barth by his experimentation with the profligacy of literary techniques and themes, Alegría with his suggestion of the imperceptibility of the origins of revolutionary acts. Yet in contrast with the texts by Robbe-Grillet and Beckett, these three novels accommodate the genre of the traditional novel, even as it accommodates itself to them.

MAKING SENSE OF THE "NEW" NOVEL

In the conventional view, the "new" novel is best characterized by one major tenet: the *denial* of meaning as classically idealized.[6] In opposition to classical expectations of serious literature, these novels do not so much engender emotions, such as pity (the inclination to approach) or fear (the tendency to flee), as raise questions by lack of information or logical coherence. The effect of these questions is to create doubt about subjectivity and the ability of the human being to claim a unified self. Of the deconstructionist penchant for calling human subjectivity into question, Nancy Hartsock (1983) has observed that, just when women discovered that they had a self, deconstruction declared that there isn't any. Questions raised by the "new" novels frustrate philosophical reflection generally, threatening to subvert all classical philosophical positions. If we inquire what the works have in common that justifies their being genred, we might well create a hypothesis for testing the postmodern novel such as the following.

Presume that the two "new" novels by Robbe-Grillet and Beckett, in radically different ways, underscore the contingency of any story that happens to be told—Robbe-Grillet by focusing on the capriciousness of perception and judgment and Beckett on the inadequacy of narrative forms for representing the life story. Each book leads the reader in one way or another to "reflect on reflection" itself. Understood as traditional novels, these stories are capricious, profligate, and devoid of meaning. Understood as "new" novels, they begin to lead us seriously to question fiction itself as one of the conditions for the possibility of renewing the meaningfulness of existence. More specifically, by understanding the full implications of the metalanguage of these difficult stories, we may also clarify and challenge the adequacy and extent of

216

those theories we employ to disclose intelligible order from our experience. Even traditional novels can profit by being tested as "new" novels.[7] This claim is partially demonstrated by recalling the modifications in the traditional novel as seen in the texts by Didion, Barth, and Alegría. Again, we see the underscoring, though not as sustained as in the "new" novel, of the contingency of the told story: Didion on the inconclusiveness of the most insignificant human event, Barth on the profligacy of literary techniques and themes, Alegría on the imperceptibility of the origins of revolutionary acts. These texts force the reader to slow down; their genre is no longer like a comfortable saddle. Instead, they provide a pothole at every step, forcing the reader to make more conscious judgments. The texts do not offer vicarious experience in the technical sense. They intensify the demand for philosophical reflection by rhetorical strategies that challenge the traditional novel's assumptions about meaning—its linear logic, the desirability and possibility of certitude, and its complacency about the adequacy of language for understanding and communication. This hypothesis has the advantage of focusing on the effects of new literature rather than on its deficiency or superiority with respect to the traditional novel. The hypothesis relates the "new" novel to contemporary epistemological issues, and the hypothesis is open to both constructive and deconstructive readings.

As postmodern fiction, these texts offer a reconsideration of human existence from the vantage point, as the philosopher Hannah Arendt has suggested, "of our newest experiences and our most recent fears" (Arendt 1958, 5). Observing that reconsideration itself is obviously "a matter of thought," Arendt also notes that the outstanding tenor of our time is "thoughtlessness—the heedless recklessness of hopeless confusion or complacent repetition of 'truths' which have become trivial and empty" (ibid). But it is not difficult to find evidence that the issue of reflection taken as the central concern of the "new" novel escapes some of the best readers who attempt to read it only in relation to the traditional novel. An example of one highly respected critic who lacks an appreciation for this complexity, Alfred Kazin, in his popular *Bright Book of Life* (1971) relegates John Barth's *Lost in the Funhouse* to a footnote on "black humor." Listing several titles, he emphasizes the "absurdist" element of such books as *Lost in the Funhouse* and dismisses it, inadequately, as "difficult to classify" fiction.

Rather than facilely dismiss these texts as absurdist fiction, we have suggested that genre testing can illuminate the predominant negativity these works have toward particular humanistic meanings and values. A first step in this direction is to suppose that these novels represent the fluctuations of consciousness as that takes place within a subject who experiences them. Whereas traditional novels generally espouse or reject this or that particular philosophy or worldview, the "new" novel can be understood to presume every reader to have some worldview, even as it steels itself against being determined by any particular worldview. The reader of postmodern texts is taken through modes of reflection, so to speak, but is not allowed to dwell on any stated meaning. Among the experiences familiar to the contemporary mind is that of a heightened exposure to multiple theories of reflection, of consciousness, and the unconscious.

Understanding these "difficult to classify" fictions as "new" novels would seem to bear important implications for the tradition of the novel. Reflecting on the postmodern novel challenges several assumptions about the traditional novel:

> The novel, written in prose, bears an apparently closer resemblance to discursive forms than it does to poetry, thus easily opening itself to first questions about philosophy or politics, and, traditionally a middle-class vehicle with a reflective social function, it bears an apparently more immediate relation to life than it does to art, thus easily opening itself to first questions about conduct. Yet a novel, like a poem, is not life, it is an image of life; and the critical problem is first of all to analyze the structure of image. (Schorer 1952, 83)

In the traditional novel, according to Mark Schorer, the relationship of both philosophy and of fiction to reality is at the heart of the critical task. But to define fiction by its relation to reality poses a problem for the "new" novel from the beginning: according to Sartre, for example, it engages the reader in a "double aspect of negativity and construction" (Sartre 1949, 279). The history of criticism is replete with attempts to deal with the problem. In the romanticist tradition, for example, creative imagination is elevated to the position of being the exclusive element of genius. Similarly, Hans Vaihinger, a contemporary philosopher, attempts to compensate for the general philosophical prejudice in favor of abstract reality in his explication of an "as if" philosophy. Unfortunately, the result of his theory has been a devaluation of both fiction and philosophy. For it is one short step to declaring both philosophy and fictions to be "fictitious," a regrettable conflation of genres.

Although the "new" novel eschews traditional thematic analysis, it nevertheless does raise traditionally philosophical questions, perhaps in spite of itself. One brief allusion to the difference between thematic and philosophical reflection can be found in Paul Ricoeur's statement that "intentionality in act is broader than thematic intentionality, which knows its object and knows itself in knowing that object; the first can never be equaled by the second: a meaning in act always precedes the reflective movement and can never be overtaken by it" (Ricoeur 1970, 378–79). Ricoeur speaks of this distinction between intentionality in act and thematic intentionality as the primacy of the "operative over the uttered." This primacy can also distinguish the "new" novel from other kinds of novels and can clarify its "predominant negativity," a negativity that is more cerebral, and perhaps therefore, in the long run, more vital than existential angst, for example, because the "new" novel questions not just the character of world but the character of understanding. Only after the primacy of the operative over the uttered is understood can the uttered further provide the basis for a thematic interpretation.

What has been lacking is attention to the method by which the operative and the uttered come to be identified in the mind of the reader. This attention is precisely what aims to be accomplished by genre and gender testing.

GENDER IMPLICATIONS FOR GENRE TESTING

In chapter 4 the initial typology used for displaying the available contemporary options for understanding genre did not provide any clear basis for choosing among them; each of the three—the traditional, the ideological, and the deconstructionist—had particular difficulties as well as distinctive merits. A basis for ordering choices among them began to emerge only when we adapted

Kristeva's (1981) typology of the three "generations" of feminist thought—which we called the liberal, the transvaluational, and the horizonal—for understanding gender.

In chapter 5 the Vendler-Gilbert-Gubar debate provided an example of both the indispensability of the first two generations of gender analysis and the misunderstandings that result when there is no systematic understanding of the aims and results of studies. Building on the distinction between literary and other kinds of reference (historical, sociological, empirical), a distinction we used to clarify the terms of the debate, we can now distinguish two kinds of theory. One relates things to other things in terms of what is the case, and the other relates things to other things in terms of what could or should be the case. The second kind of theory demands participation by the reader in constructing what could and should be the case. Although sociological, historical, and empirical theory can be of either form, from a reader-reception perspective the sui generis character of imaginative literature must be of the second kind. This demand is confirmed in the third generation of gender theory, which posits the struggle between male and female at the center of a personal appropriation of the issues manifested in the first and second generations of gender reflection.

We are now prepared to refine the criteria we have relied on for arbitrating among conflicting interpretations. Until now we have assumed that that interpretation is best which accounts for the greatest number of elements in the text and which does so at the highest level of persuasion. But these criteria lead to the expectation that there should be one best interpretation. Is one dominant interpretation the best outcome? Or is it likely that the text will be silent on certain points (the silences are called "gaps" by Wolfgang Iser [1978] and "naturalized points" by Mieke Bal [1987]) and the practical inevitability of filling the gaps will lead us to expect to have to try harder to hear differences among interpretations, given that different persons may notice different gaps/naturalized points and will fill (reconstruct) them differently? Here we have the basis for expecting that a text can be oriented in more than one way, depending on how these salient points are filled. We also have a basis for claiming that many of these different interpretations will not be idiosyncratic—rather, that they will correspond to genre differences and gender differences, as understood according to Kristeva's generational descriptions. Genre testing can nourish a plurality of interpretations and at the same time avoid both relativism and dilettantism.

Here again the two strands of our study intersect. A number of recent studies suggest that genres are often constituted on the basis of presumed gender distinctions. In her study of four biblical "love stories" (Samson and Delilah; Ruth and Boaz; Tamar, Er, Onan, and Judah; Adam and Eve), Mieke Bal (1987) has shown how the problem of representation is related to gender. In her view, it is better to assume that the biblical texts are neither sexist nor feminist but that both the author and the reader are confronted with problems of representation that are best understood through a gender analysis. The gender analysis, in turn, can be used to disclose that different genres used to frame the same events yield different meanings. The gender analysis can also bring to light shifts within a single genre. In the story of Samson and Delilah, for example, Bal finds a "shift in the concept of heroism from an instrumental view, in which the hero is sent by higher powers to represent their glory through pure physical acts, to a view wherein individualism and responsibility replace the lack of psychological concerns in the older view" (Bal 1987, 37). Most readers remember the story of Samson and Delilah as a story of betrayal by a woman, but Bal shows a pattern of heroic unfulfillment that culminates not in blaming women but in understanding how, in the story, they point up the hero's need for experience and new self-understanding. In this latter view, the story is no longer so meaningful as an epic tragedy; rather it makes better sense as an archetypal bildungsroman.[8] Both can be retained in the archives of canons and memory as a history of traces of the past in our present.

Genre testing moves the conflict to the site of judgment. Having to choose forces the reader to experience and to understand the conflict between what is desired and what has been opposed to the satisfaction of that desire, and both have the potential of being recognized as somehow—if only partially—one's own. Testing for genre forces one to reconstruct the text more than once, thus providing the opportunity to try out more than one understanding. To be able to reidentify the text is also to be able to reidentify different selves; during the process of testing, the self becomes one among several possibilities. Genre testing makes possible a plurality of identities—of the text and of the interpreters. Genre testing also becomes a means of relocating gender conflicts: through the quest for equality, through the quest for the transvaluation of values traditionally assigned to male and female, and through the consciousness of those who have struggled and continue to struggle with the problem, now for the first time as a choice among authentic values for oneself.

If this plurality of possible identities takes place in enough communities of discourse, cross-culturally related, the genres become vehicles for mediating the tensions already in public language, waiting there to be discovered and appropriated.

CONCLUSION

Interpreting and Animating Public Discourse

A father and his son were driving to a ball game when their car stalled on the railroad tracks. In the distance a train whistle blew a warning. Frantically, the father tried to start the engine, but in his panic, he couldn't turn the key and the car was hit by the onrushing train. An ambulance sped to the scene and picked them up. On the way to the hospital, the father died. The son was still alive but his condition was very serious, and he needed immediate surgery. The moment they arrived at the hospital, he was wheeled into an emergency operating room, and the surgeon came in, expecting a routine case. However, on seeing the boy, the surgeon blanched and muttered, "I can't operate on this boy—he's my son."
Douglas Hofstadter, Metamagical Themas *(1985, 136)*

Why not? Many who read this anecdote as a riddle strain for answers: Did the dead father come back to life as the surgeon? Was the dead man a surrogate father and the surgeon the boy's true father? Was the dead man or the surgeon a celibate priest? Gender testing the riddle, however, yields a straightforward answer: the surgeon was the boy's mother. Failure to test for gender is an obstacle for many readers. When they are told the answer, however, many are embarrassed for having assumed that the surgeon is male. A few readers, suspecting that the anecdote is being presented as a parable (for their benefit), continue to search for a solution that is not dependent on gender. As a riddle, however, the tension is released as soon the gendered answer is known.

Do not all texts demand some kind of gender analysis? We have argued that the quality of interpretation—indeed, often the ability to interpret at all—is sustained and enhanced by genre and gender testing.

223

The immediate origin of this book was in my experience of listening to a college audience respond to a lecture on Vietnam by Noam Chomsky in the late 1970s. Reactions to Chomsky's lecture were divided between those who were persuaded by Chomsky's argument and evidence that U.S. behavior during the war was as reprehensible as, if not more than, that of its adversaries, and those who thought Chomsky's presentation was sheer propaganda, based on distorted, if not falsified, data.

Convinced that their respective opinions were the only correct understanding of Chomsky's talk, the two groups had no common ground: they understood his presentation either as naked truth or as blatant falsehood. If the issue of genre had been raised, I wondered later, would it have been possible to discuss his lecture as a polemic? More to the point, could anything have been gained by testing what was said—testing it as propaganda, as documented report, as polemic? testing its gendered elements?

I thought of this incident last summer when I saw for the first time Peter Rockwell's series of five lithographs entitled "Reading Rots the Mind," on exhibit in the summer of 1990 in the Haverford College Library. To an educator or to a college student, this title at first glance is shocking in its blasphemy of an assumption that, for the most part, goes unquestioned in a liberal arts education. But on second thought, the title seemed very much in accord with the premise of this book: namely, that uncritical reading, that is, reading uninformed by genre testing and gender questions, does indeed rot the mind, by lulling and locking it into complacency and a single vision.

The major obstacle to genre testing, on occasions like the Chomsky lecture, where genre testing could have opened some space for critical thinking beyond initial reactions, is that what is lost by *not* testing is not obvious. In *The Critical Difference* Barbara Johnson credits literature with making what is crucially lacking apparent: what literature often seems to tell us is the consequences of the way in which what is not known is not *seen* as unknown. She concludes with a statement, part of which I quoted in the introduction: "It is not, in the final analysis, what you don't know that can or can't hurt you. It is what you don't *know* you don't know that spins out and entangles that perpetual error we call life" (Johnson 1980, xii). Prescinding for a moment from her analogy of life as error—a distinctively deconstructionist spin on the subject of the whole—we may nevertheless read her statement as pertaining to differences of genre and gender as well. If one does not *know* that the text can be read differently, one is likely to cling to the one naive, immediate, unreflective, uncritical reading as the only one possible or worth supporting. To extrapolate from Johnson, a naive reading can hurt you not only by depriving you of a fuller, more adequate understanding of a text; a naive reading can deprive you as well of a community of interpreters.

We have argued that a different reading of a text is frequently the result of its being read as a different genre and in the light of gender issues. Some gestures in this direction can be noticed in the recent efforts by the legal profession to "thicken" certain kinds of interpretations by borrowing methods of literary criticism for reading legal briefs. The discipline of history likewise employs fictional texts to extend and to challenge more conventional historical forms, such as eyewitness accounts, chronicles, journals, diaries, and treatises.

Yet several of the disciplines' own histories prevent, rather than encourage, genre testing for more than one reading. Such prevention occurs whenever a discipline in effect canonizes certain genres to the exclusion of others and insists upon reading unorthodox genres in the same way as those it has canonized. Narrative is relegated to the popularization of science, for example, and excluded from having a legitimate function in "true" science. The primacy of the genre treatise in late nineteenth-century theology is in contrast to the plurality of genres in the earlier and later history of that discipline. Analytic philosophy similarly assumes that argument is a kind of "super-genre" that precludes the need to consider the exigencies of any other.

Not surprisingly, such exclusionary practices with respect to genre are gender issues as well. Science and philosophy continue to be the province of male academics. Except by engaging in something like genre and gender testing, how will they realize the necessary transformations?

I once wagered with a philosopher that many of the impediments to effective public discourse could be overcome by increasing the number of genres that are used. Avoiding my claim, he demurred, saying that a multiplicity of genres does not guarantee the truth of an argument. I heard in his response the appeal of a timeless truth—if not timeless, one that pretended to transcend genre and gender considerations. But I continue to think that competence in making truth claims is most likely to develop in a context of a plurality of genres and genders as distinct from one . . . or even two.

Just evoking more than one genre or questioning gender differences in a particular situation will not by themselves alter the level or effects of debate in a time (any time) when we have become unused to thinking critically and publicly about any texts. Nevertheless, it is highly probable that only if we recognize different kinds of texts and the differences in them that come to light through gender analysis can texts enrich rather than erode our discourse.

The reader oblivious to gender and genre as framing the text will be framed in one way or another.

Notes

Introduction

1. Nancy K. Miller (1980) alludes to the nebulous understanding of the relationship between gender and genre when she remarks of the exclusion of Colette from Philippe Lejeune's major study of autobiography in France: "It seems, perhaps, unregenerate bad will that despite the caveat implicit in 'Colette's' jibe at the male reader expecting to find autobiography seeping through the pages of women's literature, we so reluctantly accept her exclusion from the French autobiographical canon. This resistance comes not so much from doubts about the legitimacy of Lejeune's criteria (as they do or do not apply to Colette) but from a hesitation about embracing wholeheartedly any theoretical model *indifferent* to a problematics of genre as inflected by gender" (p. 260). That the relationship between genre and gender, once made explicit, is also an uneasy one can be seen in the debates over *écriture féminine,* for example, as summarized in Dallery 1986.

2. Many still believe that genre reflects the motivation of the author and that motivation is based in sexual difference. In *The Book of J* (1990) Harold Bloom, an American deconstructionist critic, cites the presence of irony in one of the four major strands of the Hebrew Torah as his principal reason for arguing that its author was a woman. He claims that the genre of the text has been misread by most readers over the centuries as a devotional, pietistic document when in fact the text is, in his reading, quite irreverent. Since women had sufficient motives for such irreverence toward a male deity, he argued, it is reasonable to think that the Yahwist was a woman. But this direct association of gender and genre ignores other uses of irony by male authors. See also chapter 3.

3. See esp. pp. 108–9. Lloyd's account is exceedingly fair: she shows how the best-intentioned corrections of the philosophical tradition—for example, by Descartes—fall back into a dichotomization of male reason and female unreason.

4. Berdache are "third sex" (or male gender-reversed) sacred persons who act as shamans among the Urok of California, the Mohave, the Lakota, and the Araucanians of Chile. See Baum (forthcoming). Foucault (1980) thought that Barbin, a hermaphrodite, broke the essentialist link between sexual anatomy and gender. See also Butler 1990: 23–24.

5. Cf. Sontag's (1966) essay distinguishing pornographic *literature* from pornography.

Notes to Introduction

6. See Modleski 1982, esp. pp. 11–12. Modleski's main point is that a critical double standard is operative by which critics find popular literature written for primarily male audiences worthy of study and that written for primarily female audiences trivial.

7. I use the adjectival form *genric* to emphasize the functions of the concept of genre in interpretation. The conventional form *generic* has come to connote aspects such as nonspecificity and common variety, aspects unrelated to the process of interpretation. The term *generic* recalls only the taxonomic function of genre, whereas *genric* points also to its productive function.

8. The title of this collection, *The New Feminist Criticism,* suggests, by omitting the word *literary,* that the study of women's writing is not self-contained in literary criticism. The collection does not make an argument for that suggestion. Indeed, the contributors seem ignorant of the possibility of criticism, for example, from the perspective of religion. See, for example, Showalter's (1985) enigmatic statement, "It is time for feminist criticism to decide whether between religion and revision we can claim any firm theoretical ground of our own," where she seems to mean by religion, "the separatist fantasies of radical feminist visionaries" (p. 247).

9. In the decade of the 1960s, genre came to the center of the critical scene with the publication of E. D. Hirsch, Jr.'s *Validity in Interpretation* (1967). Soon after, a new journal, *Genre,* was founded, and Hirsch and his respondents contributed a decade of debate, debate that centered largely on the issue of authorial intentionality.

Since 1968 several critics seem to agree that the concept of genre is in need of reformulation. The major problem to be overcome is the almost exclusive association of genre with classification. In studies of specific genres, many critics have tried to reformulate an understanding of genre in other than classificatory terms. In his investigation of the lyric, for example, William Elwood Rogers (1983) suggests that only a "reflexive" notion of genre—one that makes explicit the role of the interpreter—can overcome objections to the concept. Rogers, like Hirsch, argues against Croce's (1953) dichotomization by calling for a reflexive notion of genre—one that would assert the role of genric considerations by the interpreter at every stage of interpretation and that assumes genric functions in the act of authoring a text. Rogers' explication of this phenomenon continues to dichotomize literary genre from scientific categories, with the result that his own epistemological basis for genre is misdirected in some of its essential elements. My own epistemology can be found in *Metaphoric Process: The Creation of Scientific and Religious Understanding* (1984), co-authored with Allan M. Russell, a physicist. See also Adena Rosmarin 1985 for evidence that those who treat individual genres find it necessary to address the issue of genre in general to provide an adequate basis for treating individual genres. Heather Dubrow begins her little book *Genre* (1982) with a wide-ranging essay on the functions of genre before two chapters of summary analysis of genre theory from Aristotle to Arnold and in the twentieth century. In her *The Resources of Kind: Genre-Theory in the Renaissance* (1974), Rosalie Colie illuminates the relationships among English Renaissance genres and between genric conventions and their historical implications. Alastair Fowler (1982) has written the most comprehensive historical-critical study of genre, which includes chapters on genric names,

228

signals, labels, systems, modulation, hierarchies, and canons. Finally, Claudio Guillén (1971) explores genre within the question of literary change. The picaresque is his focus for reflecting on the uses of literary genre and on the relationships between genre and countergenre.

Chapter 1

1. This example is adapted from one used in Barton 1984, and from a conversation with Renée Schoen-René.

2. Almost any passage of James Joyce's *Finnegans Wake* (1939) provides an example. Here, a courier teacher is conducting a little group of tourists: "(Stoop) if you are abcedminded, to this claybook, what curios of signs (please stoop), in this allaphbed! Can you rede (since We and Thou had it out already) its world? It is the same told of all. Many. Miscegenations of miscegenations. Tieckle. They lived und laughed ant loved end left" (18).

3. Marginalized people frequently parody the behavior and thought of the dominant class. Parody can both destroy and construct meaning. Parody that is simultaneously a criticism and a construction characterizes the following passage from Daly (1978, 29): "the Methodolatry of patriarchal disciplines kills creative thought. . . . The products are more often than not a set of distorted mirrors, made to seem plausible through the mechanics of male bonding. . . . Gynocentric Method requires not only the murder of misogynistic methods (intellectual and affective exorcism) but also ecstasy, which I have called *ludic cerebration*."

4. The term *genre* does not always appear in English translations of *The Poetics*. One might argue that Aristotle's emphasis is on what we can know by comparing and contrasting different modes of imitation: "Epic poetry and Tragedy, as also Comedy, Dithrambic poetry, and most flute-playing and lyre-playing, are all, viewed as a whole, modes of imitation. But at the same time they differ from one another in three ways, either by a difference of kind in their means, or by differences in the objects, or in the manner of their imitations" (Aristotle [1st century B.C.E.] 1954, 1:1447a). Aristotle's *Poetics* nevertheless illustrates the intrinsic role of generic considerations in literary meaning. For Aristotle's and Plato's theories of genre, see chapter 2.

5. Some of the major participants in the *Genre* debate were Monroe Beardsley ("Textual Meaning and Authorial Meaning"), Gale Carrithers, Jr. ("How Literary Things Go: Contra Hirsch"), John Huntley ("A Practical Look at E. D. Hirsch's *Validity in Interpretation*"), Merle E. Brown ("Interpretation of Poetry"), George Dickie ("Meaning and Intention") and Arthur Efron ("Logic, Hermeneutic, and Literary Context"). Efron (1968), perhaps better than any other participant, pinpointed the major failure of Hirsch's approach: namely, its refusal to come to terms with the ambiguity and complexity of literary meaning. Efron wondered why there is "such a widely diffused need for a guarantee of a continuing 'exploration' which can make no discoveries? . . . The reasons are more than those of bad logic and the weakness of wanting things one's own way; in the Twentieth Century the real is almost too disturbing to touch. Yet there is nothing else to touch" (p. 214). Efron thinks that "meaning is definite in the few great works" that a critic works with extensively, but his own critical principles are drawn from "contextualism" (a combination of hermeneutic and

formal logic), as developed by John Dewey and Stephen C. Pepper. For all their disagreements with Hirsch, none of the debaters denies his thesis that genre is intrinsic to literary meaning.

6.   Hirsch has since shifted his attention from genre to the teaching of writing. The issue of genre, oddly enough, does not come up in his widely read *Cultural Literacy: What Every American Needs to Know* (1987). Indeed, one might argue that the thesis of this book—that learning "what literate people know" is a necessary basis for a living cultural tradition—is flawed because of its lack of attention to genric differences.

7.   The issue, in other words, is not to identify the genre of a work correctly, but to come to an understanding of what genres inform the work and how the work changes by reading it in the light of different genres. A critical understanding of the text requires this process of reading a text in the light of multiple genres; the process gives the reader the opportunity to be aware of the demands that the text makes for being understood in a particular way as well as to arbitrate those demands through a recognition of other possibilities.

8.   See also Gerhart and Russell's (1984, 38, 64–68, 127–29) reinterpretation of first and second naïveté.

9.   See, for example, Jonathan Monroe 1987 for an analysis of the "polemical function" of poetry in the contemporary network of genres. He writes: "The prose poem today is a genre that does not want to be itself" (p. 15). Later he refers to the prose poem as "the literary genre in which [the class struggle] manifests itself most explicitly in terms of the ongoing struggles *among* genres" (p. 19).

10.   For a reader-reception theory treatment of foremeanings, see Hans-Robert Jauss 1982a, 1982b.

11.   Heilbrun (1988) has a telling insight into Harlequin romances from her experience of reading Peter Ackroyd's (1984) biography of T. S. Eliot after having read several biographies of women. She is struck by the "ease of men's lives" in the sense that for males there are "so many possible narratives," whereas for women writing their own lives, "the price is high, the anxiety is intense, because there is no script to follow, no story portraying how one is to act, let alone any alternative stories." Heilbrun finds it easy to settle into the T. S. Eliot biography because she knows from the genre of male biographies that "of all the choices life might offer him, Eliot would find those that suited." She reflects that romances, "which end when the woman is married at a very young age, are the only stories for women that end with the sense of peace, all passion spent, that we find in the lives of men" (Heilbrun 1988, 38–39). For detailed reader-reception analyses of Harlequin romances, see Radway 1986, 128–31; Snitow 1986, 134–40; Light 1986, 140–45; and Coward 1986, 145–48.

12.   *Alice* has also been read as a philosophical work of logic on the subject of nonsense by Pitcher (1971) and as a social critique.

13.   See Mary Daly's (1978) analysis of this story as one of "female rape and dismemberment" in which the Goddess (the tree) is made into "a willing participant in her own mutilation, which makes her 'happy' " (p. 90). The reaction to Daly's reading by students who have read and loved this story as children is initially one of shocked disbelief and then gradual agreement.

14.   See, for example, Paul Ricoeur's (1973a) account of Jürgen Habermas's

criticism of Gadamer. Whereas Gadamer sees distancing from tradition as a negative phenomenon, Ricoeur sees it as also potentially productive. See also Thompson 1981, 66–68, where Ricoeur's position is seen as mediating between a hermeneutics of tradition (Gadamer) and ideology critique (Habermas).

15. See Hempfer 1973 for a detailed analysis and an anatomy of theories of genre that opposes theories that have nominalist premises to those that spring from a realist position. In his conclusion Hempfer advocates an evolutionary model for genre theory.

16. These quantitative data are based on entries in the index to Watt 1957. Feminist examples currently offer clear examples of changes in genre and in public revision of values given to particular genres. For all their contribution to clarity, however, ambiguity flourishes. See Jardine and Menke 1991: "Many of us, as feminists, are increasingly unsure of who and where we are (actresses or audiences?) with regard to the master narratives of patriarchal history" (p. 2). Even though the statements in this book are in the genre of interview, the editors suggest that they are better understood in the genre not of "personalities" but of "scenes."

17. For the classic debate between Benjamin and Lukács on the role of Marxist theory in literary criticism, see Bloch et al. 1977. See also, Jameson 1981, Eagleton 1976, and Benjamin 1968. For a literary development of Louis Althusser's Marxist theory, see Macherey 1978.

18. See, for example, Dan Ben-Amos 1976. For examples of genric considerations applied to the disciplines, see Geertz 1980 and chapter 5.

19. This skepticism is characteristic of deconstructionist criticism, which is discussed in chapter 3. See also Miller 1979: "If the word 'deconstruction' names the procedure of criticism, and 'oscillation' the impasse reached through that procedure, 'undecidability' names the experience of a ceaseless dissatisfied movement in the relation of the critic to the text" (p. 252).

20. See especially Ricoeur's work on metaphor (1977), on narrative (1984–88), and on ideology and utopia (1986).

21. Lang (1975, 140) argues for a concept that would be a "counterpoise to the concept of aesthetic distance."

22. For a comparison of two studies of the genre of "woman's language," see Brown 1980, in which she compares a study of a society in which "women's language" is more polite than men's with her own study of a Mayan community in which "men's language" is more polite. Her conclusion is that men are seen by members of both societies as superior to women.

23. Ricoeur (1960) holds that it is inappropriate to "juxtapose" philosophical discourse and myth, "as if one ends where the other begins." Nor is it possible to "transcribe" myth directly into philosophical discourse. He explores a third way, "a creative interpretation of meaning" in which "the symbol gives; but what it gives is occasion for thought, something to think about" (pp. 348–49).

Chapter 2

1. *Webster's Ninth New Collegiate Dictionary* gives the etymology of *gender* as "ME *gendre,* fr. MF *genre, gendre,* fr. L. *gener-, genus* birth, race, kind,

Notes to Chapter 2

gender—more at KIN." It gives the etymology of *genre* as "F, fr. MF *genre* kind, gender—more at GENDER."

2.   Judith Kegan Gardiner (1985, 127–28) argues that the analysis of popular literature is at once a psychological analysis of its audience and an analysis of genre. Michel Foucault (1978, 21) locates the origins of the link between sexuality and literature in the pre-seventeenth-century religious injunction to tell all: "the task of passing everything having to do with sex through the endless mill of speech."

3.   The genre of the lyric, for example, has frequently been regarded as the province of the feminine. For an analysis of a single moment in the histories of the lyric and of the feminine gender, see Jones 1986.

4.   There were interesting variations on this pattern. In mid-eighteenth-century France, for example, "classic" began to have two meanings: (1) texts written in the second half of seventeenth-century France (called the Golden Age), which were looked upon as an ideal, and (2) texts taken as pedagogical models in the schools. Dejean (1991) finds that women authors of the Golden Age were included in the first meaning of classic (and continued to be read by adults) but were excluded from the second meaning of classic (and therefore were unknown to or regarded as less than ideal by younger generations). In her study of American literature, Judith Fetterley (1978) observes that, because of "the pervasive male bias of [American] literature, . . . the experience of being American is equated with the experience of being male" (xii). Although Fetterley's study focuses on the issue of the politics of literature (or who does and does not possess power), genre issues are implicit, such as in her reference to "the structure of romantic love" (xv).

5.   Woolf (1979, 44) cites the ambiguity of knowing about women writers: "Thus, if we wish to know why at any particular time women did this or that, why they wrote nothing, why on the other hand they wrote masterpieces, it is extremely difficult to tell. Anyone who should seek among those old papers, who should turn history wrong side out and so construct a faithful picture of the daily life of the ordinary women in Shakespeare's time, in Milton's time, in Johnson's time, would not only write a book of astonishing interest, but would furnish the critic with a weapon which he now lacks. The extraordinary woman depends on the ordinary woman."

6.   According to Todd (1986, 130–32), Williams and Wollstonecraft were friends, and some of Wollstonecraft's novels seem to be based on her experience of this and other female friendships. Todd explores the differences between male and female sensibility in eighteenth-century writing and the reasons for the devaluation of the concept.

7.   For an expanded discussion of the three classical genres and a far-ranging systematic treatment and application, see also Genette 1979, 1–6, and 1986, 89–160.

8.   Aristotle *Poetics* 1450.15: "Tragedy is essentially an imitation, not of persons but of action and life, of happiness and misery. All human happiness or misery takes the form of action; the end for which we live is a certain kind of activity, not a quality."

9.   Cf. Mieke Bal's (1987) interpretation of the Samson and Delilah story, which avoids seeing the woman as lethal.

10.   See, for example, Crane 1953, 3–38.

11.   Terry Eagleton (1983) brings a similar criticism to bear on the hermeneutical critics: namely, that they assume that "works of literature form an 'organic unity'. . . . Hermeneutics does not generally consider the possibility that literary works may be diffuse, incomplete, and internally contradictory" (p. 74). Eagleton overlooks, however, the possibility that epistemologically to consider a work diffuse, incomplete, or internally contradictory is to posit a disunity that may depend on unity for its intelligibility.

12.   For a feminist version of Eliot's project, see Gilbert and Gubar 1986.

13.   For the clearest statements of the German classical tradition, see, for example, Goethe 1949, A. W. Schlegel 1965, and F. Schlegel 1968. For the genius of classical French theory, see Brunitière 1890. For a study of recent genre theory in Germany, see Zutshi 1981.

14.   See Genette 1979 and 1981. For a succinct exposition of Genette's work, see Terry Eagleton 1983, 105–6.

15.   Recall also, however, that New Criticism found the "new novel" difficult, if not impossible, to interpret.

Chapter 3

1.   See, for example, Leon Wieseltier's "Unlocking the Rabbis' Secrets" (1989, 3): "For Jewish culture, the task was to find an image that will not become an idol. A word is such an image. A text is a holy thing that will not be worshiped. For the Jew, therefore, words became images, and the sign of a text became a spiritual experience." For the hermeneutical and ontological implications of the text as a "bridge" between imagining and thinking, see Hart 1968, 230–31: "Historical reality does not proceed through the mind, givingly or withholdingly, as water through a conduit. Responses of the mind are geared into the giving and withholding of historical being. Thus both the intension and extension of an event are unintelligible apart from appropriate cognitive acts."

2.   On the significance of the Hebrew Testament and Christian Testament being "bound" (not least by publication) together, see Ricoeur 1974, 381–401.

3.   Moore (1989, 72) later argues that "New Testament reader-response criticism is a more narrowly focused and more unified phenomenon than its nonbiblical counterpart." Still later, he emphasizes the reader-oriented literary study of the New Testament with his caption "Tracking the Reader-in-the-Text" (ibid., 104).

4.   Religious interpretation of texts is not confined either to scriptural texts or to genres explicitly designated as religious, usually because of their affinity with scriptural texts—for example, religious poetry, mystery and miracle plays, prayers. For a brief account of the complexity of designating a text as religious, see Gerhart 1990. Nor is biblical interpretation of scripture necessarily religious, either explicitly or implicitly. Some sociological, historical, and political analyses of texts are designed to deconstruct previous religious interpretations, to correct, or to ignore religious implications altogether. Whatever else it also does, the field of biblical hermeneutics affords an open field of common texts—open because it is affected by new interpretations, by new relationships with other genres, and by newly discovered ancient texts. The interpretation of the Bible

233

in the long run is a prime testing ground for the extent and limits of the ways human beings attempt to make sense of their experience of ultimacy.

5. It is worth noticing that the publication was collaborative—a significant arrangement if it differed from most male scholarship of the period. To see the extension of insights from *The Women's Bible* into contemporary scholarship, compare the treatment of one incident in *The Women's Bible* and in Higgins 1978. Following is a comment from *The Women's Bible* on the Garden of Eden temptation scene in Genesis: "Compared with Adam [Eve] appears to great advantage through the whole drama. . . . The conduct of Eve from beginning to end, is so superior to that of Adam. . . . It takes six verses to describe the [fall] of woman, the fall of man is contemptuously dismissed in a line and a half" (Stanton et al. 1895, 25–26). Higgins, in turn, also sees the first man as passively accepting the fruit in contrast to the woman, who is "active, intelligent, and decisive" (Higgins 1978, 254). More recently, two panels entitled "Rethinking *The Women's Bible*" have been held at the 1989 and 1990 annual meetings of the American Academy of Religion and the Society for Biblical Literature.

6. See John Barton 1984, esp. 45–60. See also his different readings of the Book of Ecclesiastes from the perspectives of form criticism and redaction criticism.

7. De Man's scholarly reputation has been threatened by his affiliation with a Nazi-sponsored Belgian newspaper during World War II. For a discussion of issues raised by this affiliation, see especially Norris 1988 and also Lehman 1991 and Loesberg 1991.

8. As Kierkegaardian scholarship of the last ten years has demonstrated so well, Kierkegaard was a master of rhetoric and used several genres expertly— so well, indeed, that his rhetorical skill was frequently misunderstood by earlier scholarship.

9. See, for example, Jameson 1981, 28–29. Jameson occasionally resorts to a positivist Marxist position. In his defense of Marxist insights as "the ultimate semantic precondition for the intelligibility of literary and cultural texts" (75), for example, he lists three concentric frameworks: political history, the social order, and history as production and destiny. The third (and largest) interpretive framework is limited to the concept of the ideology of form, which pertains exclusively to modes of production (75–76). But when Jameson raises questions about different versions of Marxism, he goes beyond a positivist stance.

10. See Booth 1975 for a sensitive assessment of "learning where to stop" in interpreting the genre of irony. Booth argues that even while the genre undermines some truths, others must be in fact presumed in order to avoid an infinite regress of negation.

Chapter 4

1. That there may be nothing that is self-evident about gender is implied by Denise Riley (1988) when she shows historically that it is essential both to concentrate on and to refuse the identity of "women." Similarly, in a lecture at Hobart and William Smith Colleges on 26 April 1991 Françoise Meltzer argued that minority groups such as women or blacks have a need both for political

identity, in order to gain legal rights, and for critical theory, to overcome the dangers of essentialism.

2. In her essay "Is There a Woman in This Class?" (1986), the title of which parodies and critiques the anecdote that gave rise to the title of a book by Stanley Fish, *Is There a Text in This Class?* (1980), Mary Jacobus analyzes the notion of gendered writing. Going beyond both Anglo-American and French feminism on the issue, she concludes with a different question, "Is there a text in this woman?" (109).

3. For an understanding of genre that at the same time corrects and reconstructs the concept "theory," see Rosmarin 1985.

4. Methodologically, the constructed history of genre is the "thread from the past appearance to the present experience" of the concept of genre. See Jauss 1970, 8.

5. I understand the ideological view to include theories of discourse, such as those of Michel Foucault, Louis Althusser, and Henri Pecheux, and of deconstructionists such as Jacques Derrida. These theorists have appropriated genre theory, usually implicitly, for their own purposes. The usefulness of their work for ours should become clear by the end of the chapter. See also Snyder 1991, who argues that it is precisely through the text's "participation in genre" that it acquires an ideological status. Snyder holds, against Cohen 1988, that "only the generic [and not individual texts] can possess ideologies" (Snyder 1991, 206). Cf. Eagleton 1976, esp. 11–43, for an alternative view of ideology to the one presented here.

6. Fowler's book is the most comprehensive representative of the traditionalist view.

7. Ghanic fairytales are so interpreted in Stewart 1979.

8. The ninth edition of *Webster's New Collegiate Dictionary* has reduced the logical inconsistency of the term. The citation is from the seventh edition.

9. Within literary criticism, the second definition presupposes evaluative judgment within a kind or genre. Some formalists maintain that evaluative judgments are not the proper business of criticism, i.e., that the work of the critic is purely descriptive and interpretative. But this position has been discredited in ideological criticism.

10. On the issue of originality and uniqueness in literary texts, see "The Work of Art in the Age of Mechanical Reproduction," in Benjamin 1968; in science, see references to "private science" in Holton 1973.

11. See Jauss 1970, 34–36, for a well-documented account of the reception of *Madame Bovary* at the time of its publication.

12. See also Gerhart and Russell 1987, 299–316. An example of the radical disjunction presumed by literary critics to exist between scientific and literary understanding can be found in the work of the New Critic R. S. Crane, as explicated in Booth 1979, 53:

No generalization of whatever kind applies to human makings in the way that scientific generalizations apply to particulars. To be sound, a scientific generalization must cover particulars in such a way that, if I know the generalization, I will know the particular. . . . An adequate general definition of a pig or a pomegranate will enable me . . . to predict the essential qualities of every pig or pomegranate . . . when dealing with works of art [however,] we have no way of proceeding from predetermined categories to knowledge about particulars: . . . "Euripides' *Tyro* is a lost work; it was a tragedy; what do you know of it?' "

Booth does not comment on this overstatement of the difference between scientific and artistic understanding, yet his own analysis at other points in his text, for example, in his discussion of Ushenko's cone (31–33, 92–97), indicates his awareness that scientific understanding is far more complex than Crane conceives it to be and that artistic understanding is more than the "stimulation of chaotic warfare" that the premise of uniqueness would require it to be.

13.   Besides the claim to uniqueness, the issue of originality has also traditionally been more important in the literary/artistic tradition than in science. In his study of ways of knowing within the disciplines, Stephen Toulmin (1972, 398) points out that "originality" in matters of technical innovation has been confused with "having something new to say." Whereas the notion of "unique" has created a virtual mystique, the notion of "originality" has been variously qualified in literary criticism. T. S. Eliot, in his famous essay "Tradition and the Individual Talent" (1929), for example, studies the way innovation affects and is affected by that which we come to know as literature. Harold Bloom, in *The Anxiety of Influence: A Theory of Poetry* (1973), as a second example, treats innovation as an oedipal conflict between poet and predecessors.

14.   Empirical studies of literature can be implicitly empiricist even though they limit their research to contemporary responses to literature and readily acknowledge the limitations of their results. In the absence of considerations of other generations or cultures, their results tend to be reified as normative for all times.

15.   Mitchell's question recalls Burke's (1961) argument that the business of the critic is to arbitrate among what he calls "god-terms."

16.   Deconstruction has been defined by J. Hillis Miller as "an investigation of what is implied by this inherence in one another of figure, concept, and narrative" (Miller 1979, 230)—and of genre, we might add. This inherence makes it impossible, according to the deconstructionists, to affirm *the* meaning(s) of a given text. All meanings are arbitrary, dependent on a system of language that is itself arbitrary and characterized by the absence of meaning rather than its presence. Any determinate meaning is therefore open to contradiction and reversal.

17.   See also Thomas Foster's (1986, 221–47) interpretation and use of Kristeva's theory.

18.   New genres are typically understood in relation to existing genres, both to identify them *as* new and to establish their legitimacy among other reigning models.

19.   I am endebted to A. M. Russell for this example.

20.   In his *Anatomy of Criticism: Four Essays* (1969, 243–340), Northrop Frye differentiates genres according to their rhythms, their forms, and their rhetoric. In his *Beyond Genre: New Directions in Literary Classification,* Paul

Notes to Chapter 5

Hernadi (1972, 165) analyzes the "genres of genre criticism" in terms of expression, concepts, pragmatic images, structural concepts, and mimetic concepts. His "anatomy" is organized on a dialectic of vision and action.

21. The disadvantages of attaching genres to disciplines outweigh the advantages of doing so.

22. For the importance of genre in "refiguring" the sense and reference of the text, see Tracy 1987, 44–46.

Chapter 5

1. Gilbert and Gubar quote Vita Sackville-West as saying that "she had experienced herself, she remembered, as inhabited by several sexes." Virginia Woolf expressed similar sentiments: "How many different people are there not—Heaven help us—all having lodgment at one time or another in the human spirit? Some say two thousand and fifty-two. . . . [Orlando] had a great variety of selves to call upon, far more than we have been able to find room for, since a biography is considered complete if it merely accounts for six or seven selves, whereas a person may well have as many thousand" (quoted in Gilbert and Gubar 1989, 324–25).

2. Cf. a related study, *The Conversation of the Sexes: Seduction and Equality in Selected Seventeenth- and Eighteenth-Century Texts* (1986) by Roy Roussel. Roussel, like Gilbert and Gubar, proposes a straightforward thesis: namely, that men's access to feminine experiences and women's access to masculine experiences may be blocked "by the way society arbitrarily assigns masculine qualities exclusively to males and feminine qualities to females" (p. 4). But Roussel hastily withdraws the possible conclusion that the blocking could be overcome by the achievement of equality of men and women. Instead, he confines his insightful study to what males perceive as feminine.

3. An interesting problem arises whenever discourse that appears to be sociological, historical, or scientific is claimed to be otherwise and made to undergo literary analysis. Some law schools currently ask their students to perform literary analysis of texts to broaden their sensibility and appreciation for ambiguity.

4. Generic scholarship has also flourished since the mid-1960s in the field of speech communication theory. In their *Form and Genre: Shaping Rhetorical Action* (1978) Karlyn Kohrs Campbell and Kathleen Hall Jamieson make four propositions regarding genre in rhetorical criticism: (1) Genres are "constellations of recognizable forms bound together by an internal dynamic." Genres are distinguished by the fusion of forms rather than by individual elements. (2) These forms can occur in isolation in other speech situations, but their "recurrence in constellation" is focused on in generic scholarship. (3) Rhetorical genres are constituted by "strategies"—substantive and stylistic forms selected for use in particular kinds of situations. (4) The combination of substantive and stylistic elements, necessitated by situation, are combined by an internal dynamic, which itself remains stable even if the other elements permutate over time (Campbell and Jamieson 1978, 9–32). Campbell and Jamieson's presuppositions by and large prevail in the field of speech communication theory.

5. The unwillingness to investigate the process of going beyond "pure" genres is not unique to film studies. Betty Roserberg defines the genre fiction as "patterned fiction." According to Roserberg, each genre follows rules governing plot and characters—and abides by some taboos—acknowledged by the authors and required by the publisher. This is not to say that a maverick author may not "flout the rules and still be published; this is, however, the exception" (Roserberg 1986, xix). She holds that the purpose of genre fiction is entertainment: "to divert and amuse, to hold the mind in enjoyment. Reading for pleasure is carefree; purposeful reading to improve the mind is not within its province" (ibid., xviii). Genre fiction includes westerns, thrillers, romances, science fiction, fantasy, and horror. The conjunction of gender and genre in film studies is relatively rare. Feminist studies of film that treat genre issues are McCormick 1991, and Penley, Lyon, Spigel, Bergstron 1990.

6. For studies of the changing models for scientific reporting, see Bazerman 1988, especially chapter 4 on "the relations between the existing book publication of scientific arguments and the newly emerging journal article" (63). For a historical view of scientific reporting, see chapter 3, "Reporting the Experiment: The Changing Account of Scientific Doings in the *Philosophical Transactions in the Royal Society, 1665–1800.* See also Black 1984, Gross 1988, and Nash 1990.

Chapter 6

1. See the notion of carnivalesque structure and the dialogical novel in Bakhtin 1973.

2. See also Charles 1977 and Ricoeur 1988, 3: 164–66, 315–16.

3. See Derrida, "The End of the Book and the Beginning of Writing" (1974, 6–26).

4. See also Barton 1984, who claims that, strictly speaking, "literary" pertains to the "internal claims" a text makes (as distinct from historical and theological claims). This sense seems somewhat contradictory to his other use of the term in the basic sense of "literary competence." Literary competence does not mean that someone is necessarily "good" at English, French, etc., but that a person is "in command of the conventions governing the use" of English, French, etc. If linguistic competence is the ability to recognize the meaning of sentences not heard before and to produce new sentences, then literary competence is the ability to recognize genres and to interpret new genres. Nevertheless, Barton limits his application of genric competence to those literary critical approaches *least* likely to yield radically new interpretations. In my own adaptation of Chomsky's notion of competence, I include deconstructionist criticism as well as formalist, structuralist, redactionist, and form criticism.

5. Merely to attend to gender issues does not ensure having a critical gender consciousness. Ivan Illich's *Gender* (1982), for example, is basically an argument in favor of traditional preindustrial gender roles, even though it purports to address the economic inequity between women and men in the contemporary world.

6. See also Chris Weedon 1987, who explores the complexity of the problem of genre for contemporary readers:

It is possible to trace the formative power of patriarchal, class and racial interests not just in modes of reading and the constitution of the canon, but in what is available to be read at all. In the case of much widely available fiction, it is possible to determine a convergence of capitalist interests in profit and broader hegemonic interests in the reproduction of the relations of production and reproduction in class, gender and racial terms. Two obvious examples of this are pornography and romance. The one is marketed for men, the other for women. Both deal with the nature of gender and gender difference. Both constitute gendered forms of subjectivity for the reader in ways that leave existing gender norms and the sexual division of labour intact (Weedon 1987, 170).

These gender issues cut across the panoply of genres popular at any given historical time. For demographic data on readers of Harlequin and other novels, see Radway 1986.

7.   "I am understanding everything until I encounter a contradiction or non-sense" (Schleiermacher 1977, 41).

8.   But see also Booth's (1979, esp. 197–234) later valuation of pluralism vis-à-vis monism. Insofar as religion can be understood in terms of conversion to a more authentic horizon, and insofar as learning to become a "gendered" and "genred" reader as described here involves a conversion of intellect and sensibility, the latter also constitutes a new measure of commerce between the study of religion and literature. Cf. Scott 1969 and Gunn 1971.

9.   For another plot of forged letters and a study of what their effects reveal about gender, see Caplan 1985.

10.   The phenomenon of not being able to hear what another person is saying or of not expecting them to be able to understand occurs between dominant and minority races and classes as well as between persons of different genders. In her short story "Revelation" (1965) Flannery O'Connor evokes a discrepancy that involves both race and class. Mrs. Turpin is berating herself for having told a group of black farmhands about her experience in the doctor's office and having received affirmations from them that she was a sweet lady, contrary to the girl who had called her "an old wart hog from hell": "Idiots! Mrs. Turpin growled to herself. You could never say anything intelligent to a nigger. You could talk at them but not with them" (422).

11.   See also the theoretical statement of Jane Flax (1986, 54): "Gender relations thus have no fixed essence: they vary both within and over time."

Chapter 7

1.   See Booth 1979, 284–301, for a detailed summary of interpretations of *The Turn of the Screw.*

2.   Kermode (1986, 131), states that the history of the novel is the history of the antinovel. In other words, if the novel is generally conceived as the continuity of traditional meaning and the "new" novel (of any period) as the emergence of new meaning, then the antinovel, rather than the novel, provides a better record of the history of the genre—a history that is one of changes in the genre.

3. We notice a lack of genric differentiation in the description of *The Extravagant Shepherd*. The reader is not self-aware as a reader and also regards genre as an extrinsic fact. In the second description there is a dawning awareness of the relationship between the antinovel and philosophical thought.

4. Sartre's approval of the "new" novel unexpectedly contrasts, for example, with his essay "Situation of the Writer in 1947" (1949, 121, 193), in which he speaks out against surrealism for its failure to go beyond the artistic *epoche*, that is, for remaining "fixed upon the things" instead of referring to their subjective source. And while he does not mention the "new" novel in that early essay, his predilection for the "new" novel can be anticipated by his recommendation that the writer present his work to the public "in a double aspect of negativity and construction" (ibid., 18). From a later vantage point, the existentialist force of defining the "new" or "anti-" literature is evident.

5. In other words, the novel is so moving without being "realistic" that it creates an alternative reality.

6. Recall Sartre's description of the first "new" novels.

7. Theory is a condition for the possibility to hear anew, sometimes to hear for the first time. Testing older texts in the light of new genres may disclose elements not noticed before. Theory is also always on its way to becoming an ideology because of the Faustian ambition to preserve the world as *we* want it. When Goethe's Faust says to Mephistopheles, "If ever I should say to any moment, 'Do stay with me—you are so good,' you may take my soul," he illustrates something that an ideologue is apt to forget, namely, that the drive to be politically correct or to subsume everything into the terms of one theory can quickly degenerate into a drive to preserve the status quo. "Politically correct" as a goal becomes its own undoing because it sets up an external test for exclusiveness. Meanwhile, the dichotomy between what is unreflectively defined as "correct" and its contrary is widened, since it remains external to the person making the judgment.

8. This shift in genre is comparable to that of a customer relations employee who shifts from the frame of responding to customer complaints to the frame of receiving customer suggestions for improving her business. This change is not merely in attitude but in structural elements as perceived by the reader.

References

Adebayo, N. 1985. "Protest and Commitment in Black American and African Literatures." In *Proceedings of the Xth Congress of the International Comparative Literature Association, 1982*. New York: Garland.

Alegría, Fernando. 1980. *Chilean Spring*. Pittsburgh: Latin American Literary Review Press.

Alter, Robert. 1981. *The Art of Biblical Narrative*. New York: Basic Books.

Althusser, Louis, 1970. "Ideology and Ideological State Apparatuses: Notes toward an Investigation." In *Lenin and Philosophy and Other Essays*. New York: Monthly Review Press.

Arendt, Hannah. 1958. *The Human Condition*. Chicago: University of Chicago Press.

Aristotle. [4th century B.C.E.] 1954. *The Rhetoric and the Poetics of Aristotle*. New York: Random House.

Ash, Timothy Garto. 1989. "Refolution: Springtime of Two Nations." *New York Review of Books* 36 (15 June).

Ashworth, William B., Jr. 1984. *Theories of the Earth, 1644–1830: The History of a Genre*. Kansas City: Linda Hall Library.

Augustine. 1942. *The Confessions*. Edited by F. J. Sheed. New York: Sheed & Ward.

Aune, David. 1986. "The Apocalypse of John and the Problem of Genre." *Semeia* 36:33.

Austin, Bruce A., and Thomas F. Gordon. 1988. "Movie Genres: Toward a Conceptualized Model and Standardized Definition." *Current Research in Film* 3: 12–33.

Bacon, Francis. [1597] 1986. "Of Studies." In *The Norton Anthology of English Literature*, 5th ed., edited by M. H. Abrams et al. New York: Norton.

Bakhtin, Mikhail. 1973. *Problems of Dostoevsky's Poetics*. Translated by R. W. Rotsel. Ann Arbor: University of Michigan Press.

———, 1986. *Speech Genres and Other Late Essays*. Translated by Vern W. McGee. Austin: University of Texas Press.

Bakhtin, Mikhail, and P. N. Medvedev. 1978. *The Formal Method in Literary Scholarship: A Critical Introduction to Sociological Poetics*. Translated by Albert J. Wehrle. Baltimore: Johns Hopkins University Press.

References

Bal, Mieke. 1985. *Narratology: Introduction to the Theory of Narrative*. Translated by C. van Boheeman. Toronto: University of Toronto Press.

——, 1984. "The Language of Subjectivity." *Poetics Today* 5:337–76.

——, 1987. *Lethal Love: Feminist Literary Readings of Biblical Love Stories*. Bloomington: Indiana University Press.

——, 1989. "Literature and Its Insistent Other." *Journal of the American Academy of Religion* 57:373–83.

Balakian, Anne, ed. 1985. *Proceedings of the Xth Congress of the International Comparative Literature Association, 1982*. New York: Garland.

Barth, John. 1969. *Lost in the Funhouse*. New York: Bantam.

Barthes, Roland. 1974. "The Struggle with the Angel: Textual Analysis of Genesis 32:23–33." In *Structural Analysis and Biblical Exegesis*, edited by Roland Barthes et al. Pittsburgh: Pickwick Press.

Barton, John. 1984. *Reading the Old Testament: Method in Biblical Study*. Philadelphia: Westminster Press.

Baum, Robert M. "Traditional Religions of the Americas and Africa." Unpublished manuscript.

Bazerman, Charles. 1988. *Shaping Written Knowledge*. Madison: University of Wisconsin Press.

Beaujour, Michel. 1980. "Genus Universum." *Glyph* 7:15–31.

Beckett, Samuel. 1967. *Stories and Texts for Nothing*. New York: Grove Press.

Ben-Amos, Dan. 1976. *Folklore Genres*. Austin: University of Texas Press.

Benjamin, Walter. 1968. *Illuminations: Essays and Reflections*, edited by Hannah Arendt. New York: Harcourt Brace Jovanovich.

Birch, Cyril. 1974. *Studies in Chinese Literary Genres*. Berkeley and Los Angeles: University of California Press.

Black, Joel Dana. 1984. "The Scientific Essay and Encyclopedic Science." *Stanford Literature Review* 1:119–48.

Bloch, Ernst, et al. 1977. *Aesthetics and Politics*. London: NLB.

Bloom, Harold. 1973. *The Anxiety of Influence: A Theory of Poetry*. New York: Oxford University Press.

——, 1979. "Introduction." In *Deconstruction and Criticism*. New York: Seabury Press.

——, 1990. *The Book of J*. Translated by David Rosenberg. New York: Grove Weidenfeld.

Booth, Wayne C. 1961. *The Rhetoric of Fiction*. Chicago: University of Chicago Press.

——, 1975. *The Rhetoric of Irony*. Chicago: University of Chicago Press.

——, 1979. *Critical Understanding: The Powers and Limits of Pluralism*. Chicago: University of Chicago Press.

——, 1988. *The Company We Keep: An Ethics of Fiction*. Berkeley and Los Angeles: University of California Press.

Borges, Jorge Luis. 1962. "Pierre Menard, Author of the Quixote." In *Labyrinths*. New York: New Directions.

Brown, Penelope. 1980. "How and Why Are Women More Polite: Some Evidence from a Mayan Community." In *Women and Language in Literature and Society*, edited by Sally McConnell-Ginet, Ruth Borker, and Nelly Furman. New York: Praeger.

References

Brunetière, Ferdinand. 1890. *L'evolution des genres dans l'histoire de la littérature*. Paris: Hachette.

Bultmann, Rudolf. 1941. "Kerygma und Mythos." In *Offenbarung und Heilsgeschehen*. Munich: A. Lempp.

Burke, Kenneth. 1961. *The Rhetoric of Religion*. Boston: Beacon Press.

Butler, Judith. 1990. *Gender Trouble: Feminism and the Subversion of Identity*. New York: Routledge, Chapman & Hill.

Buscombe, Edward. "The Idea of Genre in American Cinema." 1986. In *Film Genre Reader*, edited by Barry Keith Grant. Austin: University of Texas Press.

Buss, Martin. 1979. *Encounter with the Text: Form and History in the Hebrew Bible*. Philadelphia: Fortress Press; Missoula, Mont.: Scholars Press.

Campbell, Karlyn Kohrs, and Kathleen Hall Jamieson. 1978. *Form and Genre: Shaping Rhetorical Action*. Falls Church, VA.: Speech Communication Association.

Caplan, Jay. 1985. *Framed Narratives: Diderot's Genealogy of the Beholder*. Minneapolis: University of Minnesota Press.

Charles, Michel. 1977. *Rhetoric de la lecture*. Paris: Seuil.

Childs, Brevard. 1979. *Introduction to the Old Testament as Scripture*. Philadelphia: Fortress Press.

Chomsky, Noam. 1965. *Aspects of the Theory of Syntax*. Cambridge: MIT Press.

———, 1968. *Language and Mind*. New York: Harcourt Brace.

Cohen, Ralph. 1988. "Do Postmodern Genres Exist?" In *Postmodern Genres*, edited by Marjorie Perloff. Norman: University of Oklahoma Press.

Coleman, Alexander. 1985. "Cutting a Film and Making *Ficciones*." In *Proceedings of the Xth Congress of the International Comparative Literature Association, 1982*. New York: Garland.

Colie, Rosalie. 1974. *The Resources of Kind: Genre-Theory in the Renaissance*. Berkeley and Los Angeles: University of California Press.

Collins, Adela Yarbro. 1986. "Introduction: Early Christian Apocalypticism: Genre and Social Setting." *Semeia* 36: 1–11.

Collins, J. J. 1979. "Preface" and "Introduction: Morphology of a Genre," *Semeia* 14:iii–iv, 1–19.

Coward, Rosalind. 1986. "Female Desire: Women's Sexuality Today." In *Feminist Literary Theory: A Reader*, edited by Mary Eagleton. London: Basil Blackwell.

Crane, R. S. 1953. *The Languages of Criticism and the Structure of Poetry*. Toronto: University of Toronto Press.

———, 1967. *The Idea of the Humanities and Other Essays, Critical and Historical*. Chicago: University of Chicago Press.

Croce, Benedetto. 1953. *Aesthetic as Science of Expression and General Linguistic*. Translated by Douglas Ainslie. New York: Noonday Press.

Crossan, John Dominic. 1975. *The Dark Interval: Towards a Theology of Story*. Niles, Ill.: Argus Press.

———, 1983. *In Fragments*. San Francisco: Harper & Row.

———, 1985. *The Four Other Gospels*. San Francisco: Harper & Row.

Culler, Jonathan. 1975. *Structuralist Poetics: Structuralism, Linguistics, and the Study of Literature*. Ithaca, N.Y.: Cornell University Press.

References

Dallery, Arleen B. 1989. "The Politics of Writing (the) Body: Ecriture Féminine." In *Gender/Body/Knowledge: Feminist Reconstructions of Being and Knowing,* edited by Alison M. Jagger and Susan R. Bordo. New Brunswick, N.J.: Rutgers University Press.

Daly, Mary. 1978. *GynEcology: The Metaethics of Radical Feminism.* Boston: Beacon Press.

Dejean, Joan. 1991. "Classical Reeducation: Decanonizing the Feminine." In *Displacements: Women, Tradition, Literatures in French,* edited by Joan DeJean and Nancy K. Miller. Baltimore: Johns Hopkins University Press.

De Man, Paul. 1979. *Allegories of Reading.* New Haven, Conn.: Yale University Press.

———, 1982. Introduction to *Toward an Aesthetic of Reception,* by Hans-Robert Jauss. Minneapolis: University of Minnesota Press.

Derrida, Jacques. 1974. *Of Grammatology.* Translated by Gayatri Spivak. Baltimore: Johns Hopkins University Press.

———, 1980. "The Law of Genre." *Glyph* 7:176–232.

———, 1987. *The Post Card: From Socrates to Freud and Beyond.* Chicago: University of Chicago Press.

Didion, Joan. 1977. *A Book of Common Prayer.* New York: Simon & Schuster.

Dilthey, Wilhelm. [1870] 1968. "Die Entstehung der Hermeneutik." In *Gesammelte Schriften,* vol. 5. Stuttgart: Teubner; Göttingen: Vandenhoeck & Ruprecht.

Doty, William. 1972. "The Concept of Genre in Literary Analysis." In *The Genre of the Gospels: Studies in Methodology, Comparative Research, and Compositional Analysis.* Missoula, Mont.: Society of Biblical Literature.

Dubrow, Heather. 1982. *Genre.* The Critical Idiom Series, no. 42. London: Methuen.

Eagleton, Mary, ed. 1986. *Feminist Literary Theory: A Reader.* London: Basil Blackwell.

Eagleton, Terry. 1976a. *Criticism and Ideology.* New York: Schocken.

———, 1976b. *Marxism and Literary Criticism.* Berkeley and Los Angeles: University of California Press.

———, 1983. *Literary Theory: An Introduction.* London: Basil Blackwell.

Eco, Umberto. 1984. *Postscript to the Name of the Rose.* San Diego: Harcourt Brace Jovanovich.

Efron, Alfred. 1968. "Logic, Hermeneutic, and Literary Context." *Genre* 1:214–29.

Eliade, Mircea. 1981. *Autobiography.* Vol. 1, *Journey East, Journey West.* San Francisco: Harper & Row.

Eliot, T. S. 1932. "Tradition and the Individual Talent." In *Selected Essays, 1917–32.* Rev. ed. New York: Harcourt Brace.

———, 1943. "The Dry Salvages." In *Four Quartets.* New York: Harcourt, Brace & World.

Ellmann, Mary. 1968. *Thinking about Women.* New York: Harcourt Brace Jovanovich.

Erlich, Victor. 1969. *Russian Formalism: History, Doctrine.* Paris: Mouton.

Falk, Marcia. 1988. "The Song of Songs: Introduction and Commentary." In *Harper's Biblical Commentary,* edited by James L. Mays. San Francisco: Harper & Row.

References

Fetterley, Judith. 1978. *The Resisting Reader*. Bloomington: Indiana University Press.

Flax, Jane. 1986. "Postmodernism and Gender Relations in Feminist Theory." In *Feminist Theory in Practice and Process*, edited by Micheline R. Malson et al. Chicago: University of Chicago Press.

Foster, Thomas. 1986. "History, Critical Theory, and Women's Social Practices: 'Women's Time' and *Housekeeping*." In *Feminist Theory in Practice and Process*, edited by Micheline R. Malson et al. Chicago: University of Chicago Press.

Foucault, Michel. [1966] 1970. *The Order of Things*. New York: Random House.

———, 1979. *The History of Sexuality*, vol. 1. New York: Random House.

———, 1980. Introduction to *Herculine Barbin, Being the Recently Discovered Memoirs of a Nineteenth-Century Hermaphrodite*, translated by Richard McDougall. New York: Colophon.

Fowler, Alastair. 1971. "The Life and Death of Literary Forms." *New Literary History* 2:199–216.

———, 1982. *Kinds of Literature: An Introduction to the Theory of Genres and Modes*. New York: Cambridge University Press.

Friere, Paulo, 1978. "Conscientization." In *Conversion: Perspectives on Personal and Societal Transformation*, edited by Walter E. Conn. Staten Island, N.Y.: Alba.

Frye, Northrop. 1969. *Anatomy of Criticism: Four Essays*. New York: Atheneum.

Furman, Nellie. 1989. "His Story Versus Her Story: Male Genealogy and Female Strategy in the Jacob Cycle." *Semeia* 46:141–49.

Gadamer, Hans-Georg. 1975. *Truth and Method*. New York: Continuum.

———, 1976. *Philosophical Hermeneutics*. Translated and edited by David E. Linge. Berkeley and Los Angeles: University of California Press.

Gardiner, Judith Kegan. 1985. "Mind Mother: Psychoanalysis and Feminism." In *Making a Difference: Feminist Literary Criticism*, edited by Gayle Greene and Coppélia Kahn. London: Methuen.

Gates, Henry Louis, Jr. 1988. *The Signifying Monkey: A Theory of Afro-American Literary Criticism*. New York: Oxford University Press.

Geertz, Clifford. 1980. "Blurred Genres: The Refiguration of Social Thought." *The American Scholar* 49:65–79. Revised version in *Local Knowledge*. New York: Basic Books, 1983.

Genette, Gérard. 1977. "Genres, 'Types,' Modes." *Poetique* 8:389–421.

———, 1979. *Narrative Discourse*. Ithaca, N.Y.: Cornell University Press.

———, 1981. *Figures of Literary Discourse*. New York: Columbia University Press.

———, 1982. *Palimpsestes: La litératur au second degré*. Paris: Seuil.

———, 1986. "Introduction à l'architexte." In *Theorie des genres*, edited by Gérard Genette et al. Paris: Seuil.

Gerhart, Mary. 1983. "Genre as Praxis: An Inquiry." *PreText* 4:273–94.

———, 1990. "Whatever Happened to the Catholic Novel? A Study in Genre." In *Morphologies of Faith: Essays in Religion and Culture in Honor of Nathan A. Scott, Jr.*, edited by Mary Gerhart and Anthony C. Yu. Atlanta: Scholars Press.

References

————, 1991. "Another Troy for Her to Burn: the True Story of Euripides' Helen." In *Radical Pluralism and Truth: David Tracy and the Hermeneutics of Religion,* ed. by Werner Jeanrond and Jennifer Rike. New York: Crossroad, 121–41.

Gerhart, Mary, and Allan M. Russell. 1984. *Metaphoric Process: The Creation of Scientific and Religious Understanding.* Fort Worth: Texas Christian University Press.

————, 1987. "A Generalized Conception of Text Applied to Both Scientific and Religious Objects." *Zygon* 22:299–316.

Gilbert, Sandra M. 1985. "What Do Feminist Critics Want? A Postcard from the Volcano." In *The New Feminist Criticism,* edited by Elaine Showalter. New York: Pantheon Books.

Gilbert, Sandra M., and Susan Gubar. 1986. "Tradition and the Female Talent." In *Poetics of Gender,* edited by Nancy K. Miller. New York: Columbia University Press.

————, 1988–89. *No Man's Land.* 2 vols. New Haven, Conn.: Yale University Press.

————, 1990. "Feminism and Literature: An Exchange," *The New York Review of Books,* 16 August: 58–59.

Goethe, Johann Wolfgang von. 1949. "Naturformen der Dichtung." In *Werke.* Vol. 2, *Noten und Abhandlungen zu besserem Verständnis des West-östlichen Divans.* Hamburg: Christian Wegner.

Gollim, Richard. 1989. "How to Read a Film." Unpublished paper presented at American Academy of Religion national meeting, Anaheim, Calif., November 20, 1989.

Grant, Barry Keith, ed. 1986. *Film Genre Reader.* Austin: University of Texas Press.

Gross, Alan. 1988. "Discourse on Method: Rhetorical Analysis of Scientific Texts." *Pre/Text* 9: 169–85.

Guillén, Claudio, 1971. *Literature as System: Essays toward the Theory of Literary History.* Princeton, N.J.: Princeton University Press.

Gunkel, Hermann. 1901. *The Legends of Genesis.* Chicago: University of Chicago Press.

————, 1928. "The Religion of the Psalms." In *What Remains of the Old Testament and Other Essays.* New York: Macmillan.

Gunn, Giles B. 1971. *Literature and Religion.* New York: Harper & Row.

Gunn, Janet Varner. 1982. *Autobiography: Toward a Poetics of Experience.* Philadelphia: University of Pennsylvania Press.

Habermas, Jürgen (1963) 1974. *Theory and Practice.* Translated by John Viertel. London: Heinemann.

Hamburger, Käte. 1973. *The Logic of Literature.* 2d ed. Translated by Marilyn Rose. Bloomington: Indiana University Press.

Hampson, Daphne. 1990. *Theology and Feminism.* London: Basil Blackwell.

Hart, Ray L. 1968. *Unfinished Man and the Imagination: Toward an Ontology and a Rhetoric of Revelation.* New York: Herder and Herder.

Hartman, Geoffrey. 1981. *Saving the Text: Literature/Derrida/Philosopher.* Baltimore: Johns Hopkins University Press.

Hartsock, Nancy. 1983. "The Feminist Standpoint: Developing the Ground

246

References

for a Specifically Feminist Historical Materialism." In *Discovering Reality: Feminist Perspectives on Epistemology, Metaphysics, Methodology, and Philosophy of Science*, edited by Sandra Harding and Merrill B. Hintikka. Dordrecht: D. Reidel.

Hauser, Arnold. 1957. *The Sociology of Art*. 4 vols. New York: Random House.

Havelock, Eric A. 1967. *Preface to Plato*. New York: Grosset & Dunlap.

Hegel, Georg Wilhelm Friedrich. [1807] 1977. *Hegel's Phenomenology of the Spirit*. Translated by A. V. Miller. Oxford: Clarendon Press.

Heidegger, Martin. [1927] 1978. *Being and Time*. Oxford: Basil Blackwell.

Heilbrun, Carolyn G. 1988. *Writing a Woman's Life*. New York: Norton.

Hellholm, David. 1986. "The Problem of Apocalyptic Genre and the Apocalypse of John." *Semeia* 36:13–64.

Hempfer, Klaus W. 1973. *Gattungstheorie: Information und Synthese*. Munich: Wilhelm Fink.

Hernadi, Paul. 1972. *Beyond Genre: New Directions in Literary Classification*. Ithaca, N.Y.: Cornell University Press.

Higgins, Jean. 1978. "Anastasius Sinaita and the Superiority of the Woman." *Journal of Biblical Literature* 97:253–56.

Hinden, Michael. 1973. "Lost in the Funhouse: Barth's Use of the Recent Past." *Twentieth-Century Literature* 19 (April): 107–18.

Hirsch, E. D., Jr. 1967. *Validity in Interpretation*. New Haven, Conn.: Yale University Press.

———, 1987. *Cultural Literacy: What Every American Needs to Know*. Boston: Houghton Mifflin.

Hofstadter, Douglas. 1985. *Metamagical Themes*. New York: Basic Books.

Holton, Gerald. 1973. *Thematic Origins of Scientific Thought*. New York: Cambridge University Press.

Horkheimer, Max, and Theodor Adorno. 1972. "Odysseus; or, Myth and Enlightenment." In *The Dialectic of Enlightenment*. New York: Continuum.

Humm, Maggie. 1986. *Feminist Criticism: Women as Contemporary Critics*. New York: St. Martin's Press.

Illich, Ivan. 1982. *Gender*. New York: Pantheon Books.

Iser, Wolfgang. 1978. *The Act of Reading: A Theory of Aesthetic Response*. Baltimore: Johns Hopkins University Press.

Jackson, W. T. H. 1985. *The Challenge of the Medieval Text*. Columbia: University of Missouri Press.

Jacobus, Mary. 1986. "Is There a Woman in This Class?" In *Reading Women: Essays in Feminist Criticism*. New York: Columbia University Press.

Jameson, Fredric. 1981. *The Political Unconscious: Narrative as a Socially Symbolic Act*. Ithaca, N.Y.: Cornell University Press.

Jardine, Alice A., and Anne M. Menke, eds. 1991. *Shifting Scenes: Interviews on Women, Writing, and Politics in Post-68 France*. New York: Columbia University Press.

Jauss, Hans-Robert. 1978. "Theses on the Transition from the Aesthetics of Literary Works to a Theory of Aesthetic Experience." In *Interpretation of Narrative*, edited by Mario J. Valdés and Owen J. Miller. Toronto: University of Toronto Press.

References

———, 1982a. *Aesthetic Experience and Literary Hermeneutics*. Minneapolis: University of Minnesota Press.

———, [1970] 1982b. "Literary History as a Challenge to Literary Theory." In *Toward an Aesthetic of Reception*. Minneapolis: University of Minnesota Press.

Johnson, Barbara. 1980. *The Critical Difference: Essays in the Contemporary Rhetoric of Reading*. Baltimore: Johns Hopkins University Press.

———, ed. 1982. *Pedagogical Imperative: Teaching as a Literary Genre*. Special issue. *Yale French Studies* 63 (December).

Jones, Ann Rosalind. 1986. "Surprising Fame: Renaissance Gender Ideologies and Women's Lyric." In *The Poetics of Gender*, edited by Nancy K. Miller. New York: Columbia University Press.

Kamuf, Peggy. 1980. "Writing Like a Woman." In *Women and Language in Literature and Society*, edited by Sally McConnell-Ginet, Ruth Borker, and Nelly Furman. New York: Praeger.

Kauffman, Linda S. 1986. *Discourses of Desire: Gender, Genre, and Epistolary Fiction*. Ithaca, N.Y.: Cornell University Press.

Kauffmann, Stanley. 1987. "The Same, Only Different." *The New Republic*, 5, 12 January, 24–25.

Kayser, Wolfgang. 1959. *Das sprachliche Kunstwerk: Eine Einführung in die Literaturewissenschaft*. Bern: Francke.

Kazin, Alfred, 1971. *Bright Book of Life*. Boston: Little, Brown.

Keller, Evelyn Fox. 1985. *Reflections on Gender and Science*. New Haven, Conn.: Yale University Press.

Kent, Thomas. 1986. *Interpretation and Genre: The Role of Generic Perception in the Study of Narrative Forms*. Lewisburg, Pa.: Bucknell University Press.

Kermode, Frank. 1968. *The Sense of an Ending*. New York: Oxford University Press.

Kinneavy, James. [1971] 1980a. *A Theory of Discourse: The Aims of Discourse*. New York: Norton.

———, 1980b. "A Pluralistic Synthesis of Four Contemporary Models for Teaching Composition." In *Reinventing the Rhetorical Tradition*, edited by Aviva Freedman and Ian Pringle. Conway, Ark.: L & S Books.

Kintgen, Eugene R. 1983. *The Perception of Poetry*. Bloomington: Indiana University Press.

Kolb, Elene. 1989. "When Women Finally Got the Word." *New York Times Book Review*, 9 July.

Kolodny, Annette. 1975. *The Lay of the Land: Metaphor as Experience and History in American Life and Letters*. Chapel Hill: University of North Carolina Press.

———, 1985. "Dancing through the Minefield." In *The New Feminist Criticism*, edited by Elaine Showalter. New York: Pantheon Books.

Krieger, Murray. 1969. *The New Apologists for Poetry*. Bloomington: Indiana University Press.

———, 1976. *Theory of Criticism: A Tradition and Its System*. Baltimore: Johns Hopkins University Press.

Kristeva, Julia. 1980. "The Bounded Text." In *Desire in Language*. New York: Columbia University Press.

References

————, 1981. "Women's Time." Translated by Alice Jardine and Harry Blake. In *Feminist Theory: A Critique of Ideology,* edited by Nannerl O. Keohane, Michelle Z. Rosaldo, and Barbara C. Gelpi, 5–19. Chicago: University of Chicago Press.

Labov, William. 1972. *Language in the Inner City: Studies in the Black English Vernacular.* Philadelphia: University of Pennsylvania Press.

Lacoue-Labarther, Philippe, and Jean-Luc Nancy. 1980. "Genre." *Glyph* 7:1–14.

Lang, Berel. 1975. *Art and Inquiry.* Detroit: Wayne State University Press.

————, 1984. *Revolution in Poetic Language.* Translated by Leon Roudiez. New York: Columbia University Press.

Lasch, Christopher. 1976. "The Narcissist Society." *New York Review of Books* 23:5–13.

————, 1979. *The Culture of Narcissism.* New York: Norton.

Leach, Edmund. 1969. *"Genesis as Myth" and Other Essays.* London: Grossman.

Leach, Edmund, and Stephen Aycock, eds. 1983. *Structuralist Interpretation of Biblical Myth.* Cambridge: Cambridge University Press.

Lehman, David. 1991. *Signs of the Times.* New York: Poseidon Press.

Lemaire, Ria. 1986. "Explaining Away the Female Subject." *Poetics Today* 7:729–43.

Lévi-Strauss, Claude. 1970. *The Raw and the Cooked: An Introduction to the Science of Mythology.* New York: Harper & Row.

Light, Alison. 1986. " 'Returning to Manderley': Romance Fiction, Female Sexuality and Class." In *Feminist Literary Theory: A Reader,* edited by Mary Eagleton. London: Basil Blackwell.

Lloyd, Genevieve. 1984. *The Man of Reason: "Male" and "Female" in Western Philosophy.* Minneapolis: University of Minnesota Press.

Loesberg, Jonathan. 1991. *Aestheticism and Deconstruction.* Princeton: Princeton University Press.

Lonergan, Bernard. 1957. *Insight: A Study of Human Understanding.* London: Longmans, Green.

————, 1972. *Method in Theology.* New York: Herder and Herder.

McConnell-Ginet, Sally. 1980. "Linguistics and the Feminist Challenge." In *Women and Language in Literature and Society,* edited by Sally McConnell-Ginet, Ruth Borker, and Nelly Furmon. New York: Praeger.

McConnell-Ginet, Sally, Ruth Borker, and Nelly Furman, eds. 1980. *Women and Language in Literature and Society.* New York: Praeger.

McCormick, Richard. 1991. *Politics of the Self: Feminism and the Postmodern in West German Literature and Film.* Princeton: Princeton University Press.

Macdonell, Diane. 1986. *Theories of Discourse: An Introduction.* London: Basil Blackwell.

Macherey, Pierre. 1978. *A Theory of Literary Production.* Translated by Geoffrey Wall. London: Routledge & Kegan Paul.

McKeon, Michael. 1987. *The Origins of the English Novel.* Baltimore: Johns Hopkins University Press.

Malson, Micheline R., et al., eds. 1986. *Feminist Theory in Practice and Process.* Chicago: University of Chicago Press.

References

Mayr, Ernst von. 1963. *Animal Species and Evolution.* New York: Cambridge University Press.

Meltzer, Francoise. 1987. *Salome and the Dance of Writing: Portraits of Mimesis in Literature.* Chicago: University of Chicago Press.

Miller, Casey, and Kate Swift. 1976. *Words and Women.* New York: Anchor Press.

Miller, J. Hillis. 1979. "The Critic as Host." In *Deconstruction and Criticism.* New York: Seabury Press.

Miller, Nancy K. 1980. "Women's Autobiography in France: For a Dialectic of Identification." In *Women and Language in Literature and Society,* edited by Sally McConnell-Ginet, Ruth Borker, and Nelly Furman. New York: Praeger.

Mitchell, W. J. T., ed. 1982. *The Politics of Interpretation.* Chicago: University of Chicago Press.

Modleski, Tania. 1982. *Loving with a Vengeance: Mass-Produced Fantasies for Women.* New York: Methuen.

Moers, Ellen. 1963. *Literary Women.* New York: Oxford University Press.

Monroe, Jonathan. 1987. *A Poverty of Objects: The Prose Poem and the Politics of Genre.* Ithaca, N.Y.: Cornell University Press.

Moore, Stephen D. 1989. *Literary Criticism and the Gospels.* New Haven, Conn.: Yale University Press.

Morson, Gary Saul. 1981. *The Boundaries of Genre: Dostoevsky's "Diary of a Writer" and the Traditions of Literary Utopia.* Austin: University of Texas Press.

Moulton, James. 1899. *The Bible as Literature.* London: Service & Paton.

Murdoch, Iris. 1977. *The Fire and the Sun: Why Plato Banished the Artists.* Oxford: Clarendon Press.

Muschg, Walter. 1969. *Die dichterische Phantasie: Einführung in Eine Poetik.* Bern: Francke.

Nash, Christopher. 1990. *Narrative in Culture: the Use of Storytelling in the Sciences, Literature and Philosophy.* London: Routledge.

Nietzsche, Friedrich. 1983. "On the Advantages and Disadvantages of History for Life." In *Untimely Meditations.* Trans. by R. J. Hollingdale. Cambridge: Cambridge University Press.

————, 1978. *Thus Spoke Zarathustra: A Book for All or None.* Translated by Walter Kaufmann. Harmondsworth: Penguin Books.

————, 1956. *The Birth of Tragedy.* Translated by Francis Golffing. Garden City, N.Y.: Doubleday.

Norris, Christopher. 1982. *Deconstruction: Theory and Practice.* London: Methuen.

————, 1988. *Paul de Man.* London: Routledge.

Nussbaum, Felicity. 1986. "Toward Conceptualizing Diary." In *Studies in Autobiography,* edited by J. Olney. New York: Oxford University Press.

O'Connor, Flannery. 1965. *Everything That Rises Must Converge.* In *Three by Flannery O'Connor.* New York: Signet.

O'Flaherty, Wendy Doniger. 1988. *Other People's Myths: The Cave of Echoes.* New York: Macmillan.

Orsini, G. N. G. 1975. "Genre." In *The Princeton Encyclopedia of Poetry and*

References

Poetics, edited by Alex Preminger. Princeton, N.J.: Princeton University Press.

Penley, Constance, Elisabeth Lyon, Lynn Spigel, and Janet Bergstrom, eds. 1990. *Close Encounters: Film, Feminism and Science Fiction.* Minneapolis: University of Minnesota Press.

Percy, Walker. 1961. *The Moviegoer.* New York: Knopf.

Perloff, Marjorie, ed. 1988. *Postmodern Genres.* Norman: University of Oklahoma Press.

Pitcher, George. 1971. "Wittgenstein, Nonsense, and Lewis Carroll." In *English Literature and British Philosophy,* edited by S. P. Rosenbaum, Chicago: University of Chicago Press.

Plaskow, Judith. 1979. "The Coming of Lilith: Toward a Feminist Theology." In *Womanspirit Rising,* edited by Carol Christ and Judith Plaskow. New York: Harper & Row.

Plato. 1961. *The Collected Dialogues of Plato,* edited by Edith Hamilton and Huntington Cairns. Bollingen Series, no. 71. Princeton, N.J.: Princeton University Press.

Poe, Joe Park. 1987. *Genre and Meaning in Sophocles' "Ajax."* Frankfurt am Main: Athenaum.

Poggioli, Renato. 1965. *The Spirit of the Letter: Essays in European Literature.* Cambridge: Harvard University Press.

Polzin, Robert. 1989. "1 Samuel: Biblical Studies and the Humanities." *Religious Studies Review* 15:297–306.

Pratt, Mary Louise. 1977. *Toward a Speech Act Theory of Literary Discourse.* Bloomington: Indiana University Press.

Propp, Vladimir. 1958. *Morphology of the Folktale.* Bloomington: University of Indiana Press.

Rad, G. von. 1965. *Theologie des Alten Testaments.* 4th ed. Vol. 2. Munich: Kaiser.

Radway, Janice A. 1986. "Women Read the Romance: The Interaction of Text and Context." In *Feminist Literary Theory: A Reader,* edited by Mary Eagleton. London: Basil Blackwell.

Ricoeur, Paul. 1960. *The Symbolism of Evil.* Boston: Beacon Press.

———, 1970. *Freud and Philosophy.* New Haven, Conn.: Yale University Press.

———, 1971. "What is a Text? Explanation and Interpretation." In *Mythic-Symbolic Language and Philosophical Anthropology,* edited by David Rasmussen. The Hague: Martinus Nijhoff.

———, 1973a. "Ethics and Culture: Habermas and Gadamer in Dialogue," *Philosophy Today* 17:153–65.

———, 1973b. "The Hermeneutical Function of Distanciation." *Philosophy Today* 17:129–41.

———, 1974. *The Conflict of Interpretations.* Evanston, Ill.: Northwestern University Press.

———, 1976. "Language as Discourse." In *Interpretation Theory: Discourse and the Surplus of Meaning.* Fort Worth: Texas Christian University Press.

———, 1977. *The Rule of Metaphor.* Toronto: University of Toronto Press.

References

———, 1981. "Science and Ideology." In *Hermeneutics and the Human Sciences*. Cambridge: Cambridge University Press.

———, 1984–88. *Time and Narrative*. 3 vols. Chicago: University of Chicago Press.

———, 1986. *Lectures on Ideology and Utopia*, edited by George H. Taylor. New York: Columbia University Press.

Riley, Denise. 1988. *"Am I That Name?" Feminism and the Category of "Women" in History*. Minneapolis: University of Minnesota.

Robbe-Grillet, Alain. [1955] 1958. *The Voyeur*. Trans. by Richard Howard. New York: Grove Press.

———, 1965. *For a New Novel*. New York: Grove Press.

Rogers, William Elford. 1983. *The Three Genres and the Interpretation of Lyric*. Princeton, N.J.: Princeton University Press.

Rose, Ruth. 1990. "I Hear You, I Hear You." *New York Times Book Review*, 5 August.

Roserberg, Betty. 1986. *Genreflecting: a Guide to Reading Interests in Genre Fiction*. Littleton, Colo.: Libraries Unlimited.

Rosmarin, Adena. 1985. *The Power of Genre*. Minneapolis: University of Minnesota Press.

Rougement, Denis de. 1956. *Love in the Western World*. Princeton: Princeton University Press.

Roussel, Roy. 1986. *The Conversation of the Sexes: Seduction and Equality in Selected Seventeenth- and Eighteenth-Century Texts*. New York: Oxford University Press.

Ruether, Rosemary. 1983. *Sexism and God-Talk*. Boston: Beacon Press.

Sacks, Sheldon. 1967. *Fiction and the Shape of Belief*. Berkeley and Los Angeles: University of California Press.

Sarraute, Nathalie. 1956. *Portraite d'un inconnu*. Paris: Gallimard.

———, [1939] 1963. *Tropisms*. Trans. by John Calder. New York: George Braziller.

Sartre, Jean-Paul. 1949. "Situation of the Writer in 1947." In *What Is Literature?* New York: Philosophical Library.

———, 1956. Preface to *Portrait d'un inconnu*, by Nathalie Sarraute. Paris: Gallimard.

Schlegel, August Wilhelm. 1965. *Course of Lectures on Dramatic Art and Literature*. Translated by John Black, New York: AMS Press.

Schlegel, Friedrich. 1968. *Dialogue on Poetry and Literary Aphorisms*. Translated by Ernst Behler and Roman Struc. University Park: Pennsylvania State University Press.

Schleiermacher, Friedrich D. E. 1938. *Sämmtliche Werke*. Vol. 7, *Hermeneutik und Kritic*. Edited by F. Lucke. Berlin: G. Reimer.

Schmidt, Siegfried. 1982. *Foundations for the Empirical Study of Literature: The Components of a Basic Theory*. Hamburg: Helmut Buske.

Schorer, Mark. 1952. "Fiction and the 'Analogical Matrix.' " In *Critiques and Essays in Modern Fiction*, edited by John W. Aldridge. New York: n.p.

Schüssler Fiorenza, Elisabeth. 1983. *In Memory of Her: A Feminist Theological Reconstruction of Christian Origins*. New York: Crossroads Books.

References

Schüssler Fiorenza, Francis, et al. 1991. "Roundtable: The Influence of Feminist Theory on My Theological Work." *Journal of Feminist Studies in Religion* 7:95–126.

Scott, Nathan A., Jr. 1969. *Negative Capability: Studies in the New Literature and the Religious Situation*. New Haven and London: Yale University Press.

Segovia, Fernando. 1987. "Recent Research in the Johannine Letters." *Religious Studies Review* 13:132.

Showalter, Elaine, ed. 1985. *The New Feminist Criticism*. New York: Pantheon Books.

Simmons, William S. 1986. *Spirit of the New England Tribes: Indian History and Folklore*. Hanover, Vt.: University Press of New England.

Simons, Herbert W., and Aram A. Aghazarian, eds. 1986. *Form, Genre, and the Study of Political Discourse*. Columbia: University of South Carolina Press.

Smith, Allen Gardner. 1980. "Edith Wharton and the Ghost Story." In *Gender and Literary Voice*, edited by Janet Todd. New York: Holmes & Meier.

Smith, Barbara Herrnstein. 1978. *On the Margins of Discourse: The Relation of Literature to Language*. Chicago: University of Chicago Press.

Snitow, Ann Barr. 1986. "Mass Market Romance: Pornography for Women Is Different." In *Feminist Literary Theory: A Reader*, edited by Mary Eagleton. London: Basil Blackwell.

Snyder, John. 1991. *Prospects of Power: Tragedy, Satire, the Essay, and the Theory of Genre*. Lexington: University Press of Kentucky.

Sontag, Susan. 1966. "The Pornographic Imagination." In *Styles of Radical Will*. New York: Dell Books.

Sorel, Charles. [1627] 1654. *Le berger extravagant, ou Parmy des fantaisies amoureuses on void les impertinences des Romans and de la poesie*. Paris: Chez Toussainet duBray. Translated as *The Extravagant Shepherd; or, The History of the Shepherd Lysis: An Anti-Romance Written Originally in French and Now Made English*. London: T. Newcomb for Thomas Heath.

Spencer, Jane. 1986. *The Rise of the Woman Novelist: From Aphra Behn to Jane Austen*. London: Basil Blackwell.

Stanton, Elizabeth Cady, et al. 1895–98. *The Woman's Bible*. Vol. 1, *Comments on Genesis, Exodus, Leviticus, Numbers and Deuteronomy*. Vol. 2, *Comments on the Old and New Testaments from Joshua to Revelation*. New York: European Publishing Co.

Stegmuller, Wolfgang. 1976. *The Structure and Dynamic of Theories*. New York: Springer.

Stewart, Susan. 1979. *Nonsense: Aspects of Intertextuality in Folklore Literature*. Baltimore: Johns Hopkins University Press.

Strain, Charles R. 1978. "Toward a Generic Analysis: An Essay-Review of Walter Rauschenbusch, *Christianity and the Social Crisis*." *Journal of the American Academy of Religion* 46:525–43.

Strelka, Joseph P. ed. *Theories of Literary Genre*. 1978. Yearbook of Comparative Criticism, 8. University Park, Penn.: The Pennsylvania State University Press.

Stubbs, Patricia. 1979. *Women and Fiction*. Brighton: Harvester Press.

References

Suelzer, Alexa. 1968. "Modern Old Testament Criticism." In *The Jerome Biblical Commentary*, edited by Raymond Brown, Joseph Fitzmyer, and Roland E. Murphy. Englewood Cliffs, N.J.: Prentice-Hall.

Suleiman, Susan. 1980. "Introduction: Varieties of Audience-Oriented Criticism." In *The Reader in the Text: Essays on Audience and Interpretation*, edited by Susan Suleiman and Inge Crosman. Princeton, N.J.: Princeton University Press.

Szondi, Peter. 1987. *Theory of the Modern Drama*. Edited and translated by Michael Hays. Theory and History of Literature, vol. 29. Minneapolis: University of Minnesota Press.

Talbert, Charles H. 1977. *What Is a Gospel? The Genre of the Canonical Gospels*. Philadelphia: Fortress Press.

Tannen, Debra. 1990. *You Just Don't Understand: Men and Women in Conversation*. New York: Morrow.

Thiher, Allen. 1984. *Words in Reflection: Modern Language Theory and Postmodern Fiction*. Chicago: University of Chicago Press.

Thompson, John B. 1981. *Critical Hermeneutics: A Study in the Thought of Paul Ricoeur and Jürgen Habermas*. Cambridge: Cambridge University Press.

Todd, Janet. 1986. *Sensibility: An Introduction*. London: Methuen.

———, 1988. *Feminist Literary History*. New York: Routledge, Chapman & Hall.

Todorov, Tzvetan. 1975. *The Fantastic: A Structural Approach to a Literary Genre*. Translated by Richard Howard. Ithaca, N.Y.: Cornell University Press.

Tolbert, Mary Ann, ed. 1983. *The Bible and Feminist Hermeneutics*. Chico, Calif.: Scholars Press.

Tompkins, Jane P. 1985. "Sentimental Power: *Uncle Tom's Cabin* and the Politics of Literary History." In *The New Feminist Criticism*, edited by Elaine Showalter. New York: Pantheon Books.

Toulmin, Stephen. 1972. *Human Understanding*. Vol. 1, *The Collective Use and Evolution of Concepts*. Princeton, N.J.: Princeton University Press.

Tracy, David. 1981. *The Analogical Imagination*. New York: Crossroad.

———, 1983. "The Context: The Public Character of Theological Language." In *Speaking of God*, edited by John B. Cobb, Jr., and David Tracy. San Francisco: Harper & Row.

———, 1987. *Plurality and Ambiguity: Hermeneutics, Religion, Hope*. San Francisco: Harper & Row.

Trible, Phyllis. 1973. "Eve and Adam," *Andover Newton Quarterly* 13: 251–58.

———, 1978. *God and the Rhetoric of Sexuality*. Philadelphia: Fortress Press.

Tudor, Andrew. 1986. "Genre." In *Film Genre Reader*, edited by Barry Keith Grant. Austin: University of Texas Press.

Viëtor, Karl. 1952. *Geist und Form*. Bern: Francke.

Vendler, Helen. 1990. "Feminism and Literature," *New York Review of Books*, 31 May, 19–25.

———, 1990. "Reply," *New York Review of Books*, 16 August, 59.

Walter, Bettyruth. 1988. *The Jury Summation as Speech Genre*. Amsterdam: John Benjamins.

References

Watt, Ian. 1975. *The Rise of the Novel.* Harmondsworth: Penguin Books.

Weedon, Chris. 1987. *Feminist Practice and Poststructuralist Theory.* London: Basil Blackwell.

Wellhausen, Julius. [1878] 1983. *Geschichte Israels.* Translated as *Prolegomena to the History of Ancient Israel.* Gloucester: Peter Smith.

Weissenberger, Klaus. 1978. "A Mythological Genre Theory." In *Theories of Literary Genre,* edited by Joseph Strelka. Yearbook of Comparative Criticism, vol. 8. University Park: Pennsylvania State University Press.

————, 1985. *Prosakunst ohne Erzahlen: Die Gattungen der Nicht-fiktionalen Kunstprosa.* Tübingen: Max Niemeyer.

Wieseltier, Leon. 1989. "Unlocking the Rabbis' Secrets." *New York Times Book Review,* 19 December, 3.

Wilson, Thomas. 1553. *The Arte of Rhetoric.* London: Richard Grafton.

Wimsatt, William, Jr., and Cleanth Brooks. 1967. *Literary Criticism: A Short History.* New York: Random House.

Winner, Thomas G. 1978. "Structural and Semiotic Genre Theory." In *Theories of Literary Genre.* See Strelka.

Wolfe, Gary, ed. 1983. *Science Fiction Dialogues.* Chicago: Academy Chi.

Woolf, Virginia. 1979. *Women and Writing.* London: Women's Press.

Zipes, Jack. 1983. *Fairy Tales and the Art of Subversion: The Classical Genre for Children and the Process of Civilization.* New York: Wildman Press.

Zutshi, Margot. 1981. *Literary Theory in Germany: A Study of Genre and Evaluation Theories, 1945–1965.* Bern: Peter Lang.

Index

Names

Index

Index

Index

Subjects

Index